D1539150

THE BROTHERHOOD

STEPHEN KNIGHT

THE
BROTHERHOOD

*The Secret World of
the Freemasons*

GRANADA
London Toronto Sydney New York

Granada Publishing Limited
8 Grafton Street, London W1X 3LA

Published by Granada Publishing 1984
Reprinted 1984

Copyright © Stephen Knight 1984

British Library Cataloguing in Publication Data

Knight, Stephen
  The brotherhood.
  1. Freemasons
  I. Title
  366'.1   HS395

ISBN 0-246-12164-5

Printed in Great Britain by
Richard Clay (The Chaucer Press) Ltd, Bungay, Suffolk

For Ma and Pa,
with love

Contents

Acknowledgements

I am free to name only a small number of the many hundreds of people who have helped me with advice and information. Most of those who helped did so only on the understanding that I would say nothing that could lead to their identification. Among these were many Freemasons who feared recrimination from other members of the Brotherhood. Others included government officials, politicians, judges, policemen of all ranks, lawyers, churchmen, past and present officers of MI5 and MI6, and people from every sector of society touched on in the book.

Some of those I can name gave me valuable assistance; some contributed a fact or an idea, did some typing, obtained press cuttings or read my notes and gave encouragement here and there. To all of them, and to all those who must remain unnamed, I am grateful. Without such people a book of this kind could not be contemplated.

Two men must be singled out for special mention: Simon Scott, managing editor of New English Library whose idea this book was and who supported me with unflagging enthusiasm all through the research and writing only to have the project snatched from him at the last moment; and my friend and agent Andrew Hewson who has never, even at the busiest moments, been unavailable.

Thank you, Simon and Andrew, and thank you, Rev Saul

Amias, Arthur Andrews, Judy Andrews, Andrew Arbuthnot, Henry Bach, Ken Barrow, Mark Barty-King, David Beal, Shirley Bennett, Victor Bretman, Ron Brown, Lord Carrington, Swami Anand Chandro, Lewis Chester, Elena Chiari, Kit Clarke, Nigel Coombs, Bill Cotton, Bernard Courtenay-Mayers, Martin Cresswell, Lord Denning, John Dickie, Athena Duncan, Robert Eagle, John Farmer, Peter Fenwick, Ray Fitzwalter, David Floyd, Laurie Flynn, Hamish Fraser, Simon Freeman, Paddy French, Sir Martin Furnival Jones, Robin Gauldie, Charles Goodman, Chris Green, Graham Greene, Karen de Groot, Martin Gwynne, Lord Hailsham, Peter Harkness, Anne Hearle, David Hearle, Cecil Rolph Hewitt, Brian Hilliard, Rt Rev Michael Hollis, Sir Geoffrey Howe, Harry Jackson, Andrew Jennings, John Johnson, Richard Johnson, Lord Elwyn Jones, Fred Jones, Ralph Jones, Tony Judge, Richard Kelly, Alistair Kelman, Rev Peter King, Robin Kirby, Philip Knightley, Feliks Kwiatowski, Barbara Land, Benedict Law, Rev John Lawrence, Leo Long, Andreas Lowenfeld, Sir Robert Mark, Tony Matthews, Doreen May, Sir Anthony Meyer, Austin Mitchell, Gerard Moate, Lesley Newson, Angus Ogilvy, Lord Justice Ormrod, June Outridge, Barry Payton, Alison Peacock, Chapman Pincher, Ronald Price, Roy Purkess, Philip Ray, Merlyn Rees, David Richardson, James Rushbrooke, Bob Satchwell, Paul Scudamore, Gustavo Selvi, Gitta Sereny, Ian Sharp, Lord Justice Sebag Shaw, John Shirley, Martin Short, Colin Simpson, Harold Smith, T. Dan Smith, Antonio de Stefano, Charles Stratton, Wendy Sturgess, Stewart Tendler, Timothy Tindal-Robertson, Peter Thomas, Peter Throsby, Fr John Tracey, SJ, Liz Usher, Alex Vincenti, Nick Webb, Peter Welling, Sir Dick White, Richard Whittington-Egan, Sir George Young.

Prologue

Freemasonry, although its leaders strenuously deny it, is a secret society. And few of its members – judges, police, politicians and royalty among them – realize that every time they attend a meeting they break the law, and (at least technically) lay themselves open to a minimum of two years' imprisonment. Under the Unlawful Societies Act of 1799 – unlikely, of course, ever to be enforced – Freemasons are permitted to hold meetings only if yearly returns providing names, addresses and descriptions of brethren are submitted to local Clerks of the Peace. This is rarely done, so most gatherings in masonic Lodges are held in breach of this law.

In England and Wales alone Freemasonry has more than 600,000 initiates, with a further 100,000 in Scotland and between 50,000 and 70,000 in Ireland. All the members of this extraordinary Brotherhood are male. All except those who are second-, third-, or fourth-generation Freemasons, who may join at eighteen, are over the age of twenty-one. All have sworn on pain of death and ghastly mutilation not to reveal masonic secrets to outsiders, who are known to brethren as the 'profane'.*

---

*From the Latin *pro* (before) and *fanum* (the temple); i.e. one outside the temple, not initiated to the rites performed within.

The headquarters of the Brotherhood in England and Wales is in London, where the massive bulk of Freemasons Hall squats at the corner of Great Queen Street and Wild Street like a gigantic elephant's footstool. This is the seat of the United Grand Lodge of England, the governing body of the 8,000-plus Lodges in England and Wales. These Lodges, of which there are another 1,200-odd under the jurisdiction of the Grand Lodge of Scotland and about 750 under the Grand Lodge of Ireland, carry out their secret business and ritual in a deliberately cultivated atmosphere of mystery in masonic Temples. Temples might be purpose built, or might be rooms in hotels or private buildings temporarily converted for masonic use. Many town halls up and down the country, for example, have private function rooms used for masonic rituals, as does New Scotland Yard, the headquarters of the Metropolitan Police.

The Grand Lodges control what is known as 'craft' Freemasonry, and brethren often refer to the Brotherhood as 'the Craft'. Craft Freemasonry covers the three degrees of Entered Apprentice, Fellow Craft and Master Mason. The vast majority of Freemasons rise no higher than Master Mason, and most are under the impression that there are no higher degrees. Even many of those who go on to become Royal Arch Masons, governed not by Grand Lodge but by Grand Chapter, have no idea that the masonic ladder extends a further thirty rungs above those on the third who believe they have already reached the top.

There is an important distinction to be made between *Freemasonry*, which is the movement as a whole, and *Freemasons*, which describes any number of individual Masons. This appears self-evident, but confusion of the two ideas has led to some gross misunderstandings. Take the death of Captain William Morgan in America in 1826. There is evidence to suggest that Morgan, having revealed certain masonic secrets in his book *Freemasonry Exposed*, was kidnapped and murdered by Freemasons. There have been suggestions that Mozart, a Mason, was poisoned by members of the Brotherhood, allegedly for betraying masonic secrets in *The Magic Flute*. And in 1888, the Jack the Ripper murders in the East End of London were perpetrated according to masonic ritual. Purely because people, wilfully or innocently, have regarded the words *Freemasons* and *Freemasonry* as interchangeable, these deaths have frequently been blamed, not on various individual Free*masons*, but on the whole Brotherhood. Some people, even today, look upon Freemasonry as an underground movement devoted to murder, terrorism and revolution. Hence, we read of Freemasonry as a worldwide conspiracy and watch, through the clouded vision of certain woefully mistaken writers, the whole of world history since the Renaissance unfold according to masonic machinations.

Freemasonry is not a worldwide secret society. It is a secret society that, originating in Britain, now has independent offshoots in most of the non-Communist world. And although the British Grand Lodges recognize more than a hundred Grand Lodges (forty-nine of them in the USA), they have no control over them, and most reflect the character and political complexion of the country in which they operate. Far from being revolutionary, there is no organization more reactionary, more Establishment-based, than British Freemasonry. Its members derive benefit from the Brotherhood only so long as the status quo is maintained.

Nevertheless, Freemasonry has a potent influence on life in Britain – for both good and ill.

The Brotherhood's stated aims of morality, fraternity and charity are well known. Indeed, circumspect and even secretive about all of Masonry's other doings, the average member of the Brotherhood will be eloquent on the generous donations made by United Grand Lodge and individual Lodges to charity, both masonic and profane. In 1980, for instance, Grand Lodge gave away £931,750, of which just over £300,000 was for non-masonic causes. In addition, many thousands of Masons and their relatives have benefited from the Royal Masonic Institution for Girls ('for maintaining, clothing and educating the daughters of Freemasons'), the Royal Masonic Institution for Boys, the Royal Masonic Benevolent Institution, the Royal Masonic Hospital ('for Freemasons, their wives, widows and dependent children'), and the Masonic Foundation for the Aged and the Sick.

On the other hand, there can be no doubt that many others have suffered because of Freemasonry entering into areas of life where, according to all its publicly proclaimed principles, it should never intrude. The abuse of Freemasonry causes alarming miscarriages of justice. It is one of the aims of this book to look at some of the effects of this abuse.

The Brotherhood is neither a commendation nor a condemnation of Freemasonry. Nor is it another wearisome and misnamed 'exposure' of Masonry's no longer secret rituals. Those rituals, or most of them, can be found in public libraries. In this respect the book differs from the vast majority of books written on the subject in the past 260 years. There is much here that will be unknown to the general reader, but all the verifiable facts I have obtained are presented in full, whether they are favourable or unfavourable to Masonry. Where I enter into speculation – and I do this as little as possible – I make it clear.

I am a journalist. From the beginning, I have thought of this investigation into Freemasonry in modern society as an extended piece of journalism. It is a factual report researched intensively over a relatively short period but because I was working without the benefit of a secretary or researchers the report does contain gaps. My network of contacts within Freemasonry, although extensive, represented a tiny fraction of all the Freemasons in this country. And the secret workings of Freemasonry, its use in manipulating this deal here, in getting someone promotion there, in influencing the actions of police, lawyers, judges, Civil Servants, is meat for a lifetime of study. I have therefore had to concentrate on some areas of society at the expense of others. I have devoted most time and energy to the areas of greatest concern. I trust readers will understand if this plan leaves questions where they feel there should be answers. I shall welcome comments, information and observations from anyone who has something to say. The updating process is already in hand and I expect to be able to expand and revise for as many editions as the public requires. Perhaps a better sub-title might therefore be *Freemasonry: An Interim Report*, because in addition to being wide-ranging and complicated (though always intensely fascinating), the nature of Freemasonry is changing – and the investigator has to face the problem of organized secrecy and 'disinformation'.

This latter can be crass and easily spotted, like the information passed to me covertly by a high-ranking Freemason posing as a nark, which said that at a certain degree a Candidate was required to defecate on a crucifix. This absurd sort of tactic is aimed at the gullible anti-Mason who is on the lookout for scandal and sensation, and who will believe anything that shows the Brotherhood in an unfavourable light. Such writers do exist, and in some number as I have found in the ten months I have had to prepare the report. These are the people who repeat what they are told without checking on facts and sources, and who ignore all evidence which runs counter to their own argument. And it is they who fall for the kind of disinformation tactic which several Freemasons attempted to practise upon me.* The crucifix story is just one example. There are others – including the yarn, gravely whispered to me in the corner of the Freemasons Arms just along the road from Freemasons Hall in London, that Prince Charles had been secretly initiated into a north London Lodge that practised Black Magic; and the fabrication, in support of which someone with access to Grand Lodge notepaper forged some impressive correspondence, that both main political parties had approached Grand Lodge prior to leadership elections to discuss the person most favourably looked upon by the Masons.

Nonsense.

Had I accepted any of this disinformation and published it, as was the intention of those who went to such lengths to feed it to me, the whole of this book would have been open to ridicule. What the disinformers evidently most desired was that *The Brotherhood* should be dismissed as irresponsible and unreliable and quickly forgotten.

I began my enquiry with two questions: Does Freemasonry have an influence on life in Britain, as many people believe? And if so, what kind of influence and in which areas of society? I felt from the beginning that it was important, if possible, to approach the subject from a position of absolute neutrality. In my favour was that I was neither a Mason nor an anti-Mason. But I had studied the subject in the early 1970s for my book *Jack the Ripper: The Final Solution*, and had received a large volume of letters from readers of that book, containing information, questions, theories and arguments on a range of topics associated with Freemasonry. So I did not have the open mind of one completely ignorant. I had already reached certain conclusions. Because of this, as the hundreds of Masons I have

---

*These individuals acted, I don't doubt, without the knowledge of Grand Lodge, which always prefers to ignore the very existence of outside enquirers.

interviewed since the spring of 1981 can testify, I probed all the more deeply for evidence that might upset those conclusions, in order to obtain as balanced a view of Freemasonry in modern Britain as I could.

But when I began writing, I very quickly discovered the impossibility of complete neutrality. I had seen, heard and discovered things that had made an impression upon me. It would have been a negation of my responsibility to the reader to deny her or him access to these impressions: I was, after all, carrying out the enquiry on behalf of those readers. Inevitably, I have reached conclusions based on the mass of new data now available to me.

Two months after I began research on this book, the United Grand Lodge of England issued a warning in its Quarterly Communication to Lodges, reminding brethren of the rule in their 'Antient Charges' concerning the ban on discussing internal affairs with outsiders. One Royal Arch Mason of thirty years' standing told me it was the first of its kind in his experience. The Quarterly Communication, according to one informant, is 'the method by which Freemasonry at its supreme level gets down to the lower levels'.

The Communication of 10 June 1981 contained this:

We have nothing to hide and certainly nothing to be ashamed of, but we object to having our affairs investigated by outsiders. We would be able to answer many of the questions likely to be asked, if not all of them, but we have found that silence is the best practice. Comment or correction only breeds further enquiry and leads to the publicity we seek to avoid. We respect and do not comment on the attitudes of other organizations. It is unfortunate that sometimes they are less respectful of ours. If therefore any of you is approached by any reporter . . . you will only be carrying out our practice if you gently decline to comment. Do not be drawn into argument or defence, however . . . Remember the Antient Charge, 'Behaviour in Presence of Strangers, Not Masons': *You shall be cautious in your words and carriage, that the most penetrating stranger shall not be able to discover or find out what is not proper to be intimated; and sometimes you shall divert a discourse, and manage it prudently for the honour of the worshipful fraternity . . .*

This warning was issued by no less a figure than the Pro Grand Master, Brother the Rt Hon the Earl Cadogan, sitting as president of the Brotherhood's Board of General Purposes. The reminder of possible disciplinary action against Freemasons who contravene Antient Charge VI.4 was not provoked solely by the United Grand Lodge's concern about my own enquiries. London Weekend Television had recently discussed in its *Credo* programme whether Freemasonry was compatible with Christianity, and the fact that several Freemasons of grand rank* had taken part in the programme had caused a storm within the Brotherhood.

A non-Mason such as I, working for information against this kind of organized secrecy, newly reinforced by stern warnings, would be hard put to obtain anything in certain areas of the subject without the assistance of at least some genuinely motivated 'moles'.

I was fortunate to have established within a few months an entire network of moles. The information this led me to was as startling as it was disturbing.

After my first book appeared in 1976, the London *Evening News*, which serialized it, received a letter from the Freemason director of a chain of bookshops, stating that he was so enraged by evidence I had produced linking Freemasons to the Jack the Ripper case that not only would he physically attack me if we should ever meet (referring to me as 'this specimen'), he would never stock the book and would do all in his power to wreck its

---

*Past or present holders of office in the United Grand Lodge are brethren of grand rank.

distribution to shops not owned by him. To some extent he succeeded. Although after the serialization it was in high demand, and quickly climbed to the top of the bestseller lists, I was soon receiving letters from would-be readers asking where it could be bought. Despite continuing demand for the book (it was reprinted in 1977, 1978, 1979, twice in 1981 and again in 1982) it cannot be found in branches of this particular chain. Many Freemason managers of other bookshops refuse point-blank to stock it.

Many previous books on Freemasonry have been published. Many, chiefly those by Masons themselves, are still in print after several years. It is interesting to see how many outsiders' works on the Brotherhood have gone quickly out of print despite continuing demand for them.

It is inevitable that many Freemasons will object to this book, if only because it overturns some cherished masonic beliefs. At least readers will be aware of the reason why, if it is in demand, all manner of excuses will be made by some booksellers for not stocking it.

One final point, which shows how easy it is to see masonic conspiracy where in reality there might be none. The episode is recounted in some detail because it has already been referred to in the press but not in the detail necessary for a balanced judgement to be reached. It dramatically affected *The Brotherhood*, so it is fitting that *The Brotherhood* should set the record straight.

Although the book is now being published by Granada, it was originally commissioned by New English Library. It was the idea of Simon Scott, managing editor of NEL. Scott approached my agent, Andrew Hewson, in the spring of 1981 after reading my *Jack the Ripper*, and suggested that I was the person to write it. We met, I produced a synopsis and specimen chapter, and *The Brotherhood* was commissioned. I began work in September 1981 and delivered the typescript to Scott in June 1982. It was to be the lead non-fiction title in NEL's spring 1983 catalogue.

From the first, Scott made it clear that only a handful of people within New English Library would know of the project. At the time the book was commissioned, NEL was owned by a remote American cartel which did not care what its English subsidiary published so long as it showed a profit at the end of the year. Nevertheless, Scott and editorial director Nick Webb took the precaution of confiding in their managing director, a non-Mason, and getting his full backing for the book. Scott told me that to avoid the possibility of sabotage by any hostile Freemasons within or associated with the company, *The Brotherhood* would not be entered in any schedule. Even the advance payment was obtained from the accounts department under an innocuous and misleading project title. At the time these seemed to me excessive cloak-and-dagger activities, although I knew that the publishing world had traditionally been rife with Freemasonry.

Shortly after I started work on the book, NEL was taken over by Hodder & Stoughton, whose chairman and managing director - two brothers eminent in publishing - were Philip and Michael Attenborough, also non-Masons.

After the takeover, NEL retained its own separate management structure with its existing managing director, and in practice no editorial control was exercised over NEL books by the Hodder management. So alarm bells began to ring in Webb's mind when, shortly after I delivered the typescript, Michael Attenborough asked to see it. He had not done this with any previous NEL book. Although Scott and Webb were anxious to get the book legally vetted, edited and delivered to the printer as soon as possible, and constantly pressed Attenborough for any comments he wished to make, he continued to sit on the typescript. This was baffling to Scott and Webb. The delay was by now beginning to jeopardize plans for a spring 1983 publication. Finally, after holding the script for nearly seven weeks, Attenborough asked Scott to gut the book and produce a precise summary of its content. This was done. The weeks continued to roll by, with no word from above. When Scott was in Frankfurt and Webb in New York, word came that the project was to be squashed. Scott flew back to London and a series of frantic transatlantic calls took place between him and Webb, then Webb and Attenborough. But by the time Webb was able to catch a plane home the deed was done. *The Brotherhood* was killed.

Scott's anger knew no bounds. He fought and fought for the book, even making it a resigning issue, but Attenborough was adamant. Then Attenborough told Scott that although neither he nor his brother was a Freemason, their father – John Attenborough CBE – was a senior member of the Brotherhood, and in deference to him they would not publish it.

I went to see Michael Attenborough at his Bedford Square office in January 1983, when the book was safely placed with Granada. He said he was delighted the book would be published.

'Are you?' I asked. 'Then why didn't you publish it yourself?'

He spent some time in obvious discomfort explaining that it had not been a pleasant decision and was one he genuinely regretted having to make, but that he did not feel that the sales force would be completely behind the book and it was not a title which Hodder felt it could publish with enthusiasm.

Yet I knew that the sales force had expressed great interest in the book and were looking forward to handling it. I told him so.

I was with him for three quarters of an hour, and

eventually he admitted something which he seemed nervous of confessing: he loved his father. John Attenborough, according to his son, is a devoted Freemason and a devoted Christian. In view of what I say in the book about the incompatibility of the two religions,* he and brother Philip realized they would cause their father very great pain by publishing *The Brotherhood*. Attenborough assured me that his father had not seen the script and he had not discussed the project with him.

If the incident does not demonstrate the direct power of Freemasonry over the Fourth Estate, it does offer a vivid example of the devotion that Freemasonry so often inspires in its initiates, a devotion that is nothing less than religious. So it was that the Attenboroughs made their decision to throw away £8,000 in advance royalties and thousands more in legal fees and in terms of time spent on the project by the editorial, design, subsidiary rights, promotion, sales and other departments rather than wound their father.

Stephen Knight
January 1983

---

*I use the word advisedly. See Chapter 25 – 'The Devil in Disguise?' – below.

PART ONE

Workers' Guild to Secret
Society

CHAPTER 1

Origins

Some Freemasons claim great antiquity for Freemasonry. This is reflected in the masonic calendar which is based on Archbishop Ussher's seventeenth-century calculation that the Creation must have taken place in the year 4004 BC. For convenience, the odd four years are ignored and Anno Lucis (in the Year of Light, when Freemasonry is deemed to have begun) is four thousand years ahead of Anno Domini – so a masonic certificate of initiation bearing the date A.L. 5983 was issued in A.D. 1983. The implication is that Freemasonry is as old as Adam.

Throughout the eighteenth and nineteenth centuries, masonic writers produced vast numbers of books seeking to show that their movement had a continuous history of many hundreds, even thousands, of years. Some claimed that the ancestors of the Brotherhood were the Druids or the Culdees; some claimed they were the pre-Christian Jewish monks, the Essenes. Others insisted that Freemasonry had its origins in the religion of ancient Egypt – an amalgam of the briefly held monotheism of Ikhnaton (c. 1375 B.C.) and the Isis–Osiris cult.

Modern masonic historians are far more cautious. It is now accepted that Freemasonry as practised today goes back little more than three centuries. What is true, though, is that the philosophic, religious and ritualistic concoction that makes up the speculative element in Freemasonry is drawn from many sources – some of them, like the Isis–Osiris myth, dating back to the dawn of history. Rosicrucianism, Gnosticism, the Kabbala, Hinduism, Theosophy and traditional notions of the occult all play a part: but despite the exhaustive literature – one scholar estimates that some 50,000 items of Masonry had been published by the 1950s – it is impossible to determine what comes from where and when, if only because Freemasonry on its lower and more accessible levels is opposed to dogma. There is therefore no authoritative statement of what Masons believe or what the Brotherhood stands for in the first, second and third degrees, to which the vast majority of members restrict themselves. Even a 33° Mason who has persevered to attain all the enlightenment that Freemasonry claims to offer could not – even if he were freed from his oath of secrecy – provide more than a purely personal view of the masonic message and the meaning to be attached to masonic symbolism, since this remains essentially subjective.

The comparatively short documented history of Free-masonry as an institution is nevertheless quite extra-ordinary. It is the story of how a Roman Catholic trade guild for a few thousand building workers in Britain came to be taken over by the aristocracy, the gentry and members of mainly non-productive professions, and how it was turned into a non-Christian secret society enjoying association with offshoot fraternal societies with millions of adherents throughout most of the non-Communist world.

In many cultures and at many times humankind has been drawn to the esoteric – the conception that the great truths about life and how to control social and natural phenomena are secrets and can only be known to initiates, who pass on their privileged knowledge to the elect from generation to generation. As one highly placed Mason told me, 'Truth, to the initiate, is not for everyone; pearls must not be thrown before swine.' Equally, throughout history men have joined together in secret groups to further purely worldly ambitions. All such groups also involve initiation – the initiation ceremony involving fearful oaths of secrecy. For secrets to remain secret there must be certain and effective sanctions. Secret societies formed for essentially practical ends have commonly had religious and moral elements. The religious element creates awe and so adds to the effectiveness of the oath of secrecy. The moral element determines the fraternal way that the organization's members treat each other, which might bear small resemblance to the way they treat outsiders.

Freemasonry is both a speculative, philosophic – even religious and mystical – system, and a fraternity of those organized to help each other in material matters. For some Masons it is entirely the former, for others entirely the latter, but for most it is a mixture of the two.

Masonic historians seem as uncertain as non-Masons about who first saw in the obsolescent mediaeval Christian masonic guild an organization that could be taken over and converted into a quasi-religious, quasi-secular secret society. What evidence there is indicates that this evolution began very slowly and almost by chance, and that it was only later that the potential of the masonic guild as a clandestine power base was perceived. In other words, it appears that the original interest of the gentry in the masonic lodges stemmed from curiosity, antiquarian interest, and a kind of fashionable search for an unconventional, exclusive social milieu – rather like a jet-set fad for frequenting working men's pubs.

There are a number of reasons why the masonic guild should have attracted this genteel interest. First, the working (or 'operative') masons' craft guild was ripe for takeover: structured in the heyday of Gothic architecture in the thirteenth century,* by the end of the sixteenth century the craft was dying. King's College Chapel at Cambridge, perhaps the last truly great English Gothic building, had been completed about 1512. Secondly, the highly skilled stonemasons of the Gothic age were peculiar in that many were itinerant workers, moving from church site to cathedral site as work was to be found. They had no regular headquarters like other trades, gathering in temporary lodges on site to discuss their affairs. And, as they often did not know each other as did permanent residents of mediaeval towns, they needed some method of recognition, some way of maintaining a closed shop to protect their demanding and highly esteemed profession against interlopers who had not undergone the rigorous apprenticeship necessary to acquire the mason's skills. These, as Professor Jacob Bronowski termed them, were the 'industrial aristocrats'.

There were thus cosmopolitan romance, an exclusivity and an organized secretiveness about the masons' guild, which became increasingly moribund as baroque replaced Gothic architecture. All of this had potential fascination for men of education.

Modern Freemasonry probably originated in Scotland. The earliest known instance of a non-stonemason, a gentleman, joining a masons' lodge is John Boswell, Laird of Auchinlech, who was a member of the Lodge in Edinburgh in 1600. Apparently the first English gentleman to join an English Lodge was Elias Ashmole, founder of Oxford's Ashmolean Museum. An antiquarian deeply interested in Rosicrucianism, he joined in 1646. Masonry became so fashionable that as the seventeenth century progressed the 'acceptance' (the collective term for non-stonemasons)

*The term 'lodge' was first used, so far as can be discovered, in 1277.

became the majority in the masonic Lodges. For example, in 1670 the Aberdeen Lodge had thirty-nine 'accepted' members while only ten remained 'operative' masons. But it was not long before the novelty in participating in the quaint and venerable doings of artisans wore thin. Men of fashion saw no reason to prolong association with working men, and they began to form their own gentlemen's Lodges. Freemasonry was launched.

CHAPTER 2

Metamorphosis

The 'speculative' Masons inherited seven fundamental points from their 'operative' predecessors:

(1) An organization with the three grades of members: Apprentice, Fellow or Journeyman, and Master Mason.
(2) A unit termed a Lodge.
(3) Legendary histories of the origins of the masonic craft set out in the 100-odd manuscripts containing the so-called 'Old Charges', the oldest being the Regius manuscript of 1390, which was in verse.
(4) A tradition of fraternal and benevolent relations between members.
(5) A rule of secrecy about Lodge doings, although the Old Charges themselves were simply lists of quite ordinary rules for the guild, which members were enjoined to keep 'so help you God'. As befitted a Christian grouping there were no blood-curdling oaths.
(6) A method of recognition, notably the Scottish 'mason word' traced back to 1550: unwritten but variously rendered as *Mahabyn*, *Mahabone* or even *Matchpin*.

(7) A thoroughly Christian foundation – the Old Charges are permeated with mediaeval Roman Catholicism.

With the demise of the original 'trade union' purpose of the organization and with the eclipse not only of Roman Catholicism due to the Reformation but also the waning of Christianity with the rise of science, what was left towards the end of the seventeenth century was the framework of a secretive association, likened by one authority to a peasant's cottage ripe for extensive development as a luxury weekend home for the well-to-do.

Serious masonic historians themselves deplore the lack of documentation about the three or four critical decades before the foundation of the Grand Lodge of England in 1717. But it was during these years that the course Freemasonry was to follow was set. It was evidently then that a few men among the small number (possibly only a few hundreds in all) of 'accepted' Masons must have come to see the potential of a secret society cutting across class divisions to embrace aristocrats, gentry, professional men and elements of the expanding middle class. It was to be a brotherhood which would put a string to pull into the hand of every member, and strings enough in the hands of its shadowy controllers to manipulate events – like puppet masters behind the scenes. But who these people were and just how consciously they planned or, as some have said, even plotted, is shrouded in mystery.

One thing united a majority of politically conscious people at this time: the need to preserve the gain of the Civil War of 1642-51 – the limitation of the power of the King. The 'accepted' Masons of the last quarter of the seventeenth century would appear to have been largely drawn from the type of people most anxious to preserve and to increase the steadily growing influence in society and government of men of quite moderate wealth and standing.

Whether Lodges as such or Masons as Masons took part in the initiative to invite William of Orange and his consort Mary to become joint sovereigns in 1688 is not known, but the suggestion is plausible. All that is certain is that by the early years of the eighteenth century a number of Masons had set their sights high: they sought a maximum of reputability. In 1716, according to Dr James Anderson (of whom more later), 'the few Lodges at London resolved . . . to chuse a Grand Master from among themselves, till they should have the honour of a *Noble Brother* at their Head'. The stage was set for the system of tame aristocratic and royal figureheads that we know today, which confers an aura of indisputable approbation on everything to do with Freemasonry. When Grand Lodge was founded, George I had been on the throne only three years. The prominent in Masonry were poised to have a hand in the manipulation of the new Hanoverian dynasty.

Before the foundation of Grand Lodge in 1717, moves to transform the old guild into a true secret society were well under way. As the normal trade union business of operative masonic Lodges dwindled and eventually ceased, so the element of ritual based on the readings of the Old Charges – their legendary stories about the origins of the masons' craft and their injunctions to members to obey the traditional rules – was transformed. Lodge ritual, initiations and speculative dissertations became the main business of actual Lodge meetings. At the same time, fraternal conviviality – which in the old days of operative masonry had probably been confined to a tankard or two after meetings in a local ale house – soon became a major feature of masonic society. Much was eaten, much was drunk, and much was discussed in the privacy of masonic meeting places (usually taverns) after the rather dry formal doings in Lodge were over. The 'better' the Lodge – in the sense of social class – the 'better' the conversation and the more lavish and expensive the entertainment. Masonry was already on its way to mirroring and reinforcing the class system and the emerging social order based on strictly constitutional monarchy. Whatever it was to become overseas, where no Civil War, no Glorious Revolution had yet taken place, Masonry in England was alreaded headed towards a conservative future. The sights of its prime movers were already set on a movement underpinning a type of society admirably suited to its purposes: a stable society with limited social mobility in which a secret inner 'Old Boy' association could provide an environment where considerable benefit could be gained by members who knew how to 'play the masonic organ'.

To achieve this end, though, the confidentiality of the old guild had to be reinforced. The transformation into a secret society meant the institution of formal oaths accompanied by penalties. But once again, before the establishment of Grand Lodge, very little is known of the development of ritual, particularly the oaths. There is evidence that rituals based on various incidents in legendary masonic history were tried out in different Lodges – rituals perhaps based on stories of Noah's Ark and the Tower of Babel alluded to in some Old Charges. It is also probable that rituals based on the story of the building of King Solomon's temple, the principal subject of present-day rituals, were 'worked' (the masonic word meaning the acting out of the Brotherhood's ceremonies). But why this subject was chosen when the legends in the Old Charges give no special prominence to the story of Solomon's temple, no one has been able to explain satisfactorily.

Formal oaths of secrecy to be sworn by individual initiates appear in a number of Old Charges containing 'new orders', but as these were published five years after the establishment of Grand Lodge they are possibly spurious.

Either way, no horrific sanctions are mentioned. Even so, the inclusion of an oath in the initiation rituals can be regarded as a crucial step in the creation of a secret society from the old guild.

CHAPTER 3

Schism and Reunion

In 1717 Freemasonry enters properly into history. Four London Lodges alone formed Grand Lodge and owed allegiance to it. What is interesting is that a none-too-well-off gentleman, Anthony Sayer, was installed as Grand Master. The upper classes kept a low profile. They backed the creation of a central organization welding individual Lodges together, but evidently wanted this done before they assumed control. Of the four original London Lodges, the first three contained not one 'Esquire' between them, whereas Lodge Original No 4 was made up of seventy-one members of whom, in 1724, ten were nobles, three were honourable, four were baronets or knights, and two were generals.

In 1718 Sayer was replaced after barely a year by George Payne, a 'man of more substance', being a member of Original No 4. But he too had only one year in office – another interim while the upper classes moved in on the small gentry just as the small gentry had moved in on the 'operative' artisans a century earlier.

The third Grand Master was the Reverend John Theophilus Desaguliers, a Doctor of Law, a Fellow of the Royal Society and chaplain to Frederick, Prince of Wales, whom he admitted to the Brotherhood in 1737. He was of French extraction. A headhunter for Freemasonry, he not only visited Edinburgh to encourage the Scots along the organizational path the London Masons were following, but visited The Hague in 1731, where he admitted the Duke of Lorraine to the Brotherhood. The Duke married Maria Theresa in 1736 and become co-Regent when she acceded to the Austrian throne in 1738. How far the Duke contributed to the masonic heyday under Joseph II when Mozart, Haydn and a host of other notables were Freemasons is not known. But the cosmopolitan Dr Desaguliers certainly appears to have sparked the missionary zeal of British Freemasonry which eventually carried the movement to almost every country in the world.

Desaguliers too only held office a short time. In 1721 he gave way to the long awaited first noble Grand Master, the Duke of Montague. But, unlike his predecessors, Desaguliers was not usurped: the evidence suggests that he was the prototype of the long line of powerful masonic figures who preferred the shade to the limelight, the reality of power to mere appearances.

By 1730 when the Roman Catholic Duke of Norfolk was installed (prior to the first papal condemnation of Freemasonry in 1738), there had been nine Grand Masters, six of them nobles. The first royal Grand Master was the Duke of Cumberland, younger son of George II, who was installed in 1782, with an Acting Grand Master, the Earl of Effingham, as his proxy. In 1787 both the Prince of Wales (the future George IV) and his brother William (the future William IV) were initiated. The patronage by the Royal Family of the new secret society was thenceforth assured. Queen Elizabeth II is the present Grand Patroness.

But all the while the royals were being courted to become titular leaders of Masonry, the process of transformation of the old masons' guild continued. The Brotherhood was de-Christianized and the rituals of the various workings became formalized. Throughout the eighteenth century more and more pagan elements were brought in to replace the discarded faith.

The de-Christianization was largely accomplished by the *Constitutions* of Dr James Anderson, a Scottish Freemason who became a member of Original Lodge No 4. Anderson, a genealogist and a far from accurate historian, appears to have been put up to the task of settling the new form of the Craft by Dr Desaguliers who in 1723 presented the first version (there was a second version in 1738) to Grand Master the Duke of Montague when he, Desaguliers, had discreetly retired to the second position, that of Deputy Grand Master.

In Anderson's constitution listing the new 'Charges of a Free-Mason', the first is the most striking and had the most far-reaching consequences. It stated: ''Tis now thought more expedient only to oblige them [members of the Brotherhood] to that Religion to which all men agree, leaving their particular opinions to themselves.'

Anderson, in a long and fanciful historical preamble tracing Freemasonry back to Adam and quite unwarrantably naming many previous English monarchs as Masons, seeks to reconcile this radical departure with the spirit and tradition of the old guild by announcing, without any historical justification, that in ancient days masons had been charged in every country to be of the religion of that country where they worked – this despite the fact that virtually all the extant Old Charges were quite explicit in their Christianity.

The only reference to Christ is in Anderson's preamble when, referring to the Roman Emperor Augustus, he notes 'in whose Reign was born God's Messiah, the great Architect of the Church'. In 1815 even this historical preamble was omitted from the *Constitutions* following the Union of the 'Antients' and the 'Moderns', described later, and during the years between 1723 and 1813 the invocation of the name of Christ in the endings of prayers gradually died out. In masonic quotations of scripture (e.g. 1 Peter ii 5; 2 Thess. iii 2; 2 Thess. iii 13) the name of Christ came very pointedly to be deleted from the text. So, to Christians, the apostasy became complete. Masonry became vaguely Voltairean Deist, the 'Great Architect of the Universe' came to be invoked, and prayers ended with 'so mote it be'.

After so much activity a period of comparative neglect now followed during which the politican and littérateur Horace Walpole, himself a Mason, wrote in 1743: 'the Freemasons are in . . . low repute now in England . . . I believe nothing but a persecution could bring them into vogue again'.

There was ribaldry and mockery, and Hogarth, also a Mason, joined in making fun in his engravings of the self-indulging, self-important image the Brotherhood had earned itself. There was no persecution. Instead there was schism, partly in reaction to the de-Christianization of the Craft and other changes in its practice. Masons calling themselves 'the Antients', who had not formed part of the Grand Lodge of 1717, created in 1751 a rival Grand Lodge, also manned by aristocrats, which stood for the link with Christianity and certain other aspects of the old tradition which the 'Moderns', loyal to the 1717 Grand Lodge, had tampered with. The two Grand Lodges vied with each other to recruit provincial Lodges. To complicate matters there were also what the great masonic historian J. Heron Lepper called the 'Traditioners' who, while remaining under the jurisdiction of the London 'Modern' Grand Lodge, nevertheless did not follow its lead entirely.

There was another, later to prove most important, bone of contention between the Antients and the Moderns – the position of a masonic degree and associated working termed the Holy Royal Arch. This time it was the Moderns who objected to something new: some of the Antients had instituted this 'fourth degree', one of the first mentions of which is in 1746 when a prominent Irish Antient was 'exalted' to it. The Moderns claimed that this was a departure from unalterable tradition because the old craft, like other guild crafts, had known only a hierarchy of three degrees – Apprentice, Journeyman or Fellow, and Master Craftsman. Despite the Moderns' objections, the Royal Arch ritual grew steadily in popularity. Perhaps the turning point in the dispute came as a result of Thomas Dunckerley, a natural son of George II, a keen Mason and a Traditioner among the Moderns, coming out as an enthusiast for Royal Arch, to which he was exalted – as Masons term initiation to the Royal Arch – according to his own report in 1754. Dunckerley looms large in masonic history and other prominent Moderns soon came to share his enthusiasm.

Eventually, in 1813, tired of their long quarrel, Antients and Moderns were reconciled, the Duke of Kent, Grand Master of the Antients, giving way to the Duke of Sussex, Grand Master of the Moderns, who thus became the first Grand Master of the United Grand Lodge of England. The Moderns gave way on Royal Arch, saving face by having it declared that this was no fourth degree but simply a culmination of the other three degrees, which completed the making of a Master Mason. The Antients for their part gave way to the Moderns in accepting the total de-Christianization of the Brotherhood.

The Union's acceptance of Royal Arch workings is of great importance, for it completed in all essentials the structure of Freemasonry as it exists today. Just as the Moderns de-Christianized the movement, so with the acceptance of Royal Arch the Antients succeeded in introducing the undeniably occult – notably the invocation of the supposedly rediscovered long-lost name of God, discussed later in this book.

It is perhaps because the Freemasonic God, as revealed to Royal Arch Masons, is so far from being 'that Religion to which all men agree' that it was determined that Holy Royal Arch workings should not be conducted in Lodges but separately in 'Chapters' under the control of a Grand Chapter and not of Grand Lodge. In practice, the officers of Grand Lodge and of Grand Chapter overlap and today both bodies have their seat at Freemasons Hall in Great Queen Street, Holborn. Moreover, Chapters usually meet in the Lodge temples to which they are attached, albeit on different evenings. Today about one in five Freemasons are Royal Arch 'Companions', these constituting a more fervent, more indoctrinated, closer-knit inner circle. With the acceptance of Royal Arch, the way was open for the conferment of the bewildering mass of further even more exclusive degrees that now characterizes world Free-masonry.

During the period from the beginning of the seventeenth century to the time of the Union of Antients and Moderns in 1813, the rituals crystallized and came to approximate each other, although to this day there are a large number of somewhat different workings. The main rituals settled around the legend of King Solomon's temple. The myth mimed in the Master Mason's degree is the murder of Hiram Abiff, claimed to have been the principal architect of the temple, for refusing to reveal masonic secrets. The would-be Master Mason has to 'die' as Hiram Abiff and be 'resurrected' into Masonry. According to the myth mimed in the Royal Arch ceremony, a crypt is found in the foundations of the ruined temple in which is discovered the 'omnific word', the lost name of God. With the rituals, the oaths too became settled in the form they have today. Should he reveal the secrets of the Brotherhood, the Apprentice accepts, among other penalties, to have his tongue torn out; the Fellow Craft to have his heart torn from his breast; the Master Mason to have his bowels burned to ashes; and the exaltee to the Royal Arch accepts 'in addition' to have the top of his skull sliced off. But, as the rituals themselves express it, the 'more effective penalty' for doing anything displeasing to Masonry is to be shunned by the entire Brotherhood, a penalty adequate to bring a man to ruin, the more certainly so as Freemasonry expanded in every profession and every branch of society.

CHAPTER 4

Across the Seas and Down the Centuries

The Irish Grand Lodge was formed in 1725 and the Scottish the following year. The Scots proved at least as fervent missionaries as the English. As already mentioned, the movement had spread to the Continent at least by the third decade of the eighteenth century, often in very high society. Frederick the Great of Prussia is claimed to have been initiated in 1738, although one must be careful of accepting masonic claims of membership by the illustrious. There is no proof, for example, that Christopher Wren, often hailed as one of the brethren, was ever a member. Masonry, its undefined Deism so close to that of Voltairean rationalism, was soon the rage among the pre-revolutionary freethinkers in France: ironically, it may have been planted there by Jacobite exiles around 1725.

Freemasonry remains a power to be reckoned with in many European countries, France and Germany in particular. The French Grand Master today is Air Force General Jacques Mitterand, the President's brother, and Freemasonry's influence in politics is profound. François Mitterand owes much of his success in the 1981 election to influential Freemasons. Masonry has been closely identified with the Socialists for most of the last seventy years. According to Fred Zeller, Grand Master of the Grand Orient of France in 1971 and 1973, the 1974 presidential election would have been won by the Socialists had Valéry Giscard d'Estaing not become a Freemason and colluded with sympathetic forces in the Brotherhood, which eventually persuaded French Freemasons that it was in their best interests to vote for Giscard. He was initiated into the Franklin Roosevelt Lodge in Paris the year of the election.

Italian Freemasonry, later to play a significant role in the unification of the country (Garibaldi was a Freemason), was established in Rome by Jacobite exiles in 1735 and was already a force by 1750. Masonry among Roman Catholic prelates was one reason for the repeated papal condemnations.

No country was too small for attention: Holland, Switzerland and Sweden all had keen and influential memberships in the eighteenth century. Continental Masonry reached as far as Russia: Tolstoy in *War and Peace* describes the different motivations of upper-class Masons during the Napoleonic Wars.

Freemasonry crossed the Atlantic to the colonies of the old empire very early on: George Washington's initiation was in 1752. Today, the dollar bill bears not only Washington's likeness but also the all-seeing-eye symbol of Freemasonry. Washington refused to become head of Masonry for the whole of the newly formed United States, and US Freemasonry came to be organized on a state-by-state basis. Today, each state has its own Grand Lodge. Royal Arch Chapters come under state Grand Chapters, the first mention of Royal Arch appearing in Virginia records of 1753. A few states followed the British lead and spread the Brotherhood abroad. For example, before the Second World War there were Lodges in China under Massachusetts jurisdiction, and it was Massachusetts that warranted the first Canadian Lodge in 1749.* No fewer

*The oldest masonic Lodge room in the USA dates from 1760 and is at Prentiss House, Marblehead, Massachusetts.

than nine Canadian Grand Lodges were eventually formed. The United States proved a home from home for the Brotherhood. Eight signatories to the Declaration of Independence – Benjamin Franklin, John Hancock, Joseph Hewes, William Hooper, Robert Treat Payne, Richard Stockton, George Walton and William Whipple – were proven Masons, while twenty-four others, on less than certain evidence, have been claimed by the Brotherhood. Seventeen Presidents have been Masons: Washington, Madison, Monroe, Jackson, Polk, Buchanan, Andrew Johnson, Garfield, McKinley, both Roosevelts, Taft, Harding, Truman, Lyndon Johnson, Gerald Ford and Ronald Reagan. Seventeen Vice-Presidents including Hubert Humphrey and Adlai Stevenson have also been brethren.

But the British – the founders of Masonry – remained throughout the nineteenth and twentieth centuries the chief propagandists for the movement. Undaunted by the loss of the first empire and with it direct control over American Masonry, the British took Masonry with the flag as they created their second empire – the one on which the sun never set. For some years membership of the Lodges set up in the empire (grouped in 'Provinces' under English, Scottish or Irish jurisdiction) was confined to Europeans, apart from a handful of Indian princely exceptions. But after 1860, at first Parsees, then other Indians were brought into the Brotherhood. In British West Africa and the West Indies there were 'black' Lodges as well as 'white' Lodges (as in the USA), and eventually mixed Lodges were formed.

Associating the native upper and middle classes on a peculiar, profitable and clandestine basis with their white rulers, some historians believe, did much to defuse resentment of imperial domination. Despite his colour, any man rather better off than the mass of the people – who were not sought as members – could, by being a Freemason, feel that he belonged in however humble a way to the Establishment. Just how far Masonry reached is shown by the fact that on the small island of Jamaica there were no fewer than twelve Lodges, some in townships of little more than a couple of streets.

Freemasonry of itself is simply a secret environment tended by its various Grand Lodges, an exclusive society within society, there to be used by its members largely as they wish. Hence its influence, political, and social, can be quite different at different times and places. In the eighteenth century Masons were thin on the ground, but enough aristocrats, men of fashion and influence, were Masons to give the top Masons influence disproportionate to their numbers. And of course royal involvement ensured, as it does today, the impression of total reputability. Because of this, Freemasonry has been able to ignore all legislation dating from 1797 concerning secret societies and illegal oaths. Although regarded as subversive in some countries where the environment was less amenable, in eighteenth-century Britain the Brotherhood had the effect already alluded to – of reinforcing the development of constitutional monarchy under which its own Establishment could thrive.

Among the middle classes, though, Masonry was then too sparse in most areas to play any crucial role in local affairs. There was none of the tight-lipped apprehensive silence so common today. People could afford to ridicule the movement, and there was a lively trade in anti-masonic pamphlets. In fact, masonic 'exposures' may have done much to develop and harmonize the still unprinted rituals.

But the advantage of Masonry, in terms of cult, diversified friendships and straight worldly interest, had become evident to many. With the Union of 1813 the movement began to snowball: for the more Masons there are in any area or profession the more important it is to be a

Mason if one is not to risk losing out, as a non-member of the 'club', in one's business, one's profession and one's preferment.

Another factor was important: with the Industrial Revolution, social mobility began to increase. And Masonry, providing a ladder extending from the lower middle class to the Royal Family itself, offered great advantages to those who could learn how to climb it. There was also the loneliness of the new urban way of life: Freemasonry provided an enormous circle of instant acquaintances in most walks of life. Then too, the English public schoolboy could continue to be public schoolboy in the intimacy of the Craft.

At the end of the eighteenth century only about 320 English Lodges had been warranted. About twice as many more were formed in the next half century, No 1000 in 1864. This number was doubled in the next twenty years, No 2000 being warranted in 1883. The next twenty years maintained this rate of growth with Lodge No 3000 opening in 1903, in which year Winston Leonard Spencer Churchill, the MP for Oldham, was initiated to a masonic career that was to last more than sixty years. All this nineteenth-century explosion resulted essentially from recruitment from the middle and professional classes.

With the First World War, which led to so many of quite humble background seeking better status, the rate of growth speeded dramatically. Lodge No 4000 was formed in 1919, and No 5000 only seven years later in 1926. The Second World War, for similar reasons, led to another such period of extraordinarily rapid growth – Lodge No 6000 being formed in 1944 and No 7000 in 1950.

In 1981, Lodge No 9003 was warranted. Even allowing for Lodges that have been discontinued, taking average Lodge membership at around sixty men, a membership of at least half a million can reasonably reliably be estimated for England alone. Official masonic estimates, as already stated, put the total for England and Wales at around 600,000.

As the recruiting ground for Freemasons is primarily the not directly productive middle and professional classes, it is clear that a very high proportion of these people, occupying key roles in British society – lawyers, Civil Servants, bank managers and so on – are Freemasons. In many fields nowadays the disadvantages of being left out of the 'club' are perceived as being too serious for a great many people to contemplate, whatever they may feel personally about the morality of joining a secret society, or about the misty tenets of speculative Freemasonry.

CHAPTER 5

The Thirty-Third Degree

There is an élite group of Freemasons in England over whom the United Grand Lodge has no jurisdiction. These are the brethren of the so-called Higher Degrees, and even the majority of Freemasons have no idea of their existence.

Most Freemasons who have been raised to the 3rd Degree to become Master Masons believe they are the top of the masonic ladder. As novices they were Entered Apprentices. They were then 'passed' as Fellow Craft Masons and finally 'raised' as Masters. The very name Master has connotations of supremacy. If Master Masons have ambition it will usually be to achieve office within their Lodge – eventually, with good fortune and the passing of years, to become Worshipful Master of their mother Lodge (the Lodge to which they were first initiated into Masonry). Those who have their eyes fixed on higher office will aim for rank in their Provincial Grand Lodge or in the United Grand Lodge itself. But even the Grand Master of all England is only a Freemason of the 3rd Degree. The three Craft

3°   Master Mason
    ↑
2°   Fellow Craft
    ↑
1°   Entered Apprentice

degrees form the entire picture of Masonry for most of the

The Thirty-three Degrees of Freemasonry

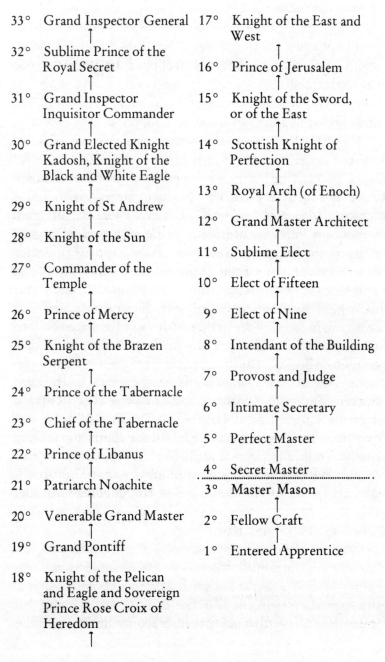

33° Grand Inspector General

32° Sublime Prince of the Royal Secret

31° Grand Inspector Inquisitor Commander

30° Grand Elected Knight Kadosh, Knight of the Black and White Eagle

29° Knight of St Andrew

28° Knight of the Sun

27° Commander of the Temple

26° Prince of Mercy

25° Knight of the Brazen Serpent

24° Prince of the Tabernacle

23° Chief of the Tabernacle

22° Prince of Libanus

21° Patriarch Noachite

20° Venerable Grand Master

19° Grand Pontiff

18° Knight of the Pelican and Eagle and Sovereign Prince Rose Croix of Heredom

17° Knight of the East and West

16° Prince of Jerusalem

15° Knight of the Sword, or of the East

14° Scottish Knight of Perfection

13° Royal Arch (of Enoch)

12° Grand Master Architect

11° Sublime Elect

10° Elect of Fifteen

9° Elect of Nine

8° Intendant of the Building

7° Provost and Judge

6° Intimate Secretary

5° Perfect Master

4° Secret Master

3° Master Mason

2° Fellow Craft

1° Entered Apprentice

600,000 'uninitiated initiates' of the Brotherhood in England and Wales.

The 'Masters', who form the largest proportion of Freemasons, are in most cases quite unaware of the thirty superior degrees to which they will never be admitted, nor even hear mentioned. This is the real picture, with the three lowly degrees governed by Grand Lodge and the thirty higher degrees governed by a Supreme Council.

These thirty degrees, beginning with the 4th (that of Secret Master) and culminating in the 33rd (Grand Inspector General), are controlled by a Supreme Council whose headquarters are at 10 Duke Street, St James's, London SW1. Nobody walking down Duke Street from Piccadilly is likely to suspect the true nature of what goes on inside the building, even if he or she happens to notice the small plate to the right of the entrance which says, 'The Supreme Council. Ring once'. Built in 1910–11, this imposing Edwardian mansion with fine neo-classical features might easily be taken for a consulate or the headquarters of some private institute. Nor do people thumbing through the S–Z section of the London Telephone Directory get any clue from the entry sandwiched between Supreme Cleaners and Supreme Die Cutters: 'Supreme Council 33rd Degree . . . 01-930 1606'.

Nobody looking at that fine but anonymous house from outside could suspect that behind its pleasing façade, beyond the two sets of sturdy double doors and up the stairs there is a Black Room, a Red Room and a Chamber of Death. To high Masons, the house in Duke Street is known as the Grand East.

Members of Craft Freemasonry – that is, all but a few thousand of England's Masons – often argue that Freemasonry is not a secret society but 'a society with secrets'. Although the argument is in the end unconvincing, it has its merits. But no such case can be made out for the wealthy society-within-a-society based at 10 Duke Street.

One of the regulations of ordinary Craft Freemasonry is that no Mason may invite an outsider to join. Anyone wishing to become a Freemason must take the initiative and seek two sponsors from within the Brotherhood.* The position is reversed for Freemasons of the 3rd Degree who wish to be elevated to the Higher Degrees. Initiation into the Rite is open only to those Master Masons who are *selected* by the Supreme Council. If a representative of the Supreme Council establishes contact with a Master Mason and concludes that he is suitable, the Candidate will be offered the chance of being 'perfected' and setting the first foot on the ladder to the 33rd Degree. But only a small proportion, even of the limited number of Freemasons who take the first step, progress beyond the 18th Degree, that of Knight of the Pelican and Eagle and Sovereign Prince Rose Croix of Heredom. With each Degree, the number of initiates diminishes. The 31st Degree (Grand Inspector Inquisitor Commander) is restricted to 400 members; the 32nd (Sublime Prince of the Royal Secret) to 180; and the 33rd – the pre-eminent Grand Inspectors General – to only 75 members.

While the Armed Forces are strongly represented in ordinary Freemasonry, the 'Antient and Accepted Rite of the Thirty-Third Degree' is particularly attractive to military men. Grand Inspectors General (i.e. members of the Supreme Council) have included Field Marshal Earl Alexander of Tunis, successively Commander-in-Chief in the Middle East and Allied Supreme Commander in the Mediterranean in the Second World War; Major-General Sir Leonard Henry Atkinson; Brigadier E. W. C. Flavell; Lieutenant-General Sir Harold Williams; Brigadier General

*This, at least, is the theory – and United Grand Lodge staunchly maintains that it is the practice. In reality most Entered Apprentices are recruited by existing Masons they know personally.

Edward Charles Walthall Delves Walthall; and scores more in the last two decades. Before his retirement in 1982 the Most Puissant Sovereign Grand Commander (the most senior Freemason of the 33rd Degree in England and Wales and Head of the Supreme Council) was Major-General Sir (Herbert) Ralph Hone, KCMG, KBE, MC, TD, and so on. There is no mention of Freemasonry in his entry in *Who's Who*, which lists every other decoration, award and distinction he has earned in his eighty-seven years, although becoming Britain's highest Freemason can have been of no little consequence to him. In masonic matters he would dispense with all the other abbreviations and simply sign himself, *Ralph Hone, 33°*. Born in 1896, he is also a Bailiff Grand Cross of the Order of St John of Jerusalem.

He was wounded during the First World War while serving with the British Expeditionary Force, went on to practise as a barrister-at-law in Uganda and Zanzibar in the 1920s, becoming Resident Magistrate in Zanzibar in 1928 and Crown Counsel of Tanganyika Territory two years later. In the thirties he was Attorney-General and Acting Chief Justice of Gibraltar, and Attorney-General of Uganda between 1937 and 1943. After serving as Chief Legal Adviser, Political Branch, and then Chief Political Officer, GHQ Middle East, he was appointed to the General Staff of the War Office in 1943. After the war he was Chief Civil Affairs Officer in Malaya for a year before becoming Secretary-General to the Governor-General of Malaya and then Deputy Commissioner-General in South-East Asia. In 1949 he was appointed Governor and Commander-in-Chief of North Borneo. At the end of five years there he spent seven years as Head of the Legal Division of the Commonwealth Relations Office. This took him into 1961 when he returned to the Bar. Among other posts at home and abroad in the next fourteen years he was a Constitutional Adviser to R. A. Butler's Advisers on Central Africa, to the South Arabian Government and the Bermuda Government. He was Standing Counsel to the Grand Bahama Port Authority until his retirement in 1975 at the age of seventy-nine. He succeeded Most Puissant Brother Sir Eric Studd, Bt, OBE, 33°, as Sovereign Grand Commander.

This, then, was the man who – at the time *The Brotherhood* was completed for New English Library – was truly Britain's highest Freemason, whatever might be said of the Duke of Kent, the current Grand Master of Craft Masonry. Page 39 shows the hierarchy over which the Most Puissant Sovereign Grand Commander presides, with the Duke of Kent's sub-hierarchy way down low.

Although in 1936, 1947 and 1967 Major-General Sir Ralph Hone held grand rank in the United Grand Lodge, and has achieved distinction in many fields, he is one of that brand of men who attain power without notoriety or fame. Few of the many hundreds of Freemasons I have interviewed had even heard of him, and of those few only five knew of him in his secret role as the highest Mason of the highest Degree. These five were all initiates of the Ancient and Accepted Rite: two Sovereign Princes Rose Croix of Heredom (18th Degree); one of the 180 Sublime Princes of the Royal Secret (32nd Degree); a 33rd Degree Grand Inspector General; and a former Grand Inspector Inquisitor of the 31st Degree who had renounced Freemasonry, in order, he said, to become 'a true and living Christian'. But beyond the fact that Major-General Sir Ralph was the preeminent member of the Supreme Council, none of them would say any more either about the man himself or about the rituals, the degrees or the administration of the Rite.

Sir Ralph's successor is Harold Devereux Still, former Grand Treasurer and Junior Grand Warden of the United

Grand Lodge of England, and Grand Treasurer and Grand
Scribe Nehemiah of the Supreme Grand Chapter of Royal
Arch Masons of England. He also attained the rank of
Grand Master of the United Religious, Military and
Masonic Orders of the Temple of St John of Jerusalem,
Palestine, Rhodes and Malta.

The Brotherhood attracts men of distinction in the
judiciary and legal profession, as will be seen later. One
such man is His Honour Judge Alan Stewart Trapnell, who
was appointed to the Circuit Bench in 1972. He is a Craft
Freemason of grand rank, having been Assistant Grand
Registrar in 1963, Junior Grand Deacon in 1971 and Senior
Grand Deacon in 1979. In 1969 he became Assistant Grand
Sojourner of the Supreme Grand Chapter of Royal Arch
Freemasons. All these details are listed in the *Masonic Year
Book*, which is now very difficult for non-Masons to come
by. What is not mentioned is that he is a Freemason of the
33rd Degree and Grand Inspector General for Middlesex.

Although Craft Freemasonry is worldwide in the sense
that it exists in most parts of the non-Communist world,
and even underground in parts of the eastern bloc, it has no
international organization. The Ancient and Accepted Rite
of the Thirty-Third Degree is the only cohesive masonic
group run on truly international lines. The Supreme
Council in London is one of many Supreme Councils in
various parts of the globe, of which the senior is the
Supreme Council of Charleston, USA, which effectively
operates a worldwide network of Freemasons in the most
powerful positions in the executive, legislature, judiciary
and armed forces as well as the industry, commerce and
professions of many nations.

The English working of the Rite – sometimes known by the
code name Rose Croix from the title of the initiate to the 18th
Degree – differs from the American in one basic respect. In
England and Wales only a few of the 33 degrees are conferred

by special ritual, while in the USA each degree has its own initiation ceremony. In this country, the 4th to 17th Degrees are conferred at once and in name only during initiation of the selected Freemason to the 18th Degree. To the few who rise higher than the 18th Degree, the 19th to 29th are conferred nominally during the ritual of initiation to the 30th Degree – that of Grand Elected Knight Kadosh or Knight of the Black and White Eagle. Degrees above the 30th are conferred singly. No initiate can rise highter than the 18th Degree without the unanimous agreement of the entire Supreme Council.

PART TWO

The Police

CHAPTER 6

The Great Debate

'The insidious effect of Freemasonry among the police has to be experienced to be believed.'

With these words, David Thomas, a former head of Monmouthshire CID, created a storm of protest in 1969 and reopened a debate that had started nearly a century before, when a conspiracy involving masonic police and masonic criminals brought about the destruction of the original Detective Department in Scotland Yard.

Since then allegations of masonic corruption within the police have been rife. The Jack the Ripper murders in the East End of London in 1888 were perpetrated according to masonic ritual and a subsequent police cover-up was led by the Commissioner and Assistant Commisioner of the Metropolitan Police, both Freemasons.

There have been allegations of charges being dropped against criminal Masons by police Masons; of unfair promotions on the basis of masonic membership and not merit; of non-Masons being hounded out of the service; of livelihoods ruined; of blackmail and violence; of discipline eroded by a system in which a Chief Superintendent, Commander or even on occasion an Assistant Chief Constable or Chief Constable can be made to kneel in submission before one of his own constables; and, in recent times, of robbery and murder planned between police and criminals at Lodge meetings.

It is almost certainly true that the corruption which led to Operation Countryman, the biggest investigation of police malpractice ever mounted in Britain, would never have arisen had a masonic City of London Police commissioner in the 1970s not turned a blind eye to the activities of several desperately corrupt Freemasons under his command.

And in the purges that took place at New Scotland Yard in the early 1970s, masonic police up to the rank of Commander were found to be involved in corrupt dealings with masonic criminals.

The debate about Freemasonry in the police began in 1877 with the sensational discovery that virtually every member of the Detective Department at Scotland Yard, up to and including the second-in-command, was in the pay of a gang of vicious swindlers. The corruption had started in 1872 when Inspector John Meiklejohn, a Freemason, was introduced at a Lodge meeting in Islington to a criminal called William Kurr. Kurr had then been a Freemason for some years. One night at the Angel, Islington, the two masonic brothers exchanged intimacies. Kurr was operating a bogus 'betting agency' swindle and was sorely in need of an accomplice within the force to warn him as and when the Detective Department had sufficient information against him to move in. Meiklejohn agreed to accept £100, nearly half his annual salary, to supply information.

The Detective Department at Scotland Yard had been set up in 1842. In the 1870s there were only fifteen detectives to cover the entire capital. These were under the command of the legendary Superintendent Frederick Williamson, described by one writer as a man of 'the strictest probity, and of great experience and shrewdness'. Under Williamson, the most senior detectives in London were Chief Inspector George Clarke, Chief Inspector William Palmer and Chief Detective Inspector Nathaniel Druscovitch – all Freemasons.

The criminal partnership of Inspector Meiklejohn, who, interestingly, was 'Countryman' in various coded messages which passed between the criminals, and William Kurr continued. Eventually Kurr teamed up with Harry Benson, a psychopathic confidence trickster who had scarred and crippled himself for life by setting himself on fire in his bed at Newgate Prison. One by one, Meiklejohn corrupted nearly all the junior officers in the Detective Department, and introduced several of his most senior masonic colleagues in the department to Benson and Kurr, and they too began to accept bribes for information and services rendered.

The enterprises of Kurr and Benson came to the attention of Superintendent Williamson after they had successfully swindled the Comtesse de Goncourt of £10,000. Williamson placed the enquiry in the hands of one of his most respected men, Chief Detective Inspector Nathaniel Druscovitch. But Druscovitch was one of those who had allowed himself to be tempted into the masonic–criminal circle, and was in the pay of the very men he was now detailed to investigate. Clarke, the sixty-year-old senior officer of the department; Palmer; and a masonic solicitor named Edward Frogatt were all drawn into the conspiracy. From there the corruption spread, its full extent lost in the tangled web of deceit woven by those involved. When the men were eventually brought to justice, the Detective Department lay in ruins and the following year, 1878, saw the complete reorganization of plain clothes investigation in the Metropolitan Police with the setting up of the modern Criminal Investigation Department.

By coincidence, it was exactly one hundred years after the arrest of Meiklejohn and his brethren in July 1877 that Scotland Yard detectives were again in the dock on serious corruption charges, when once again an Old Bailey jury heard of collusion between detectives and criminals who belonged to the same masonic Lodges.

But before going on to see how history repeated itself at the Yard (see Chapter 8, below) and the startling events that affected the unique City of London Police, taking it into its darkest period, it is important to take a look at certain episodes in the years between the imprisonment of Scotland Yard Detective Inspector Meiklejohn (Freemason) in 1877 and the imprisonment of Scotland Yard Detective Chief Superintendent Moody (Freemason) in 1977.

In my book *Jack the Ripper: The Final Solution* I demonstrate how the murders of five prostitutes in the East End of London in the late summer and autumn of 1888 were perpetrated not by one person working alone but by three men operating together for a specific purpose. Four of the five women – the man in charge of the operation had been deliberately misled about the identity of the fourth victim – shared, it was later revealed by one of the killers, a dangerous secret. They had to be silenced.

It was a period when England was perilously unstable. Many believed that revolution was just beyond the horizon. The prostitutes had learned first-hand of a secret the most potent forces in the British government had been striving to maintain for nearly four years. The Prime Minister himself believed that if the secret got out, the throne itself would be in peril. In an age of fierce anti-Catholic feeling, Prince Albert Victor Christian Edward, grandson of Queen Victoria and Heir Presumptive to the throne, had illegally married and fathered a child by a Roman Catholic commoner.

In the early part of the operation, the wife of the Prince

had been bundled off to a lunatic asylum by no less a personage than Sir William Gull, Physician in Ordinary to the Queen. All this, I hasten to add, without the Queen's knowledge. When it was realized that others had to be silenced, Prime Minister Lord Salisbury turned again to Gull, never imagining that the good doctor, who was more than a little unstable, would go to the lengths he did. Gull was a Freemason. He decided that the penal oaths he had taken as a Freemason were more than mere symbolism. Gull concluded that the only safe way to silence the women was to eliminate them. And the proper way to execute them was as traitors to the nation, in which, according to one masonic writer of the period, 'true Freemasonry is about to be more powerful than Royalty'. In other words, they would be mutilated according to the penalties laid out in masonic ritual. That his intention was carried to its conclusion is borne out by the ritualized and specifically masonic nature of the injuries inflicted on the Ripper victims. Contemporary descriptions of the mutilations contained in *The Times* and the secret Home Office file on the case, to which I had full access during my investigations, compare with the mimed murders in masonic rituals and with an illustration by Hogarth of an actual masonic murder, showing startling parallels.

The importance of the Ripper murders was not so much in the individual tragedies of the five women who died at the hands of a demented Freemason and his two toadies, although those were disturbing enough, but in the national tragedy of what followed: an official cover-up of immense proportions that confirmed that Freemasonry really was the unseen power behind the throne and government alike.

The man actively responsible for concealing the truth behind the Ripper murders was Sir Charles Warren, Commissioner of the Metropolitan Police and one of the country's most eminent Freemasons. Warren impeded the

investigation of the murders at every turn, caused endless
confusion and delays, and personally destroyed the only
clue the Ripper ever left. This was a scrawled chalk message
on a wall inside a tenement block near the site of the fourth
murder. Beneath the message was a blood-soaked piece of
cloth which Jack the Ripper had recently cut from the
apron of his latest victim. The message itself, according to a
careful copy made by a conscientious PC who was at the
scene early - which had been concealed in the Scotland
Yard files on the case for nearly ninety years before I gained
access to them - read:

> The Juwes are
> The Men That
> > will not
> be blamed
> > for nothing

The moment he was told of this, Warren, who had not
previously ventured near the East End, rushed to the place
before the message could be photographed and *washed it
away*. This has never been explained. The truth was that
Warren, who had been exalted to the Royal Arch in 1861,
had realized that the writing on the wall was a *masonic*
message.

Much of masonic ritual centres on murder. At the 3rd
Degree, the victim is Hiram Abiff, mythical architect in
charge of the building of Solomon's temple. The ceremony
involves the mimed murder of Hiram by three Apprentice
Masons, and his subsequent resurrection. The three
Apprentices are named Jubela, Jubelo and Jubelum -
known collectively as the *Juwes*. In masonic lore, the Juwes
are hunted down and executed, 'by the breast being torn
open and the heart and vitals taken out and thrown over
the left shoulder', which closely parallels the details of Jack
the Ripper's *modus operandi*.

Warren, a founder of the Quatuor Coronati Lodge of

Masonic Research and by the time of the Ripper murders a Past Grand Sojourner of the Supreme Grand Chapter, knew only too well that the writing on the wall was telling the world, 'The *Freemasons* are the men that will not be blamed for nothing.'

The City of London Police is unique. Descended from the Watch and Ward which manned the City's walls in case of attack in the thirteenth century, the force belongs to the City and is financed largely by the City. It is controlled by a Commissioner who is equal in rank and standing with the Commissioner of the thirty-times-bigger Metropolitan Police. The Commissioner of the City of London Police is appointed by the Court of Common Council of the City Corporation and he and his force are overseen by a police committee of selected Common Councilmen (elected councillors) and Aldermen. The City of London is steeped in tradition, and it is possibly the ever-present awareness of ancient customs, of the perpetual intrusion by the past into the present, that explains why Freemasonry has been so prevalent among officers in the City of London Police.

Cecil Rolph Hewitt, criminologist, author, journalist and Vice-President of the Howard League for Penal Reform, joined the City of London Police in 1921. Writing as C. H. Rolph in the weekly news magazine *Police Review* in September 1981, he said:

I saw enough chicanery and favouritism fostering Freemasonry in the police service to satisfy me that it ought to be barred. It wasn't so much that the Masons got actual preferment (though I'm sure some of them did); they *believed* they would, and the belief devalued their characters in a way that was as odd as it was disturbing.

Hewitt told me later, 'I was instructing City of London Police recruits from 1931 to about 1940, holding during

that time the dizzily rising ranks of Sub-Inspector,
Inspector and Chief Inspector. We had a school room at
Snow Hill police station, opposite Holborn Viaduct
railway terminus. I had to teach them rudimentary criminal
law, police practice, and, I suppose, some kind of social
ethics – of the kind now greeted as innovatory in the
Scarman Report. The recruits often seemed to believe that
if in due course they could join a Lodge their careers would
be assured. I sometimes found it difficult to disabuse them,
and the result was that when their time came to study for
promotion, which involves a lot of hard work and is
specially hard, in my opinion, on the relatively unlettered
types who usually join the police, they just didn't work
hard enough and they failed their exams time after time.
These pre-conceived notions about the value of Freemasonry as a means to advancement had been inherited, as
a rule, from parents or uncles, often policemen themselves.'

Hewitt left the City Police in 1946 and joined the *New
Statesman* as a staff writer the following year. He was the
editor of the Society of Authors' journal *The Author* for
four years and between 1947 and 1978 produced nineteen
books, mostly on the police, law and crime. The evidence
of one of his contemporaries in the City of London Police
is particularly valuable in building up a picture of the
degree to which the high incidence of Masonry within the
force influenced it between the 1920s and the late 1950s.
Gilbert Stone, who joined the force in 1927, was a much-
respected officer. Although a non-Mason, he is not anti-
Mason, and gave a considered and self-evidently balanced
account.

'I retired from the City Police early in 1959 as a 1st Class
Superintendent,'* he told me. 'I served under two Com-
missioners, Sir Hugh Turnbull and Sir Arthur Young, and
I am sure that neither of them were Masons. The Assistant

*This rank has since been upgraded to Chief Superintendent.

Commissioner in my early days was, I am pretty certain, a
Mason. Quite a number of senior officers were Masons and
some were not.

'I would imagine that there was a greater proportion of
CID officers of all ranks in Masonry than uniformed
officers, and I got the general impression without any
evidence to substantiate it that Masons had a better chance
of getting into the CID than non-Masons. I must say, however, that in my early days or years in the force in the late
twenties I did for about a year or so work in the CID at my
Divisional Station, doing clerical and admin work, and on
several occasions I was invited by several CID men,
including a Detective Inspector and several Detective
Sergeants who were Masons, to enter the CID, which
invitations I always declined. I mention this to show that
the CID was not the exclusive preserve of the Masons, but
I must add that I often wondered whether, if I did accept
the invitations and enter the CID, I would then have been
invited to become a Mason.

'A lot of constables were in Masonry, although I would
not like to hazard a guess on what proportion. Some
belonged when they joined the force. I think it reasonable
to assume that quite a lot of them were, or became, Masons
because it would confer some advantages, whether by
giving them an easier "ride" in the force, or because they
thought it would help them with promotion, or perhaps
both.

'There is only one case, as far as I can recollect, where a
Mason did reap an advantage by being one. He was a man
who occasionally got drunk and in that condition often
turned violent and assaulted people, including senior
officers. On more than one occasion his conduct resulted in
a disciplinary charge against him, and on each occasion he
virtually got away with it. A small fine, 19s 6d if I
remember aright, was imposed and that was that. Often he

was not charged. The general view of his colleagues, which included me, was that had he not been a Mason he would have been sacked long ago.

'On one occasion a colleague invited me to think about becoming a Mason and said that if I was interested he would be pleased to propose me, but, as you can gather, I was not interested, and no pressure was brought to bear on me.

'I personally was not affected, so far as I am aware, by not being a Mason. I met and served with some Masons who were delightful colleagues and real gentlemen. I met some Masons who were quite the opposite. And that applies equally to colleagues who were not Masons.'

Ex-Superintendent Stone introduced me to Albert Treves, 'an old colleague and friend who retired as an Inspector in the City, who was a very active Mason and was also a very charming and gentlemanly person'.

Treves told me that during his fifty years' service in and with the police, the subject of Masonry was seldom if ever mentioned to him, and to his knowledge had no influence in any way. His impression was that it was a private matter that concerned only members of the Brotherhood.

I have spoken to nearly seventy former and currently serving officers of the City force, about a third of them Masons. There can be no doubt that whatever part Freemasonry played in the distant past, by the late 1960s it was very hard for non-Masons to obtain promotion above Superintendent in the uniformed branch, and above Sergeant in the CID – even under the non-masonic Commissioner Sir Arthur Young. A masonic sub-structure had grown up, which enabled Freemasons in every department and every division to come together in secret and influence decisions in the force to a remarkable degree. But more of that later.

David Gillespie (a pseudonym) joined Essex Police in 1937 as a PC and retired as Acting Detective Chief Inspector of the same force in 1963. According to several independent statements I have received from men in this force, it has been dominated by Freemasons for generations.

'The application form didn't list Freemasonry under Special Qualifications,' Gillespie told me, 'but in fact from Inspector up to and including Assistant Chief Constable, four out of every five were practising Freemasons, all promoted by one man.'

During his career, Gillespie served at Clacton-on-Sea and the adjoining area around Holland-on-Sea, in the Staff Division CID, at Tilbury Docks, Braintree, and Rochford near Southend-on-Sea. His penultimate job was a £30,000 smuggling run, and he rounded off his career with a successful investigation into murder on the high seas.

The Chief Constable of Essex for much of Gillespie's service was Sir Francis Richard Jonathan Peel, who died in 1979. A direct descendant of Sir Robert Peel, he is remembered in the force as a remote figure who would simply rubber-stamp the decisions of his most senior men. Gillespie liked Peel and reveres his memory, but says that 'he was so intent on creating a vast gulf betwixt his ivory tower and the untouchables that he left promotion to one man'. That man, Assistant Chief Constable John Crockford, was a Freemason.

'Crockford ran the promotion field for twenty years until he retired about 1953. He was a likeable man in many ways who conferred many kindnesses, although many men in the force hated him. Despite his unchallenged power in the service, he saw himself primarily as a Freemason, and one of extremely high rank.

'Of course, not all promotions of Freemasons in my force were disreputable, but many were. The most awful in my time were Walter Stephen Pope, a ridiculous little squirt, to Super, and that of James Peters. Words fail me. They were derided even by their own kidney.

'Both these men were Masons. By police standards Pope was a little man with an inverted inferiority complex, possibly for that reason. He had a high IQ in my opinion, but he was just a police clerk who climbed. He never to my knowledge caught a crook, never saw a blow struck in anger, and never looked in at Tilbury Docks on the night of the sainted Patrick when we were struggling with the Micks and the Molls outside the Presbytery or at the Sign of the Anchor Inn.

'Pope had a hectoring voice and a pompous manner, which in all charity he probably couldn't help. He was a ridiculous figure who upset the troops in every branch he entered. I had him, for my sins, in four divisions. His leadership, of how to get the best out of his men, was pathetic. I sometimes wondered if he were quite sane. Now and then men approached me for a written application *in extremis* to get them away from him. I complied. Such reports fetched up on ACC Crockford's desk and proved successful. None of this prevented them making Pope a Divisional Superintendent.

'But the case of James Peters is if anything worse, if such were possible. Peters was an amiable half-wit. He was simply one of nature's dunderheads, a twit in any company who made one cringe. And he was a congenital liar. But he had become a Freemason at twenty-one and never missed a Lodge meeting. When he was promoted to station clerk, the resultant shock waves startled even the serried ranks of the Magic Circle, which is saying something. When the promotion was published, a certain high-ranker, another Freemason, threw the relevant Force Order B across the room in a fury. He knew Peters.

'Later, on our sergeants' training course, he confided in me that during a heart-to-heart talk, Crockford had told him his future was assured. It was. His rate of promotion after that was astonishing, and he retired at a rank very very few policemen achieve.'

Detective Superintendent David Thomas, former head of Monmouthshire CID, devoted four pages of his memoirs, *Seek Out The Guilty*, to an examination of Freemasonry in the police. Before this, criticism of alleged masonic influence in the police forces of Britain had usually come from the lower ranks. Such men as did raise the question were almost invariably dismissed by their masonic colleagues as embittered failures who used Freemasonry as a scapegoat. This was not wholly unfair. Freemasons, like Communists, Jews, Gipsies and Negroes, have frequently been used as scapegoats by those simplistic souls who like to believe all society's ills have one source: a conspiracy of aliens and subversives dedicated to the overturning of the status quo. Hitler spoke of falling into a 'nest of Freemasons', and seems to have loathed them as much as he did the Jews – certainly he persecuted them as ruthlessly. Mussolini, too, hated Freemasons and during his dictatorship many were executed. On a more moderate level, the belief that no one is promoted in the police unless he is a Freemason is frequently held by non-masonic officers who would be unsuitable for promotion anyway. Unable to accept their own failings, they all too easily subscribe to the conspiracy theory and latch on to Freemasonry as a convenient scapegoat.

On the other hand, the belief that Freemasonry often exerts an improper influence is also held by many police officers who are Freemasons – because there is no doubt at all that many Freemasons have been promoted by other Freemasons for no other reason than that they are members of the same secret Brotherhood. The blanket denial that this happens, or that it can happen, issued by the United Grand Lodge, is untruthful.

The significance of David Thomas's words was that they came from a man of unimpeachable integrity and of high standing in the police and the community. Here was no hot-headed PC, freshly rejected for promotion, flinging wild allegations round the 'nick' canteen, but a successful senior officer in retirement making a reasoned statement and calling for a Royal Commission to investigate a situation he regarded as sinister and dangerous.

During my thirty-two years' police service I saw a great deal of this secret society in action, not only in my own force but also in the many others I visited as honorary secretary of the detective conferences of No 8 Police District, which comprises the whole of Wales, Monmouthshire and Herefordshire.* Sometimes my visits took me to other areas, but wherever I went the story was the same.

'Are you on the Square?' or 'Are you on the Level?' are all naïve enquiries as to whether or not one is a Mason.

Thomas thought that of the total number of policemen in 1969, probably only a small percentage were Freemasons. 'But that small percentage forms an important and all-powerful group, the majority of whom are senior officers of the rank of Inspector, or above. Their influence on the service is incalculable.'

He assured readers that Masonry often did affect promotion, and that many sergeants and PCs became Masons for this reason. In this way, the system became self-perpetuating. Without implying that Masons will ensure the promotion of their brethren in the service, Thomas was certain that when two men of equal ability came before a promotion board, the dice would be loaded in favour of the

*The reorganization of police forces in the 1970s changed this.

Mason because of the masonic composition of many boards.

The official response to Thomas's call for a Royal Commission was predictable: like the United Grand Lodge, successive governments have adopted an ignore-it-and-it-will-go-away policy on calls to investigate any state of affairs in which Freemasonry is alleged to be playing a questionable role. An unnamed writer in the *Sunday Telegraph* said this: 'I can confirm that many detectives believe Freemasons exercise an insidious secret influence inside Scotland Yard. But it seems now the suggestion has come into the open the lie may be given to this well-entrenched belief.'

A spokesman for the Police Federation, the police 'trade union' representing all ranks up to Inspector, was quoted as saying that the Federation had never received a complaint from anyone losing promotion or being victimized for not being a Freemason. This was untrue. I have seen copies of statements of just such a nature submitted to the Federation both before and after the date of the Federation's pronouncement. Indeed, only eleven months before the publication of Thomas's book, a Northampton police Sergeant submitted a three-page typed report, every page signed by himself at the bottom and every surname typed in capitals as if it were a formal witness's statement. In it he complained of two incidents:

In March of last year I was told in no uncertain terms by Det Insp Brian JENKINS [pseudonym] that if I did not join the lodge he would personally see to it that I was never promoted above my present rank . . . On December 24 last, just before the Christmas Party, I was called in to see Chief Insp Howard FIELD [pseudonym]. He said that life could be made very uncomfortable for officers who tried to buck the system. I asked him what he meant. He said, 'You are not on the square, are you. I won't say any more than that.'

The complainant told me the Federation never replied. He said, 'Life became intolerable after that. They treated me like a leper. I was either ignored completely by most of them or they kept picking arguments with me. Complaint after complaint was made against me. It was ridiculous. I stuck it for about a year but then I just got out.'

Now a Superintendent in the North East of England, my informant achieved very rapid promotion *without* joining the Brotherhood.

The Federation spokesman who told the *Sunday Telegraph* that complaints of this nature had never been received, went on to say: 'Under modern promotion procedures it is difficult to see how it could happen. We have national promotion exams. In London, promotion up to station sergeant is decided by exams. Boards decide other promotions. It would be gross exaggeration to say Freemason members had any undue influence.'

What the spokesman did not point out was that passing a promotion examination did not mean automatic promotion. There are many PCs and Sergeants in the country who have qualified as Inspectors, but because of a dearth of vacancies at the higher ranks, they remain at the bottom. In the 26,000-strong Metropolitan Police there is a much greater chance of early promotion, as there is for an officer prepared to move from force to force; but in country forces it is often a case of dead men's shoes. And even when a vacancy arises, applicants go before promotion boards. In suggesting that examinations eliminated favouritism the Federation was therefore being less than truthful, and the reason is perhaps not hard to find. Until very recently the majority of regional representatives of the Police Federation were Freemasons. Even today, a large proportion of its civilian staff are ardent members of the Brotherhood.

There are two other allegations which have been made so frequently, and by such well-respected officers, two Assistant Chief Constables (one a Mason) included, that they should be mentioned, although it must be said that I have yet to see undeniable evidence. One claim is that masonic officers taking exams will make some kind of mark on their paper to indicate their affiliation to the Brotherhood. The most common, it is alleged, is the age-old masonic code of writing a capital 'A' in the form of the Brotherhood's Square and Compasses symbol, thus:

Alpha

This will be meaningless to a non-masonic examiner but will be immediately recognized by a fellow Mason. The other allegation, made by scores of officers of all ranks, is that masonic promotion boards sometimes slip masonic references into their conversation when interviewing. If the candidate for promotion responds correctly, it is said, his chances are immediately elevated.

The row about Freemasonry in the police blew up again in May 1972 when *Police Review* published an article by a thirty-five-year-old Sergeant of Nottinghamshire Combined Constabulary, Peter J. Welling. The article captured the feeling of many non-masonic police officers and provoked fierce opposition and loud agreement which were publicized in the daily press and on television. Welling said that from the beginning of his police career he had been made aware by members of the general public which of his police colleagues were Freemasons. In his early years in the police he thought most masonic officers were in the higher ranks.

This manifested itself in the instructions one would sometimes receive regarding one's attitude to certain members of the public who held prominent positions in public life and who committed infringements, if only minor infringements, of the law. I took this to be a legacy from the old watch committee and standing joint committee days when those governing bodies virtually held the efficiency of the Service by its purse strings. It was therefore extremely important for members of the senior ranks in the Service to have close contact, not only in committee, but also socially, with such persons who were no doubt closely aligned to the Freemasonry movement.*

However, with the progress of time, the conduct and structure of the Police Service has changed, and is continuing to change at a rapid pace. But there is an increasing awareness among junior members of the Service that, after passing the appropriate examinations, a sure way to promotion is through the Freemasonry movement. Thus there is a considerable amount of canvassing to be done which appears to be creating a split in the Service itself.

Sergeant Welling was concerned with the possible long-term effects of this. He thought that if increasing numbers of serving police officers were to join the Brotherhood, 'then a saturation point will be reached when the majority, if not all police officers, will be members'.

What consequences might this have? Welling thought the best way of finding an answer was to examine 'the terms of reference and ethics behind both the Police Service and the Freemasonry movement'. He went on:

It is a fact that when a Police Officer is appointed he takes an oath of allegiance to the Queen and the community to carry out his duties 'without fear or favour, malice or ill will'. It is not commonly known that on enrolment to a Freemasonry Lodge a Freemason also takes an oath. I do not profess to know what form this oath takes or how it is administered, but it is most certainly an oath of allegiance not only to members of his own Lodge but to

*This kind of woolly phrase is misleading. Men are either Freemasons or not Freemasons. No 'close alignment' without membership is possible.

all members of the Freemasonry movement. To assist him to recognize other Freemasons he is taught secret handshakes and other secret signs. This type of association taken throughout the country forms a formidable chain of contact and associates from all walks of life.

It was in this 'formidable chain of contact' that Welling felt the danger of Freemasonry in the police lay. 'When this country has a national police service* criticism may well be levelled by minority groups against the police that the service is not impartial. The question I ask is – how can a Freemasonry Police officer be impartial? No man can serve two masters.'

The Sergeant's suggestion was for the Police Federation and the Home Office to 'join hands' on the subject of Freemasonry and press for legislation to prohibit serving policemen from taking any oath in any secret society, and to compel new recruits to renounce affiliation to any such society 'in the same manner as he would if he was an active member of a political party'.

Two days after the publication of Welling's article, the *Sunday Telegraph* ran a long story which claimed that the Sergeant's call for a ban on Masonry in the police was 'supported by thousands of policemen'. The reporter, Peter Gladstone Smith, wrote:

Sgt Welling said to me yesterday he had very good friends who were Freemasons and he had nothing against Freemasonry outside the police. He was concerned about disciplinary proceedings when it came to complaints.

'If a person who is a Freemason complains against a police officer and that complaint is investigated by a senior officer who is a Freemason, then that cannot be an impartial enquiry.' His attitude was not 'sour grapes' and he himself was promoted early.

Cdr Ray Anning, head of Scotland Yard's new 60-strong

*Which it still doesn't have, more than eleven years on.

round-the-clock complaints branch, told me that he was not a Freemason. At the same time he believed the suggestion was 'utter nonsense'.

The *Daily Telegraph*'s crime correspondent, T. A. Sandrock, wrote a similar story the following day, which ended with this observation:

I have discussed this subject myself during many years' association with policemen, asking on hundreds of occasions if they would be restricted as Freemasons in investigations into a criminal act if the suspect was also a Freemason. Invariably their answer has been that they would continue to do their duty as police officers.

Can this distinguished journalist have imagined that if any masonic officers did feel restricted in this way, they would openly have admitted it? It was nonsense to intimate such a thing.

On the next day, Tuesday 9 May, Welling was interviewed on BBC Television's *Nationwide* programme. Also in the studio was Brian Bailey, a local government officer and former Freemason.

Presenter Michael Barratt asked Bailey, 'What do you say to these charges that a sure way to promotion in the police force is through the Freemasonry movement?'

The ex-Mason replied, 'I don't think there's any substance in this. I lapsed my membership of the masonic movement for various reasons, but it seems to me that you might as well say that if the Chief Constable is a keen Rugby enthusiast and you play a good game of Rugby, you are on the inside track.'

And then he added a comment which seems to run counter to his main argument. 'I think one gets all sorts of ideas that there are ways of getting preferment. I think that Freemasonry is just one of them. I doubt very much *these days* if there is any real substance in it.' (My italics.)

The admission that Freemasonry did have an undesirable influence 'up to about ten years ago', 'until only recently', 'not since the last war', 'up until a year or so ago', 'around five years back' has been made to me by scores of Freemasons and former Freemasons. Most are prepared to say it had an influence 'then' – never now. It is interesting to note that in a period when, according to many of my masonic informants, Masonry *was* exercising undue influence in the police, there were those who even then were denying its existence except in the past.

The 'Rugby enthusiast' point of view was taken up by Welling, who replied: 'If Freemasons were as open as a member of a Rugby club would be, then I would have no objections. It's the secrecy that surrounds the whole movement which I object to.'

Bailey did not like the secrecy either. 'One of the things I disliked in the Craft was its secrecy. I think it's bound to give rise to suspicion. It doesn't follow that this suspicion is well founded, however.'

The controversy arising from Welling's article continued in the correspondence columns of *Police Review* for the next three months.

Chief Superintendent T. W. A. Lucas, who became a Freemason after achieving senior rank in the police, said that nothing would influence him to show favour to anyone. 'Neither do I hope to seek such favour, and, while obviously I cannot speak for all, those of senior rank whom I know in many forces hold the same views.' He said:

Everyone who enters Freemasonry is, at the outset, strictly forbidden to countenance any act which may have a tendency to subvert the peace and good order of society; he must pay due obedience to the law of any state in which he resides or which may afford him protection, and he must never be remiss in the allegiance due to the Sovereign of his native land. At no time in

his capacity as a Freemason is he permitted to discuss or to
advance views on theological or political questions.*

A PC from Neath in Glamorgan wrote to say that he had
been a Freemason since 1955. He had qualified for
promotion in 1963 but was still at the lowest rank. Further
evidence that the police service was not totally the domain
of Freemasons came from John Williamson, CBE, QPM,
President of the Christian Police Association in Northampton. He said Welling's article 'moved me strangely',
and continued:

After 45 years in the service I have found that being a Christian –
that other brotherhood – stood me in better stead when it came
to promotion interviews, particularly in the old days. On one
occasion I was able to quote a verse from the 75th Psalm:
'Promotion cometh from neither the east nor the west but from
the Lord'. I have always believed that it is the worker bees that
keep the hive working and strong. I do not think that
Freemasonry was that powerful for I made my way through the
ranks to become Chief Constable of Northampton at 33. Never
was I approached by anyone to become a Mason . . . I went into
the service in 1910 fearing God and the Sergeant, and came out in
1955 fearing God.

A Freemason who signed himself T. M. T. described
Welling's article as 'a load of rubbish . . . on a subject he
obviously knows nothing about'. There were many letters
in a similar vein. 'Freemasons,' declared T. M. T., 'are the
backbone of the community. They are the most public
spirited and charitable people he [Welling] will find. That is
if he cares to look. Why has he picked on Freemasons when
there are other "secret societies" he could expose?'
One of those phrases admitting that the Brotherhood

*It is perfectly true that the Brotherhood forbids its members to discuss
business, politics or religion, but there is ample evidence from present and
past Masons that this is rarely obeyed.

had influence but only in the past reared its head in a letter
from C. P. Cheshire. This time it was: 'Since Edwardian
days Freemasonry has not had the influence ascribed to it.'
The majority of Freemasons who know anything about the
police admit that the Brotherhood has until some point in
the past – remote or recent, depending on the individuals –
exerted influence within the police forces of this country.
None of them has been able to answer satisfactorily why, at
the particular moment in history they have chosen, the
Brotherhood's influence either dwindled appreciably or
ceased altogether.

In this connection the view of *Police Review*, or at least
its then editor Brian Clark, is worthy of note:

In pre-war days [my italics] it was a power to be reckoned with in
the Police Service and in many Forces, membership of the 'square'
was virtually a qualification for promotion. The falling off of the
influence of the movement is related to the 'liberalization' of the
Police Service and the Freemasons who remain tend to be found in
the senior ranks of the Service – particularly those with pre-war
service. Young men are not interested in the pseudo religiosity of
Freemasonry and all its secret ritual.

Even if this decline in interest among young policemen
was apparent in 1972, and I have found no evidence of it, it
is most certainly untrue today. Freemasonry in the police is
as high today as ever. And while a great number of senior
officers are members of the Brotherhood, so too are many
Constables and Sergeants. Back to Clark's assessment of
the situation a decade ago:

Nepotism, through Freemasonry, may still be a factor in
promotion, albeit to a decreasing degree, but what is still a serious
matter is that Freemasons (and come to that Rotarians, Lions,
Roundtablers) tend to expect favours from fellow members who
are police officers. A few policemen have been so embarrassed by
what is expected of them that they have been obliged to dissociate
themselves from Freemasonry.

A former Sergeant of the City of London Police, Frederick E. Moore, a non-Mason, had this to say:

As a young Constable, despite my keeping an open mind on the subject, it became increasingly evident that the suspicion, not without foundation, was right: membership of one of these fraternities [i.e. secret societies] was an advantage especially for those seeking promotion, for defaulters in disciplinary cases, and when top brass belonged to your Lodge, who could go wrong?

Freemason PC Robert Glencross of Fife replied thus to Sergeant Welling's criticisms:

There are Freemasons in every trade and not only the Police and there could be those who have reached high ranks in those fields. If junior members of the service feel that the road to success is paved with handshakes they are in for a big disappointment. Among any group of people some will take advantage of whatever benefits are going but there are others who further the aim of the group itself, and one seldom hears from them.

While I am not at liberty to divulge the form of oath taken by Freemasons it in no way conflicts with an officer's duty . . . Freemasonry is not so secret that it is impossible to find out who its members are. Its secrets are there for anyone to learn who wants to join.

This last comment holds true for the Mafia and the Ku Klux Klan, of course, so does not answer Welling's point about the secrecy of Masonry breeding suspicion among the uninitiated. And as for finding out who its members are, a non-Mason has only to ask for help at United Grand Lodge to be told, 'It is not our policy to make membership lists of our Lodges available to enquirers.' (See Epilogue, page 307.)

But one point made by PC Glencross, and by a multitude of Masons before and since, is true up to a point: the oaths, or obligations to use the masonic term, if properly interpreted, should not create the kind of dual allegiance most 'profane' policemen are concerned about. (See Appendix 3.)

Eight weeks after the publication of the original article, a letter appeared from a former police officer, a non-Mason of Malvern Link, Worcestershire. 'The letters on Freemasonry in the service filled me with remorse,' began ex-Detective Chief Inspector Ralph Jones ironically.

When I joined a large force before the war three-quarters of divisional Superintendents and above belonged to the Craft, a position that still obtains. I see now that most of their appointments only *appeared* bizarre, but were really based on merit.

The tradesmen who whispered down the years, 'Met your Super last night. Don't you want your stripes?' were having me on . . . What shamed me was the revelation that all those old mates who climbed like blue meteors from PC to the top in quick time just *happened* to belong to the Craft but were in fact devoted to Christianity and charitable works. They could have fooled me.

As a practising Christian with a son an Anglican priest, I doubt if I have quite got the moral fibre to qualify. But now I realize that the parcelling out of promotions and the dispensing of rough justice on delinquents behind closed doors is merely benevolent paternalism. Long may it reign.

The fact that the Police Federation was dominated by Freemasons did not inhibit the editor of the Federation's journal *Police* from publishing this complaint from Metropolitan Police Sergeant Robin Kirby in 1977:

All my service, I have been aware that it is a distinct advantage to be a Freemason. Doors are opened, rank structures are broken down and men normally destined to perform shiftwork all their service are spirited on to 9 A.M. to 5 P.M. jobs, often never to return to the mundane vulgarity of early, late and nights.

The following issue of *Police* contained one of the most serious allegations about Freemasonry in the police to have appeared in print up to that time. Blair Watt, a Thames Valley PC for sixteen years, wrote:

I speak from personal experience of no less than three occasions on which I have been approached, and even threatened, by more senior officers who sought to influence my dealing with fellow Freemasons and relatives of fellow Freemasons, with regard to offences committed by them.

Watt said later, 'I'm either very brave or an idiot. I was approached by senior officers on quite serious offences. But it must be said that nothing came of their pressure.'

He was not prepared to name the individuals involved, he said, for fear of repercussions. Depending chiefly on whether they are Masons or non-Masons, people have said that Watt's reluctance to give full details was quite understandable, given the power of Masonry in the police, or that it indicated he was inventing the story. Watt himself died shortly afterwards, of natural causes, so a conclusive investigation of his claim is impossible.

CHAPTER 7

The Men at the Top

There are fifty-two police forces in England, Wales, Scotland and Northern Ireland. These comprise ten combined forces in England and Wales, two combined forces in Scotland, thirty-one county forces in England and Wales, six Scottish regional forces, the two London forces and the Royal Ulster Constabulary. I wrote in 1981 to every one of the fifty Chief Constables and both London Commissioners. From this survey, and from private enquiries involving more than 200 informants between the ranks of Chief Inspector and Chief Constable in forces all over the UK, I have been able to identify with certainty only fourteen as non-Masons.

These are C. James Anderton (Greater Manchester); Ronald Gregory (West Yorkshire); R. Birch (Warwickshire); A. F. C. Clissitt (Hertfordshire); G. E. Fenn (Cheshire); Robert Sim (Tayside); A. Morrison (Grampian); Sir George Terry (Sussex); Sir Kenneth Newman (Metropolitan Commissioner since October 1982); Peter Marshall (City of London); G. Charlton (Norfolk); Philip Myers (North Wales); Peter Imbert (Thames Valley); and W. G. Sutherland (Bedfordshire).

The consensus among my most reliable, high-ranking informants is that of the remaining thirty-eight Chief Constables, no fewer than thirty-three members are of the

Brotherhood. If this is correct, more than sixty per cent of all police chiefs in the UK are Freemasons. According to sources within the Police Federation, the Association of Chief Police Officers, the Scottish Police Federation, the Police Superintendents' Association, police forces all over the country and also within the Police Authority for Northern Ireland as well as retired senior police officers and former Chief Constables, this figure is about ten or twelve per cent lower than it was before the amalgamation of police forces.

Police chiefs who replied to my enquiry but refused to answer the question 'Are you a Freemason?' included C. F. Payne (Cleveland) and Alex Campbell (Dumfries and Galloway). Campbell told me, 'I consider that whether or not a man is a Freemason or for that matter whether he is an Orangeman, a member of the Black Preceptory or a member of the Ancient Order of Hibernians is a matter for him alone. Likewise his religious persuasion, be he Protestant, Roman Catholic, atheist or agnostic is a matter for him. I would point out, however, that in my police experience extending over forty-three years, irrespective of the persuasion of senior officers I have found them performing their duties and accepting their responsibilities with complete impartiality.'

Another Chief Constable told me, 'I am well aware of the traditions of Freemasonry and I agree with you there is much misunderstanding, and yet it is not always what exists that is important but other people's perception of what exists. For professional reasons I have never thought it right for a senior police officer in particular to be associated with any political, religious, social or cultural group to the extent where decisions may be seen to be biased or actually to be biased, even if subconsciously.

'I can say that from time to time decisions which have

been made concerning advancement or discipline have often been perceived, however rightly or wrongly, as having been influenced by the bonds of Freemasonry. I do believe that sometimes the "reds under the beds" theory can apply to Freemasonry as it can to politics and religion . . . It is my impression that the proportion of police officers who belong to the movement becomes higher as you reach the higher echelons of the service. I am not however suggesting that this is cause and effect, but merely noting the phenomenon.

'I think my own views could be summed up by saying that what a man does with his private life in these matters of religion, politics or culture is part of the freedom of our society, but where such beliefs manifest themselves as influencing decisions against people who are outsiders or are perceived to do so this can cause problems for those concerned.'

Another Chief Constable, a non-Mason, said, 'Free-masonry is not *so* much a problem today in the police service as it was twenty years ago. Even so, it is still a problem. It certainly still has some controlling influence, and any amount of influence is wrong. Over the years a lot of policemen have been Masons. It's not so fashionable today, although it's as strong as it ever was in one or two quarters of the country.

'Its influence in the police was strongest in the days pre-amalgamation of forces when the promotion stakes relied on this kind of thing in the days of Watch Committees and local political influence on the police. This is what I am very fearful of today – that we don't move back into the era of Watch Committees in spite of the fact that some elements of society are calling for a greater accountability of the police. Accountability is OK but if it's going to be accountability with too much political influence then it will lead us back into worse problems with Freemasonry than we have now. If it's bad now, you should have seen Masonry at work pre-1964 and pre-1947.'

One Chief Constable was particularly frank. His reputation, record and standing in the police service lend particular weight to his testimony. He told me, 'I went to London as a Chief Inspector and it was at that stage that I became a Mason, for no real reason other than the people who invited me to join were friends who I respected very very much.

'Masonry did me a great favour because public speaking didn't come easy to me. I'd lose sleep for two nights beforehand, get very tense and then make a botch of it. And Masonry – the fact that one has to get up on one's feet on occasions, the occasional after-dinner speech or vote of thanks or what-have-you – fulfilled a need that in retrospect I see was very very important to me in terms of character building.

'I joined a very small, friendly Lodge in London, and eventually within a period of about eight years I became Master of that Lodge, which was a tremendous thing. I thoroughly enjoyed it. But then when I left London and moved to B— [a provincial city force], because of the sheer logistics involved, I dropped off. I was three years in B— and gradually my attendances were declining until I got the Deputy Chief Constable's job in this force. My predecessor here was also a Mason and was very heavily involved locally. In fact he subsquently became Master of a Lodge not far from where we're sitting now. But I thought as Deputy Chief when I came here, I would not – certainly for the first year – take part in it at all. I received countless invitations to go out – genuine invitations, for no underhand motives but people genuinely wanted me to go out and visit various Lodges. But I declined this for a year. The year became two years, the two years became four years and so I've never

ever set foot in a Lodge in the area covered by this police force.

'I've also ceased to be a full member in London; although I'm still a member it's on what we call a Country List. That means if ever I do go back I pay for my meal on the night as opposed to paying a large annual subscription.

'I've not stood back because I've got any guilt complex or conscience at all about Masonry, but because of what people think of Masonry. If one is in the position to (a) influence promotions and (b) take decisions on discipline, then quite obviously one is open to the allegation that Masonry is a factor in one's decisions – although I can assure you that I've locked up Masons in my time and sent police officers and others to prison, and been very pleased to have done it.

'Masonry *is* fairly strong in the police service. In my service, which will be twenty-five years next year, therefore relatively modern, I can honestly say that I don't know of any occasion when Masonry has been a fundamental issue in promotion or any other aspect for that matter.

'I think it's not wholly to be unexpected that police are quite heavily involved because we are very conservative by nature. Like attracts like. Freemasonry is a very conservative organization, all about the Establishment, all about the maintenance of the status quo, which is bound to attract a certain sympathy with police officers.

'A lot of nonsense is talked about promotion and so on, and the way I always answer that is this: if you and I went to the same school together, or played for the same Rugby club, or our fathers did whatever together, and then we come to a situation where I am interviewing you and A. N. Other for a job, I've got to make a judgement on your characters, and I've got to take a gamble. I've got to choose the best man to manage this branch or the best man to do this job, or what-have-you. And the more I know about you that causes me to be in sympathy to your cause – the school, the Rugby club, the golf club, Freemasonry or whatever it may be, the more I will be inclined to take a chance – life is all about taking chances when you give appointments – on you as opposed to the man that I know nothing about.'

I wrote to every senior officer at New Scotland Yard in 1981 when Sir David McNee was Commissioner. With the exception of two Deputy Assistant Commissioners, Sir David and all his men ignored my letters to them about Freemasonry. One of the DACs wrote: 'I understand that several of my colleagues have not answered your letter of 21st August. Lest you get the wrong impression that this relates to Freemasonry I am replying just to state that I am not, never have been or ever will be, a Free Mason.'

His colleague told me, 'I am not a Mason, so it is *possible* to get promotion right up to Commissioner without being one. But it is unlikely. Nearly all of my colleagues and seniors are Masons. It's not enough to say that senior police officers are the kind of men who like Freemasonry, or that the sort of men who join Freemasonry are senior officer material. A lot of people at the Yard have got into positions they shouldn't be in purely and simply because they've got Masonry behind them. But if you think anything can be done about it, you're wasting your time.'

CHAPTER 8

Worshipful Masters of Conspiracy

Corruption among Scotland Yard detectives, always a problem, grew enormously during the 1960s. One cause of the trouble was that conventional methods of detection were becoming less and less effective in the face of the burgeoning crime rate. Many policemen believed in a surer way of securing convictions that necessitated a blurring of the 'them and us' divide between the law enforcers and the law breakers. The belief was that to combat crime adequately, the police had to be intimately acquainted with the ways of individual criminals and the day-to-day workings of the underworld. This meant cultivating certain smaller villains, who in return for favours could be counted upon to 'grass' on the bigger men the Yard regarded as its prime quarry. The idea was not new. London police for generations had known that brilliant detective minds which required only sketchy clues and a warm fireside to solve the most bizarre crimes were fine for 221b Baker Street and 10a Piccadilly – but in the cold reality of life at Scotland Yard, things did not work out so neatly. Real-life detectives had to some extent to depend on informers; and informers were usually criminals. In the past it had been an unpalatable necessity, never officially recognized. By the 1960s it was the norm. The system inevitably brought temptation to many police officers, who would be offered money to keep quiet about so-and-so's activities, or a cut in the takings if they made sure the regular police patrol was diverted or unavoidably delayed on a particular night when a job was planned.

The question to be asked is: were there any masonic elements in this corruption, and but for Freemasonry would the corruption have been less likely to have occurred or more easily discovered?

In forces all over England, Freemasonry is strongest in the CID. This had been particularly noticeable at Scotland Yard, and the situation remains the same today. Between 1969 and the setting-up of the famous Operation Countryman in 1978 there were three big investigations into corruption in the Metropolitan Police. These were:

(1) An enquiry into allegations of corruption and extortion by police, first published in *The Times*. This resulted in the arrest, trial and imprisonment of two London detectives in 1972.

(2) An enquiry by Lancashire Police into members of the Metropolitan Police Drug Squad. This led to the trial of six detectives, and the imprisonment in 1973 of three of them.

(3) An enquiry into allegations of corruption among CID officers responsible for coping with vice and pornography in London's West End. Over twenty detectives were sacked from the force during the three-year investigation in the early 1970s, which led eventually to the notorious Porn Squad trials.

There were corrupt masonic policemen involved in all these cases, but this report is not concerned with corrupt policemen who just happen to be Freemasons any more than it is with corrupt policemen who happen to be Roman Catholics, Rotarians or members of their local lawn tennis club. Many people see the discovery of a corrupt Freemason as proof of the corrupting influence of Masonry. This is about as sensible as condemning Christianity because a murderer is found to be a regular churchgoer. There might well be grounds for criticism of Freemasonry in the police, but where Freemasonry has clearly played no part in the corruption of an officer, where his membership of the Brotherhood is incidental, it must not be brought as evidence. Only one of the three major cases of corruption investigated in the seventies can be said to have had any serious masonic elements – the activities of the Porn Squad. This section of the Metropolitan Police was, in the words of the present Lord Chief Justice, 'involved in wholesale corruption. The very men employed to bring the corrupt to book were thriving on the proceeds of corruption.'

The worst of these men was Detective Chief Super-intendent William 'Bill' Moody, former head of the Obscene Publications Squad. Moody, an exceedingly cor-rupt policeman, was an active Freemason. He was gaoled for twelve years, the heaviest sentence meted out to the 'bent' members of the Porn Squad. Moody and ten others, who had received sentences ranging from three years upwards, were told when their appeals were dismissed that 'the individual sentences properly reflected the degree [of responsibility] and complicity and wickedness'.

Moody still protests his innocence from behind bars. Ironically, it had been Moody who in 1969 had been placed in charge of the first of the major enquiries into corruption while himself extorting vast sums of 'protection money' from Soho pornography racketeers. In one transaction alone Moody received £14,000. Almost the entire Porn Squad was in on the racket, openly collecting huge bribes – at one stage estimated at £100,000 a year – from porn shop proprietors in return for the freedom to flout the law unmolested.

Moody lived at Weybridge in Surrey. He and several

other Freemason members of the Porn Squad who lived in the area were members of the same Lodge. So, incidentally, were a number of pornographers. These included a small-time pornographer who used to work in the nearby village of Cobham; another whose home was at Walton-on-Thames; and others who lived or worked at Hampton Wick, Weybridge and Hersham.

John Shirley, co-author of *The Fall of Scotland Yard*, who gave oral evidence before the Royal Commission on Standards of Conduct in Public Life, chaired by Lord Salmon, told me, 'It's fairly certain that the basis of a corrupt network, of the corrupt relationship between that particular group of police officers and those particular pornographers, was either formed or developed within that masonic Lodge.

'The point I was trying to make to the Salmon Commission was that, yes, police officers had private lives but in the nature of it the privacy of their lives needed to be more clearly known to their superiors. If it had been spotted that Moody was a member of the same Free-masonry Lodge as a number of well-known pornographers, on whom the police would have had files, then I think the link between them would have been established much earlier than it was.'

The major breakthrough in stamping out corruption on a grand scale within the Metropolitan Police was the appointment of Robert Mark as Commissioner in 1972. As Chief Constable of Leicester until 1967 he was unhampered by long-standing personal loyalties, untainted by the years-old corruption at the Yard, and a man who loathed nothing so much as a bent copper. Within a very short time, Mark, a non-Mason, had turned Scotland Yard on its head. One of his first reforms was to set up the 'ruthlessly efficient' department A10 to investigate complaints against police officers. In *The Fall of Scotland Yard*, the authors explain:

The setting-up of A10 broke the absolute control of the CID over the investigation of all major crime, whether it occurred inside or outside the Metropolitan Police. For the first time, uniformed officers were to be empowered to investigate allegations of misconduct – whether disciplinary or criminal – not just against their uniformed colleagues but also against the CID. This was a complete reversal of the status quo, where only CID officers had been able to investigate complaints against the uniformed branch *and* their own tight fraternity.

That tight fraternity, as has been mentioned, was and is heavily masonic. And despite A10's success in ridding the Yard of suspect detectives – nearly 300 had been forced to resign by spring 1975 – it was constantly obstructed in its attempts to obtain evidence solid enough to make charges stick. Even in cases of obvious criminality, fellow officers whose evidence was vital clammed up and obstinately refused to make statements, or co-operate in any other way. Some would not speak at all. It rapidly became clear why. The 'honest' men needed as witnesses were members of the same Brotherhood as the 'bent' officers. Many shared the same Lodges.

CHAPTER 9

Operation Countryman

Operation Countryman, the biggest investigation ever conducted into police corruption in Britain, would never have come about if the Commissioner of the City of London Police between 1971 and 1977 had not been corrupted and unduly influenced by Freemasonry. Indeed, there seems little doubt that if James Page had refused to join the Brotherhood, he would not have been appointed Commissioner in the first place.

Page transferred at the rank of Superintendent from the Metropolitan Police to the tiny, 800-man City Force in 1967, at first simply for experience as Commander of B Division based at Snow Hill police station. An excellent communicator and a good host, Page brought a style of administration to Snow Hill that can rarely, if ever, have been matched in any force in the country. It was the style he had learned in the disreputable old Blackpool City Force, where he had served under disgraced Chief Constable Stanley Parr (pages 99–102). Coachloads of policemen would arrive at Snow Hill for darts matches, boozing sessions and parties of all kinds. This earned him popularity with 'the lads' in the lower ranks, most of whom, even the lowliest PCs, were encouraged to address him as 'Jim'. Two months before his forty-fourth birthday in March 1969, he was promoted to Chief Superintendent. At this stage, so far as is known, he had never set foot inside a masonic temple. Eight months later the then Commissioner, Sir Arthur Young, was seconded to the Royal Ulster Constabulary and Page transferred to Old Jewry, the force headquarters, as Acting Commissioner. Page's successor at Snow Hill, Chief Superintendent Brian Rowlands, was astonished at what he found. 'It was,' said one of the most senior officers in the force at that time, 'like running a huge pub.'

By now Page had set the pattern of his relations with the public and the force. In stark contrast to the aloof and dignified manner of the man he was standing in for, 'good old Jim' would be right in there with the lads – drinking, guffawing over a bar-room joke, out within the hallowed purlieus of the City of London opening pubs, and all too frequently getting so inebriated that he had to be carried home in a patrol car. He was liked and respected as 'one of the boys', a very different kind of respect from that enjoyed by the absent Commissioner. In the minds of senior officers, Page's extravagant *bonhomie* was marring his undoubted abilities. 'He had a very good brain,' I was told by one of the top men of the time. 'He could think on his feet in crises and was a staunch supporter of his men.'

Although a significant proportion of City policemen had been Freemasons since the twenties and there had been a masonic element in many promotions over the decades, there is no evidence that before the early 1970s the consequences had been more serious than occasional miscarriages of justice, a distortion of values, and a disgruntlement among non-Masons, inevitable whenever less able men are given preferential treatment. All this was bad enough but what flourished under Page was iniquitous.

In 1969, on the eve of Page's taking over as Acting Commissioner, a private meeting took place at his office at

Old Jewry. One of the highest-ranking officers in the force, whom I shall call Commander Dryden, had some urgent advice for his new chief. Dryden warned Page about two City police officers he knew to be corrupt. Because the Countryman investigations in the City have still not been completed – whatever offical statements say to the contrary – I shall give these men pseudonyms and refer to them as Tearle and Oates. Both were Freemasons.

'If you are ever going to run this force,' said Dryden, 'watch Oates and Tearle very closely. If you ever promote them you'll have so much trouble you won't know where to turn.'

Dryden told me, 'I'd not been long off the shop floor and was still closely in touch with events at grass roots. Everyone said that Oates and Tearle were corrupt. They would duck and dive with villains, take bribes to put in false reports on cases so that charges would be reduced or dropped altogether. One night, Oates was called to a jeweller's shop which had been found to have a broken window. He helped himself from the stock and reported that it had been missing when he arrived. Tearle was looked upon as being "swift", very shrewd and quick to make a few bob in league with criminals. A suspect man in all respects, he too would square a job up for a price.'

Dryden felt 'quite pleased' that he had alerted Page. It was a load off his mind, and he felt he'd done his duty.

So the matter rested . . . for a while.

Sir Arthur Young was due to retire on 30 November 1971, so applications were invited for his successor. The process by which the City of London Corporation appoints a new Commissioner begins with the police committee, one of twenty-seven committees whose membership is drawn from the Court of Common Council, setting up a sub-committee. The sub-committee vets applications and draws up a short list which it passes to the

main committee. Short-listed applicants are later interviewed by the entire Common Council, at which each
delivers a prepared speech on his own behalf. Voting then
takes place and the applicant with the highest number of
votes is appointed, subject to ratification by the Home
Secretary and the Queen.

Inevitably, Page applied for the job, but he knew he was
skating on thin ice. On the grounds of his now notorious
drinking habits alone, few in the force thought he had a
chance. Everyone knew that the former City Assistant
Commissioner, John Duke, had been groomed for Sir
Arthur's job and had meanwhile transferred to Essex Police
to await the day the office fell vacant. Duke had duly
applied and the force waited for his appointment to be
announced.

When the short list was down to two and Page let it be
known that he was on it, his colleagues felt sure the police
committee had already reached its decision, but had kept
Page's name on the list until the very latest stages out of
consideration for his feelings. Duke was the man. Then, to
everyone's astonishment, it came through the grapevine
that Duke was not on the short list, that Page, incredibly,
had beaten him. Still, the force were confident Page would
not be appointed because it was learned that his rival was
no less a figure than John Alderson (who resigned as Chief
Constable of Devon and Cornwall in April 1982).

Not only had Alderson been personally recommended by
Sir Arthur Young himself, his achievements cast a long
shadow over those of Page, who was almost exactly three
years his junior. Then Commandant of the Police College
at Bramshill in Hampshire, Alderson had served in the
Highland Light Infantry between 1938 and 1941, and after
five years as Warrant Officer with the Army Physical
Training Corp in North Africa and Italy, he had joined
West Riding Constabulary as a constable in 1946. He had

been promoted to Inspector in 1955, and given command of a sub-division in 1960. Between 1964 and 1966 he was Deputy Chief Constable of Dorset, after which he transferred to the Metropolitan Police as Deputy Commander, Administration and Operations. Appointed second-in-command of No 3 Police District in 1967, he was promoted again the following year to Deputy Assistant Commissioner (Training), which gave him a two-year lead-up to running the Police College from 1970. In 1971, the year he applied for the Commissioner's job in the City, he became a member of the BBC General Advisory Council. In addition he was a qualified barrister, having been called to the Bar of the Middle Temple. He was a Fellow of the British Memorial Foundation of Australia, he held an Extension Certificate in Criminology from the University of Leeds, and was a Fellow of the British Institute of Management. He had contributed to the *Encyclopaedia of Crime and Criminals* (1960), and written numerous articles for newspapers and professional publications.

This, then, was James Page's opponent. The outcome of the Common Council's vote seemed a foregone conclusion.

But neither the general run of officers in the City, nor probably even Page himself, reckoned on the power of Freemasonry within the Square Mile.

It became clear that influential Freemasons had decided that Page was the man for the job, for various reasons. For one thing, he was a known quantity. His sense of duty was more malleable than Alderson's, his loyalty to those who helped him very easy to exploit. In many ways, Page was as trusting as a child.

Page was initiated into City Livery Club Lodge No 3752, at the Masonic Temple at Sion College on the Victoria Embankment. Things were so arranged that Page was able to move through the first three degrees and rise from non-Mason to Entered Apprentice to Fellow Craft and finally to Master Mason – a process which generally takes many months – very rapidly. All Page's problems seemed to melt away as soon as he joined the Brotherhood. As the days ticked by before the crucial choice between himself and Alderson, he was awarded the Queen's Police Medal. A Home Office official told me that the recommendation had come from a most unusual quarter – Her Majesty's Inspector of Constabulary, most of whom are Masons.

'It was astonishing,' said Dryden. 'When I heard that Alderson had lost to Page, it was as big a shock as when Kennedy was shot. I can remember exactly where I was and what I was doing on both occasions. Others felt the same.'

And there the trouble, which led eventually to the multi-million-pound Countryman operation, began.

Page quickly demonstrated his unsuitability for the post, although his achievements should not be glossed over lightly. He is remembered, for instance, as Director of Police Extended Interviews between 1975 and 1977. He became a Fellow of the British Institute of Management in 1975 and an Officer of the Légion d'honneur in 1976. But he was promoted above his ability. Attending more than 600 social functions in a single year, he became known as a heavy drinker not only in the force but in other organizations and institutions within the City, both august and common. He would turn up to almost every birthday, retirement or promotion party in the force. He would even be found at the lowliest office celebrations, when for instance a uniformed constable was transferred to the CID.

James Page had much to thank Freemasonry for, and he showed his gratitude by proving an enthusiastic Mason. 'He was mad about his Masonry,' said one uniformed superintendent. Others of all ranks, some Freemasons among them, have confirmed this. When the already highly masonic City force learned of the new Commissioner's passionate commitment to the Brotherhood, many more officers joined the Lodges. Page had a simple faith in Masonry's power for good: officers who were Masons were good officers because Masonry was good.

Dryden liked Page as a man, but he did not like the way he was running the force. He did not heed the warning about the two bad apples, Tearle and Oates. Far from keeping them down and watching them with an eagle eye, he openly fraternized with them. The answer was not hard to find. Both Tearle and Oates were Freemasons, so in Page's view Dryden must be mistaken about them. Things went from bad to worse: Tearle introduced Page to his own Lodge, where as Worshipful Master he was superior in rank to the Commissioner.

Eventually, Dryden confided in Chief Superintendent Brian Rowlands, who was still in command at Snow Hill and was secretary of the National Police Superintendents' Association. They agreed something had to be done and decided to speak of their fears to Assistant Commissioner Wally Stapleton, who had influence with Page. They received a cheering reply.

'Don't worry,' said Stapleton. 'Those men will get promotion over my dead body.'

Dryden told me, 'He satisfied both of us that he had the measure of the situation, and that nothing wrong would get past him.'

Page ignored even Stapleton and subsequently promoted Tearle not once but twice. Oates later received even higher promotion.

'A lot can happen to a force in ten years,' I was told by a sorrowing Detective Sergeant at Old Jewry. Himself a Freemason since 1957, he is 'appalled' by what has happened in the City: 'I've seen Masonry used for rotten things in the force in recent years. I'd never have believed it was possible if I hadn't seen it and heard it myself. What sickens me is the filthy distortion of the principles of

Freemasonry. It's not meant to be for this, it's really not. But Masons are being promoted over the heads of non-Masons left, right and centre. I've been to most of the police Lodges in the City area and in the last few years it seems to me that the ritual and purpose of Masonry is getting less and less important. It's forbidden to talk about politics, religion or business in the Temple, but these yobbos – they shouldn't be in the police, let alone the Craft – they're using the secrecy to get into corners and decide who's next for promotion and who they can place where to their own advantage. Most of the time it's about how to protect themselves, having someone in the right place to cover up if they skive off. That's bad enough, and it's shown itself in the fallen standards of the force as a whole. But I've seen one or two things worse than that – actual criminal stuff. Nothing really terrible when you consider some of the things Old Bill Masons are supposed to have done here – I don't have any personal knowledge of that. But nevertheless I know people in the Craft who have had charges dropped as a result of little conferences at Lodge meetings: things like acts of gross indecency, taking and driving away and, once, a GBH [grievous bodily harm].'*

Page was now immersed in the whole Freemasonic life of the City, and he had been corrupted by it to the extent that the 'without fear or favour' part of his oath as a policeman no longer took precedence. I have been told by several senior officers who served under Page that there were numerous occasions when his judgement on relatively minor issues was called into question. All of them related in some way to Masonry. He was once challenged by a high-ranking officer as to why he had ordered the suspension of certain proceedings against an organization whose Freemason head had appealed to him for help. Page explained: 'I owe them

*This statement is culled from a long interview which took place on 30 September 1981.

three more years yet,' meaning that he owed his position to the Masons, and in return for that, wherever he could, he would see to it that his first allegiance was to the Brotherhood.

On at least seven occasions he is alleged to have contacted Grand Lodge for advice on how to act in purely internal matters, or *for permission* to take a course of action if it related in any way to Masonry.

Another non-Mason in the City related how he had once sat with Page on a two-man interviewing panel considering the application of a man who had already been rejected by two other forces as a police probationer. It was decided that he would be given a try, but he proved highly unsatisfactory. I have seen a four-page report in which the officer who sat with Page on the interviewing panel describes various incidents in which the PC became involved – offences as serious as threatening violence to a member of the public, absenting himself from duty while on reserve during a sensitive Old Bailey trial and later abusing an Inspector who found him drunk at home, and phoning the force control centre in the middle of the night and demanding to be put through to Page. This was roughly comparable to a drunken private in the army insisting on an audience with his General.

Convinced the probationer was unstable, the officer recommended to Page that his services be dispensed with, which is possible at any time within a PC's first two years of service. The recommendation was supported by other senior officers *and* the Assistant Commissioner.

Bearing in mind the strength of the condemnation, and the standing and integrity of the officer who made it, it was unthinkable that the recommendation could be ignored.

But the erring PC was a Freemason. The masonic cogs began to move and Page was prevailed upon to do the unthinkable. He vetoed the recommendation and simply transferred the PC to another division. Thus Page's incomplete understanding of the obligation he had taken to assist fellow Masons in distress led not only to the retention of a known dangerous element within the force, but to undermining the authority of one of the most senior men below the rank of Assistant Commissioner. In the event, the decision proved disastrous as the PC went from bad to worse, finally leaving the force after Page's own less than happy exit in 1977.

The first of three serious crimes in the City Police area, which led eventually to the Countryman investigation into police malpractice, occurred in May 1976 at the offices of the *Daily Express* when £175,000 in wages was stolen. This was followed sixteen months later by a £520,000 robbery at the City headquarters of Williams and Glyn's Bank in Birchin Lane, off Lombard Street. Six men in balaclava helmets armed with shotguns ambushed a Securicor van about to deliver the money to the bank, and blasted one of the guards in the legs. Two other members of the gang waited nearby in getaway cars. The third crime took place at the *Daily Mirror* in May 1978 when three robbers, two disguised as printers, staged a daring raid on a Securicor van after it had actually been locked inside the loading area beneath the *Mirror* building. The gang escaped with £197,000 in banknotes after shooting the driver of the van at point-blank range through the heart. He died on the way to hospital.

These crimes would never have occurred if Page had not allowed himself to be initiated into Freemasonry to assure himself of the Commissioner's job. If Page had not been a Freemason, he would not have become Commissioner in 1971. If Page had not been a Freemason, he would have heeded Dryden's warning in 1969 never to promote Tearle and Oates, when both of them were in the less influential rank of detective chief inspector. As it was, he promoted

them because he and they were part of the same Brotherhood. They achieved high rank under Page. Commander
Dryden told me: 'If Tearle and Oates had not been
promoted, others would not have been promoted because
they – Tearle and Oates – came to have influence over
other promotions. Once they were in a position of control,
they then promoted their masonic brethren, many of whom
were in on the corruption with them. This brought about
an ease of communication and a whole corrupt masonic
network was set up within the force. Tearle and Oates
colluded with some of these newly promoted Masons and
played a part in setting up the Williams and Glyn's and
the *Mirror* jobs, and they helped out after the event at the
Express. Mason police shared out around £60,000 from one
job.'

Oates and some of the worst of their accomplices have
now gone from the force, but Tearle remains, terrified that
his name will be connected publicly with the crimes in
which he has taken part if one of his former colleagues
decides there is no longer anything to be gained by
protecting him. One of the men who is thinking very
seriously of 'shopping' Tearle, Oates and the rest of the
crew told me, 'One word from me and they go down for a
long, long while.'

So far that word has not been forthcoming.

CHAPTER 10

The Brotherhood Misjudged

In 1978, following one of several appearances I made on Australian television, the studio's switchboard was jammed with calls from viewers who wanted to talk to me about the masonic aspects of the Jack the Ripper case. One man subsequently wrote to me saying, 'I have a story which confirms yours. The same secret society is still doing the same things here (Sydney). I cannot begin to even outline events that have taken place here, but misdeeds ranging from murder to cannibalism have taken place. Persons involved include some famous, wealthy and politically powerful people, including a person in one of the top political offices in Australia. This story is still current and desperately needs someone to write/expose it.

'If you are outside Australia when you get this letter, *please* write back at once, as time is getting short in many ways.'

The letter ended with the postscript, 'Help! Please.'

I had my reservations, not only because of the extreme nature of the allegations but also because of the tone and presentation of the letter, which was handwritten on flimsy lined paper. However, I was intrigued, and in view of the man's plea I decided it would do me no harm to listen and might well do him some good to have a listener. Although it was hard for me to picture Malcolm Fraser sitting down to breakfast off a human arm and orange juice, it was just possible there was a story in it somewhere. I phoned the man and we met at the Melbourne Hilton.

I sat and listened to a convoluted tale of crime and wickedness in high places, partly involving the corruption by way of 'the secret brotherhood of Freemasonry' of all levels of the police in Sydney. The allegations of criminal activity might or might not have been well founded. But apart from the fact that several unconnected cases involved men who were Masons, he offered no evidence except his own 'absolute certainty' that Freemasonry played any part at all.

Logic can very quickly go out of the window if a clear distinction is not made between incidents caused by Freemasonry and incidents merely involving Freemasons. As I have already said, the difference between the two is often ignored or not appreciated. There are several examples of alleged police malpractice involving Free-masons which show the importance of this point.

One bullish Welsh PC told me at great length how an Inspector had once intervened and stopped him when he, the PC, was dealing with a charge of obstruction against a detective sergeant of a nearby force whose private car had blocked the pavement in the town's main street for more than an hour on a busy Saturday afternoon. The Inspector and the Sergeant were Masons in the same Lodge, said the non-Mason PC.

So, here we have a clear case of one police officer with masonic loyalty to another stepping in and preventing the law taking its course. Or do we?

If the only reliable test – beyond reasonable doubt – is

applied, the PC's case does not stand up for five minutes. The PC was convinced that had the other two not been Freemasons, the incident would not have occurred. But his argument begins from the premise that Freemasonry is corrupting, and cites an example of dubious conduct on the part of a Freemason to prove it. The argument is circular and therefore specious.

The plain fact is that embarrassing incidents of this sort are being covered up all the time, and nobody takes much notice until someone says, 'They're both Masons, of course,' and everyone nods sagely and grumbles about the Great Conspiracy.

This incident would have occurred whether or not the men were Freemasons, because they were also brothers-in-law, something the PC failed to tell me when he was cracking on about masonic corruption.

Stanley Parr, the sixty-year-old Chief Constable of Lancashire, was suspended on full pay in March 1977 following a top-level enquiry into allegations of malpractice, including the misuse of his position to show favours. Ten months later he was sacked amid a welter of publicity. The case of Parr, who was a Freemason, has been quoted as one which provides strong evidence of the corrupting influence of Masonry. Unfortunately for the anti-Brotherhood lobby, this is not strictly true.

The trouble began when a Blackpool Sergeant, Harry Roby, made a complaint to an Inspector of Constabulary. Further allegations were made that certain motorists known to Parr were given preferential treatment after being accused of speeding and parking offences. The most serious suggestion was that Parr had altered a charge made against a motorist whose car had mounted the pavement on the main Blackpool–Preston road in August 1975 and killed two young mothers.

Sir Douglas Osmond, the then Chief Constable of Hampshire, was appointed to investigate and report on the allegations. He was assisted by a highly respected detective, Norman Green, who is now Assistant Chief Constable of Bedfordshire. Both men were non-Masons.

The three-month investigation resulted in the confidential 150-page Osmond Report, part of which examined the alleged undesirable associates of Chief Constable Parr. Before the reorganization of police forces in England and Wales, Parr had been Chief Constable of Blackpool. He had risen through the ranks of Blackpool City Force, and was strongly Blackpool-orientated. Even after the reorganization, when Blackpool Force had been absorbed into the new Lancashire County Force with headquarters in Preston, Parr continued to live in Blackpool and spent a great deal of his time, both on and off duty, in the town. It was the relationships which Parr maintained in Blackpool which proved his undoing. He fraternized with a number of people who were considered undesirable company for a Chief Constable, either because they were themselves criminals or associates of criminals, or because they were proprietors of businesses which required some kind of police-approved licence to operate.

These characters included the owner of a Blackpool hotel. Parr was regularly in this man's company, and the two men and their wives went on holiday to Tenerife together. One of thirty-seven disciplinary charges against Parr alleged that he had intervened improperly to prevent the hotel owner being prosecuted for traffic offences. A tribunal set up in the wake of the Osmond Report heard how the hotel owner's son had collided with another

vehicle while driving his father's Jaguar on the day the two
families returned from Tenerife. The son had told the
police who interviewed him: 'My father is on holiday in
Tenerife with Stanley Parr and I'll see Mr Parr when he
returns home tonight.' He was not prosecuted. His father,
who was the holder of a Justice's Licence and therefore
subject to police observation and supervision, was considered 'untouchable' by the local police because of his
friendship with the Chief Constable. This meant that
although he committed frequent traffic offences he was
effectively immune from prosecution.

Other acquaintances of the Chief Constable included a
'swag shop' operator, the joint owner of a large 'bingo'
business, two bookmakers, a former bookmaker, two club
owners, two amusement caterers, a holiday-camp proprietor and a licensee.

These 'unwise' relationships were formed and developed
in various organizations in Blackpool – Freemasonry
among them. The main one was Sportsmen's Aid, a
crypto-masonic organization which over a period of ten
years raised more than £70,000 for various local charities.
As the original complainant, Sergeant Roby was grilled for
two full days by Assistant Chief Constable Green. At one
point, Green, who suspected a Freemasonic link between
Parr and those who benefited from his improper conduct,
asked Roby outright what part Masonry had played in the
whole affair. To Green's surprise, Roby said, 'Oh, nothing
whatever. In fact I am a Mason myself.'

Sources close to the investigation told me that at the end
of the enquiry, Osmond and Green concluded that a lot of
people who were involved were, like Parr, Freemasons. But
they were also members of other organizations like the
Rotary Club and more particularly Sportmen's Aid. And
although Freemasonry played a part in building relationships which were not 'kept at the proper level', there was

no real reason to suspect that Freemasonry alone was to blame.

It is widely appreciated that some journalists will go to inordinate lengths to get a 'good story'. One case, involving the police and the Brotherhood, illustrates how far many people go to malign Freemasonry unwarrantably. The *News of the World* carried a story by a freelance reporter in some editions of its 3 January 1982 issue under the headline ROW OVER COP CAUGHT IN VICE TRAP. It must be said that the newspaper published the story in good faith. It ran:

A detective who is a Freemason has caused a storm in a county's police force after being caught with a prostitute in his car by the Vice Squad.

Detective Sergeant Alpha Beta [a pseudonym], who is married with a family, has been officially reprimanded by Assistant Chief Constable David East, of Devon and Cornwall force.

But a senior detective said last night: 'Ordinary policemen feel that if it were them they would have been put back into uniform or transferred.

'It has led to a sincere belief that there's one rule for Masons and another for the rest.'

The incident involving Detective Sergeant Beta, who is stationed in Paignton, happened in Plymouth's red light district.

Vice Squad officers watched as he picked up prostitute Janice Hayes, 18, in his car. Then, after he had handed over £10, they pounced.

The policemen recognized the sergeant, who was previously stationed in Plymouth, and they called in their duty inspector.

A report was made to Police HQ in Exeter and the reprimand followed.

At her bedsit home in Devonport, Janice said: 'We agreed £10 for straight sex and drove to a nearby car park.

'I hadn't even got my knickers off when there was a tap on the window. It was the Vice Squad.

'They seemed to know him and said Hello. One of them told

me to be on my way so I just ran. If it had been any other punter I'd have been done.'

When a local paper inquired about the affair, Assistant Chief Constable East wrote to the editor admitting the sergeant had been reprimanded, but asking for the story not to be used because it might damage his marriage.

A police spokesman said yesterday: 'This was an internal matter that did not involve a complaint from the public.'

When I read this story, I naturally sought further information because of its relevance to my research. I went first to the *News of the World*, and second to a reporter on the Devon News Agency who had had a hand in producing it. According to this man the story was even better – which was journalese for sensational – than was suggested in the *News of the World*.

I was told that Detective Sergeant Beta, aged thirty-seven, had been initiated to the Princetown Lodge about two years previously on the recommendation of none other than David East, his own Deputy Chief Constable (wrongly described as ACC in the newspaper report).* I was told that East was a former Worshipful Master of a Lodge in Somerset and that Beta's superiors in the CID right up the line were all brethren of his Lodge. Not only that, they had all been to a Lodge meeting together the night Beta was picked up by the Vice Squad. The journalist told me: 'After the arrest in Plymouth, the girl was sent home and after the duty inspector was called Beta was taken to Charles Cross Police Station in Plymouth and later released. No disciplinary action was taken against him and he never appeared before a disciplinary board, which he should have done. It was East's statutory duty to discipline the man but he let him off. All he got was a reprimand, which means he goes back in seniority a year. Anyone but a Mason would have

*East succeeded John Alderson as Chief Constable of Devon and Cornwall in 1982.

been back on the beat. That copper was aiding and abetting a criminal offence.'

I asked the reporter to get further details for me and he assured me that he would arrange for me to talk to someone within the police who knew all the details of the 'masonic corruption' and could provide evidence to back up what he said. Days passed. I phoned again. He told me the contact was unavailable. This state of affairs persisted for nearly two months, then the first reporter passed on to me another reporter in Torquay. I met with similar promises and an identical lack of results. Eventually I investigated the story myself. This is the truth of the case.

Detective Sergeant Beta was a Freemason, and a member of Benevolence Lodge No 666 at Princetown, Devon. A number of his colleagues and superiors were brethren in the same Lodge, and on the night of his misconduct he had been to a Lodge meeting with them. The truth about what happened in Plymouth is quite at variance with the account that appeared later in the *News of the World*, however.

One vital point is that the prostitute Janice Hayes quoted by the newspaper *was not the prostitute who was found with the detective sergeant*. Nor could the real prostitute have said, 'One of them told me to be on my way so I just ran. If it had been any other punter I'd have been done,' because the prostitute found with Beta *was* done. She was not sent on her way but was arrested and taken by the two Vice Squad officers along with Beta to the police station, where she was officially cautioned. 'Janice Hayes' was either a figment of the reporters' imagination dreamed up for the purpose of making a good story or, less likely, was another prostitute who agreed to lend her name to the untruthful quote. The reporters are known to have been talking to prostitutes in the red light district of Plymouth after Beta was found in the compromising position.

A man who consorts with a prostitute does not commit a

criminal offence. The lawbreaker is the woman, the offence 'soliciting for the purpose of prostitution'. In order to prove soliciting to the satisfaction of the courts, it is established practice all over the country that a woman be cautioned twice and only on the third time be taken before the court. An element of the offence is *persistent* soliciting. The two cautions were devised in order to prove that element. This was the first time the woman involved with Beta had been cautioned, so there was no offence by her. Logically, there was no offence by Beta. Had she committed an offence, Beta would then technically have been aiding and abetting, but no policeman or lawyer I have spoken to on the subject has heard of any man in Beta's position being charged with aiding and abetting a prostitute.

Because a policeman was involved, and because the Vice Squad officers quite properly informed their superiors, the matter came before Deputy Chief Constable David East. East was a Freemason but had not been active for years and had no connection with Benevolence Lodge No 666 or any other in Devon and Cornwall. It was up to East to decide how to deal with Beta. There had been no criminal offence by the woman, therefore none by the man, so the case was outside the ambit of the Director of Public Prosecutions. Therefore it was a matter of internal police discipline. The only offence within the disciplinary code which was even remotely relevant was discreditable conduct – bringing discredit upon the force.

When this is analysed, it is not difficult to see East's dilemma. There had been no member of the public involved, the prostitute did not know Beta was a policeman, and the only others involved were two police officers. In technical terms it would have been extremely difficult to press a charge of bringing discredit on the police when the arresting officers were the only witnesses. Adding to the difficulty were the facts that he was off-duty, in his own time, and over forty miles away from the place of his work, Torquay. Taking all this into consideration, East had little choice but to decide that it was not a case for formal discipline but for parading Beta in his office, one means at a DCC's disposal for dealing with less serious disciplinary cases, and really going to town on him verbally.

Beta was severely reprimanded by East and the admonishment was formally entered in his personal file, which meant that he was barred from promotion for three years. Having applied that not insignificant punishment, East had to decide whether to leave the officer where he was or transfer him back to uniform. There were problems. CID officers have more freedom than uniformed police. The plain clothes man is far more on personal trust, out of the immediate scope of organized routine supervision. Some officers have told me the answer was clear: Beta could not be trusted, so he should have been back in uniform without delay.

One aspect to be considered was that his wife and family knew nothing of the incident. In itself, that would be no justification for East failing to transfer Beta if a transfer was the only proper course. The main problem was that if the Sergeant was moved back to uniform on the grounds that he required greater supervision, he would have to go either to Exeter or Plymouth. A move to Exeter would mean that he would become responsible for young probationary constables. A move to Plymouth would put him right back in the midst of one of the biggest red light districts in the West Country. Bearing in mind both the nature of the incident and the punishment already meted out by East, most senior police officers – non-Masons to a man – I have tackled about this case are of the opinion that the action taken in leaving Beta in plain clothes at Torquay was the correct one.

This case has been treated at some length because it is an admirable example of how the anti-Mason's view of any incident can be coloured by his prejudices. This goes further than interpreting ordinary events in a masonic way simply because Freemasons happened to be involved – it actually leads people, as in this instance, to *invent* details that turn happenstance into masonic conspiracy.

CHAPTER 11

Birmingham City Police

What I really needed at the outset of my investigation into Masonry in the police was a masonic 'mole' who was a policeman of rank and integrity. Eventually, as has been shown, I built up a large network of such men. None was so earnest or more scathing than those contacts, Masons and otherwise, who spoke to me about Birmingham City Police.

One informant spoke of his experiences in Birmingham dating back many years. He was on the point of entering the first of the three chairs of his Holy Royal Arch Chapter. He had, he told me, been considering becoming a Knight Templar, the branch of Freemasonry which admits only Christians, but was becoming increasingly disillusioned with the abuse of Masonry within the police and had come to realize that he had to resign from one or the other.

He explained that in Birmingham City Police before the reorganization of police forces in England and Wales, it was next to impossible for non-Masons to reach any rank above Chief Inspector. The then Chief Constable, Sir Derrick Capper, was an officer of the Warwickshire Provincial Grand Lodge, and he saw to it as far as possible that non-Masons were kept to the lower and middle ranks. In Capper's time, according to my informant, it was impossible to be a civilian employee at higher level unless you were a Mason. This became the accepted way of life.

In 1974 Birmingham City Police was amalgamated with other nearby forces to become West Midlands Police. My informant continued, 'The old masonic system still pertains within the Birmingham City area. Within the wider scope of West Midlands, which now includes places like Coventry and Wolverhampton, it does not pertain. But in the City area there is not one of the divisional commanders or their deputies who is not a Freemason.'

I pressed him about his motive for talking to me. He replied, 'I've always been conscious of democracy and I just don't see why many good men who joined with me have never reached the same rank as me because they have the misfortune not to be Freemasons.'

I felt there must be something closer to home. If he had been an active Freemason for ten years, as he had told me, he must have been aware for a long time that the existence of Masonry in the police could put non-Masons at a disadvantage. I put the point to him.

'I've had to rack myself recently as to whether I'm going to stay in the job,' he said, 'or abandon Masonry. I don't find them compatible at all.

'In theory, Masons are not supposed to show favour to a man just because he's a Mason. But in practice it doesn't work that way at all. You go to a London Lodge where the Met Police meet, and the next promotions in every department are discussed. It's the same in Birmingham. You cannot possibly rise in the CID, for instance, in the old Birmingham City area, which is a considerable area, unless you're in a Lodge. And it even has to be the right Lodge. The centre of it all is the Masonic Temple at 1 Clarendon Road, Edgbaston.'

But wasn't there something more particular?

'Yes. I'm not finding it particularly good having colleagues in my rank and the two above me getting promoted because they are Masons. I don't see that it's necessary as a criterion for promotion that you're from a masonic Lodge. I'd rather have the men who qualify and get there by hard work. I have two deputies, both promoted because they're Masons. They really are shockers at their job. I suddenly realized they would never have got there if they hadn't been Masons, and that worried me considerably. That's why I'm speaking to you.'

A Birmingham Detective Chief Inspector, also a Mason who wished to remain anonymous, contacted me on 10 October 1981. He said he would try to write but probably would not. In the event he didn't and that one conversation is the only contact I had with him. Even so, he impressed me as genuine and in the light of the information given by my first informant, whose identity I do know, the DCI's conflicting comments should be noted.

He said, 'I'm not an avid Mason. I joined when I was doing a two-year stint at Scotland Yard. I was in a big town where nobody talks to you and I was lonely. I'd been along to a Ladies' Night* at a friend's masonic Lodge and been impressed with the really genuine people there. So I decided to join.

'I didn't join the Masons until I reached my present rank, so it wasn't Freemasonry that got me there. It's sheer hard work that gets you promotion, whatever non-Masons tell you. I had a lad in my department just a while ago who was transferred into uniform because he had transgressed. He was a Mason. It just doesn't make any difference. All this talk of allegiance to two masters is based on ignorance.

'I once met a retired Detective Chief Inspector in Birmingham. He was a good policeman. He'd have rated a Detective Chief Superintendent today. I met him wander-

*Most Lodges hold a Ladies' Night once a year. It is the only occasion when women (wives, daughters or girl friends) are permitted at a gathering of brethren.

ing aimlessly around the streets of the city. His wife had died, he had lost all drive, he was not looking after himself properly. His clothes were patched, he had nothing to live for. I bought him a drink and we talked. He sounded hopeless. Some years later when I had joined the Masons I saw him again – at a Lodge meeting. It had been the making of him. Someone had bumped into him just as I had done, and, being a Mason, had pointed him in the right direction. He was smart, enthusiastic about life, a completely changed man, very enthusiastic about Masonry. Freemasonry alone had given him a reason for living, and that's quite something.'

Quite something indeed. But few people would deny that there are many men, women and children in the world who benefit directly and indirectly from Freemasonry. The movement's contributions to charity, and the work of the Royal Masonic Hospital and the Masonic schools are examples of how non-Masons as well as Masons benefit from the existence of the Brotherhood. This good, and there are other examples, as will become apparent, should not be taken lightly. But neither should it be seen as an answer to those aspects of Masonry which are alleged to be bad. 'The good justifies the bad' is as dangerous a philosophy as 'The end justifies the means'.

But to return to Birmingham, one other masonic policeman who has seen no harm come from so many police officers swearing allegiance to the Brotherhood is former Superintendent David Webb, well known for his championing of 'community policing' in the Birmingham ghetto districts. He resigned from the police in December 1981 and spoke to me shortly after.

'In the City of Birmingham there are hundreds of policemen who are members of Freemasonry,' he said, 'including plenty of divisional commanders. I am a Past Master of more than one Lodge.

'I can honestly say that in the police service I've never found anyone that's ever tried to use Masonry – just the opposite. Amongst the policemen that I know in Masonry, if anyone tried that bloody game on, he'd get clonked well and truly. It's never gained me anything.'

However, hearing various allegations about Birmingham which had been reported to me by informers, he said, 'I'm not saying it *doesn't* happen, the same as when I say to people about police beating people up. I don't say it doesn't happen, but I've never experienced it.'

A Birmingham Chief Inspector, another Mason, said, 'Policemen are very isolated socially. I'll admit that my whole life, because I'm a Mason in a police Lodge, is tied up with the same people. There is a lot of jiggery-pokery among police Masons in Birmingham, I don't mind saying as long as you won't quote me on it. But I doubt if it's any better anywhere else. There's nothing specially bad about Birmingham, it's a good force. The worry is that if I know about one or two of my colleagues who are involved in one or two little – let's say, they've got some fingers in a few pies they shouldn't have—'

'You mean corruption?'

'No, nothing like that. Just *involvements* outside the force. Certain people they don't arrest for certain things. The worry is that as a Mason policeman myself, if I report them I will put my whole work and social life in jeopardy, all my friendships and work relationships will be at stake. So it's better to say nothing. That's the only problem with Masonry. You can get too involved.'

CHAPTER 12

Conclusion

An independent enquiry into Freemasonry in the police should be initiated at the earliest possible moment. Even though the majority of police, including masonic officers, are not corrupt, it is clear that corrupt police can and do use Freemasonry to effect and further their corruption. There are now so many allegations about masonic corruption within the service that even if ninety-nine per cent of them were wholly groundless - and no one who has investigated it could accept that for one moment - we are still left with a disturbing situation. Why successive Home Secretaries have ignored or refused calls for an enquiry is not known. Not all have been Freemasons, but all have had masonic advisers in the persons of their senior Civil Servants.

In September 1981 and again in April 1982 there were claims in court of criminal conduct on the part of Freemason police. At Knightsbridge Crown Court on Tuesday, 22 September 1981 an ex-Metropolitan Police Detective accused of trying to bribe a senior Drugs Squad officer said they were both members of the same masonic Lodge. The detective told the court that he had seconded the application of the Drugs Squad man - a Superintendent - to join the Lodge when they were both stationed at King's Cross Road. The Superintendent admitted that he was a member of the Brotherhood and that he had visited the Lodge when the detective was there, but denied he had ever been a member of the Lodge. And the detective denied, along with a co-defendant, paying the Superintendent £2,800 as an inducement to return sixteen million diethylpropion hydrochloride tablets. Prosecuting counsel told the court that when the attempted bribe had taken place, the conversation had been secretly recorded.

In the later case, a police informer named Michael Gervaise claimed at the Old Bailey that policemen in the same masonic Lodge as criminals involved in a multimillion-pound silver bullion robbery had warned them that they were about to be arrested. As a result of this masonic act, one of the men involved in the £3.5 million robbery fled and has never been traced. Gervaise, who had been involved in the robbery himself, told the court, 'certain officers were Freemasons. Certain criminals belonged to the same Lodge. There were eight or nine officers in the same Lodge as the people involved in the silver bullion robbery.'

Unrest about the undoubted misuse of Freemasonry by policemen is spreading and demands for an enquiry will continue to grow. The worst possible thing would be a masonic witch-hunt, and the surest way of avoiding that would be to institute a proper, sober enquiry before the issue becomes a tool in the hands of political extremists.

Many people want to see Masonry banned in the police. This would inflict damage to the personal happiness of many thousands of upright masonic policemen and to the principle of individual freedom that might outweigh any good effect. But a compulsory register on which police officers have to list their affiliation to secret societies, and their status within such societies, is the minimum requirement if a grave situation is to be improved.

PART THREE

Inside Information

CHAPTER 13

The Rabbi's Tale

Despite the ban on speaking to outsiders, many Freemasons allowed me to interview them. Some were extraordinarily frank, some going so far, having secured my
promise not to reveal their identities, as confiding the most
secret workings of the Brotherhood. Some said very little at
all. Most were prepared to give me candid answers to as
many questions as they felt were not within the areas of
secrecy. Only a few, however, had the courage to be quoted
by name and, while remaining faithful to their masonic
obligations of secrecy, spoke openly of the little-known
aspects of Masonry which, properly speaking, are not
covered by the oaths, however hysterical some grand
officers might become in insisting that everything masonic
is for Masons alone. Among these honourable men was an
eminent Freemason of long standing and grand rank: the
Rev Saul Amias, MBE, a London rabbi who was Assistant
Grand Chaplain to the United Grand Lodge in 1973. I
interviewed him at his home in Edgware in 1981.

'Before I joined Freemasonry there were members of my
community in Edgware who were members, and we used to
discuss it. A few of them were fighting to have the honour
to introduce their minister to their own particular Lodge. I
asked them to tell me about it. They said, "No, we can't
tell you, but there's nothing bad about it. It's only good,

it's only a movement to do good, and there are a lot of Jewish people in it as well as non-Jewish. There's nothing that you say a Jew shouldn't be." In fact, the late Chief Rabbi was a very foremost Mason, and it did not take away from his position as a Chief Rabbi.

'I'm not sorry that I came into the Work because apart from being a brother amongst Masons, if I have to see somebody – say in hospital – and he's a Freemason, I can talk to him and we talk about Freemasonry, take away his mind from his illness. But I don't ask. My first question isn't, "Are you a Freemason?", that would be silly. You're not supposed to do that.

'Anyhow, there's another thing that I want to say. People say Freemasons only help each other. If my brother, my blood brother, comes to me and asks me to advise him or help him, I drop everything, I go, because he's my brother. Or if there's a member of my congregation – although I'm retired they still come to see me – who says, "Look, I need help", I don't say, "Look, I'm retired, go somewhere else." I give help because I *know* him. Mr Cohen. I know him, so why should he go to strangers when he knows Mr Amias? And the same thing, if a man is a Mason, and another Mason comes to him, why shouldn't he help? It doesn't mean to say that I do not help non-Masons, or non-brothers of my family or non-members of my Synagogue.'

'There is, however, a widespread belief that Masons are helped to the detriment of non-Masons,' I said.

'This excites us very much! It's absolutely not a fact – *not* to the detriment. Look, I was looking only this morning – I got a letter from the Royal Benevolent Organization of the Freemasonry. There are about eighteen homes for old people, retired people, for Masons or their relatives, their dependants, their wives, or their widows. Right? Should we not help them? But I help other homes, non-Jewish and Jewish, for old people too. There's no saying I'll only help the masonic ones. No, not at all. But if people come to me through an organization which in this case is the organization of the Brotherhood of Freemasonry, why should I not help him? Or his widow, or whomever? There's a hospital of which I am chaplain, the Royal Masonic Hospital at Hammersmith. I go there very religiously each week. Now all those patients are Freemasons or dependent relatives, that is to say a wife or a son under twenty-one, or an unmarried daughter. So why should I not go? But it doesn't mean that I am not going this afternoon to the Edgware Hospital because I heard the wife of one of my people is there. Or tomorrow I will go to St Albans Hospital where I am a chaplain and to Napsbury Hospital where I'm a chaplain and to Hill End Mental Hospital. It's *absolutely false* to say otherwise.'

'Yes,' I said, 'it's absolutely false to say that Freemasonry *sets out* to help its members to the detriment of non-members, or that any Freemason swears in his oath to help any other Mason to the detriment of a non-Mason, but it does happen. Only this week a man senior in local government admitted to me that he doesn't see anything wrong with showing favour to his fellow Masons. He thinks this is what Freemasonry is about. If he is on a panel interviewing people for posts in the council, assuming there wasn't a great deal of difference in the ability of two applicants, he would choose the Mason every time.'

'Well, I think that's wrong,' replied Amias. 'I know it does happen. All things being equal, you are saying. But if he's not the best candidate and he chooses him as a Freemason then it's . . . un-moral, and it is against all the precepts of Freemasonry where we've got to help *people*, and we keep on stressing that we must practise outside the Lodge, not only with Freemasons, those things which we say and we do inside the Lodge. There is no question.

'It is *true* that people help their brother Masons. Let me put it this way: Freemasonry for some people, who are quiet, who don't take part in local affairs, don't go to church, don't go to Rotary, who don't belong to Toc H, or all the usual – or the tennis club, you know, people who are quiet, who perhaps haven't the opportunity – they work long hours and they haven't got the opportunity of any social work, and so on. For *them* Freemasonry is an avenue through which they walk to the path of helping . . . of unselfish deeds – that means charity, that means helping, that means lending the car to somebody, taking them into hospital, or . . . helping it might be with money, it might be with a job, as you say. It might *be*. But people don't go and say, "I'm a Mason, can you help me?"

'I cannot . . . I will *not* accept that Freemasons help *only* Freemasons to the detriment of others.'

CHAPTER 14

Five Masters and a Lewis

'A Freemason is not supposed to use Masonry for selfish reasons. But there is no doubt that a percentage of people do try. Accepting that, do you think they can succeed?'

I was speaking to a Master Mason, a retired barrister, at his home on the top floor of a Middle Temple chambers. He looked into his sherry and said, 'Oh, I should think to a very limited degree. If you join any club there are always some people who hope to gain something by their membership apart from the normal things in the club. Yes, I'm sure some people do, but it's very indirect, you know?

'You might say, "That's a nice doctor in our Lodge. Perhaps I'll go and see him when I'm ill; that chap's a nice estate agent – yes, well, who should I put my property in to sell with? Oh, well, there's Joe in our Lodge, I'll give it to him to do." That sort of thing. That does crop up. It applies to some more than others, probably solicitors more than barristers. Estate agents, doctors, tradesmen, people like that.

'This doesn't happen so much in London. It's more likely to apply in a smaller, more integrated local place – but then they know each other anyway, so I expect Freemasonry doesn't mean anything one way or the other.

'I think if someone's really hard up, then Freemasonry

comes into its own. "Joe's very hard up, can't you put a bit of business his way?", or something like that.

'I'm not a very enthusiastic Freemason. In fact I suppose I'm a very *unenthusiastic* one, because I like having the dinner with my friends but I get rather bored with the little ceremonies they go through before. I can't be bothered to learn it, anyway.'

'What happens if you don't learn it?'

'Oh, well, you just sit back and don't take an active part in it. They don't like you to write it down. Well, quite frankly, I can't be bothered to memorize it. I wouldn't mind doing it if I could have a sheet, a sort of brief in front of me. That's my attitude to it, so you can see I'm not a very good Freemason.'

A former Worshipful Master of several Lodges of the Hampshire and Isle of Wight Province, a master builder, told me how after a lifetime of devotion to Masonry, he no longer took any part in it because he had become so despondent about its deteriorating standards.

'There was a time,' he said, 'up to about twenty years ago, when it was a proud thing to be a Freemason. They didn't let just anybody into it in those days like they do now. There was a real feeling of comradeship. And we had real power then, as well.

'All the top-notch people in the community or parish or whatever would be in it – the police chief, the magistrates, the coroner, the doctors, tradesmen, solicitors, architects, builders, dentists and the like. And a lot of good men of lower station. It didn't matter what you earned, it was your *character* which mattered. That meant that if anything ever happened in the community, we would have the authority to do something about it.

'Like when, years ago in the fifties, there were some

attacks by a pervert on some young girls. I phoned up the senior policeman in the district (he was in the Lodge), and a deputation of us Masons went to see him to find out what we could do. All the Lodges in the area formed into vigilante groups and we did house-to-house searches. We found him all right and by the time we'd finished with him he was in no state to interfere with anyone again.

'But we can't do those sort of things now. All the same people are in the Lodges but they've gone namby-pamby. With all this talk about rehabilitating criminals and leaving the law to take its course. It can still happen in some places where standards haven't dropped so much, but the old fellowship and trust isn't there any more. It's got bad all over. They are even taking blacks and Jews into it now.'

A Warwickshire Mason of Provincial grand rank, a leading figure in the construction industry, had different reasons for suggesting that Freemasonry was in decline.

'If you became interested enough in Freemasonry after what I tell you tonight to want to join, and asked me to sponsor you, I would say no. If you came back to me in two years I would say no. If you came back in five or eight years I would say no. I would want to know you well for at least ten years before I would consider supporting your application for membership. That's the way it always was, but it's not like it any more with most Masons.

'Interest in the Craft has been steadily decreasing among young men for the past twenty or twenty-five years. Because Lodges wanted to reverse this trend and give recruitment a boost, they gradually began to lower their standards. Now it is very easy to become a Freemason. Some members sponsor people they hardly know, or workmates of only a few months. It is not possible to know someone enough in a short time to be certain he genuinely has the values of a real Mason. Because of that, the Craft is now full of people who have joined because of what they can get out of it, not for what the Craft can get out of them.'

'I never found Freemasonry the least bit of use to me. I don't think in this country people understand it. It has a reputation that is completely misinformed,' said one of my informants, who has been a Master Mason for thirteen years. 'Obviously, if one belongs to a club, and I wouldn't put Freemasonry much higher than a dining-club incidentally, one meets people. If one meets people who get to know you, they probably give you their business. I happen to be a barrister so I don't really seek business. I never sought business or expected to get anything out of it except comradeship.'

'And you got that?'

'I belong to a Lodge which includes most of my friends anyway, so it's just another occasion where I meet my friends.'

'Would you agree that the majority of Freemasons do put it higher than a dining-club? There's the ritual, for instance . . .'

'I've noticed people do seem to like ritual, and I've been surprised once or twice how seriously some Masons do take all that side of it . . . One of the problems with Freemasonry is that you don't really know what it is before you join.'

'Does that worry you at all?'

'No, not if you're being introduced by your friends. I mean, some people think it's a secret society, but it's not a secret society because a secret society is one that you don't know exists.'

This definition of a secret society, repeated to me so often by Freemasons I interviewed, is inaccurate. The existence of many secret societies is known. What makes them secret is that their inner workings are unknown to outsiders, and their secrets are protected by initiation ceremonies which impose penalties on those who betray secrets. There is usually some ritualistic element to the secret society. These elements in Freemasonry justify the application of the term to Freemasonry just as they do to societies which are generally thought more sinister like the Ku Klux Klan, the Italian Carbonari or the Chinese Triads, whose ritual has much in common with English Masonry.

When a man seeks admission to Freemasonry he must find two sponsors within the Brotherhood. In theory, a Mason must not approach an outsider with an invitation to join. In practice, an invitation from a friend or business associate in the Craft is the most common kind of introduction, although United Grand Lodge steadfastly denies this.

One of my contacts within Grand Lodge, a man who thinks of the secrecy with which Masonry surrounds itself as ludicrous and childish, told me what follows a would-be candidate's application to join a particular Lodge.

'We have a little preliminary committee of senior Lodge members who interview the Candidate informally, to look at him and to ask questions like, "Why do you want to come into Freemasonry?" and "Why particularly this Lodge?"

'He might say, "An uncle of mine recommended this one," or a business associate, or a neighbour spoke about it.

'The very first question he is asked is: "Do you believe in God?" and invariably they answer, Yes. Maybe they were told by other Freemasons that they'd better, but they do. I had one case only in all my long experience in Freemasonry when a man began to vacillate, saying, "I'm not really sure, I don't know . . ."

'*We wouldn't have anything to do with him.*'

It would seem, therefore, that atheistic or agnostic Candidates canny enough to know the rules in advance and to lie about their beliefs are preferred to those who have genuine doubts and are honest enough to say so. My informant continued:

'After that, we send one or two of our committee to go into his home, by appointment, to see how he lives, that he is living in a *decent* way. I mean, I'm not a judge and you're not a judge, but if we go to his house and it looks reasonable, lived in, and it's nicely decorated, we know that we've got a man of standing. And I don't mean in the material sense. I mean that he is living as a human being should. He can be very modest, in two rooms, very modest. But, you see, a man in two rooms won't be a Mason because the fees are a bit costly, and you're expected to give charity. We don't say how much, but you're expected to give. If it's a pound or a thousand pounds, you give charity. Nobody will query.

'So we go into his home. We speak to his wife, if he's married. And we ask if she approves of her husband coming into the movement.

'We see if there are children. We ask him, "What about family life?" We're entitled to ask. If you want to come into my club, I'm entitled to ask you certain questions. If you resent it then it's a shame, then you can't come in. Same everywhere. This is how we accept people. If a man is a bankrupt we don't accept him. It sometimes happens that after joining, a man becomes bankrupt. That's too bad. We ask if the Candidate has any convictions. Someone who has been fined for speeding or not putting two bob in the parking meter is not rejected, they aren't criminal acts. But if a man has had a criminal record, we don't accept him. It's a pity, because a man might perjure himself to get into Masonry and say he does not have convictions. But if he admits he has, we don't accept him because we want men of standing, or stand*ards*. Not standing so much as standards. The ones that you and I try to live up to.'

I asked if a would-be Freemason in England had to be 'whole', or was there a rule here, as there is in America, forbidding the initiation of people with serious illnesses, or those who are chairbound for any reason.

'We've got men with wooden legs, we've got men who are lame. There is a lame man at one of the Lodges I go to. No, I suppose in parts of the ceremonies which are to do with legs it may be difficult, but we make special allowances, even if they don't do exactly what is laid down in the ritual. The Lodge committee will discuss this kind of difficulty and find ways to cope with it. So, yes, we accept people with a physical disability. If you had a mental disability you wouldn't want to be a Mason, and it would be embarrassing for a mentally handicapped person, and for members of the Lodge.'

As a Lewis, or son of a Freemason, author and *Sunday Times* feature writer Philip Knightley was able to join the Brotherhood at eighteen instead of twenty-one. When I contacted him he said that he had been wanting to tell someone about his masonic experience for years. He said, 'My father had been a Mason for years. I don't know how he joined. I think he was invited by friends.

'In Australia, the Masons have to single *you* out and invite you to join – it's the opposite to the system in England. If you make the approach first then you're likely to be turned down.

'After being initiated as an Entered Apprentice in

Sydney, I was to do my Second Degree in Fiji, where I'd gone. And so I switched from the jurisdiction of the New South Wales Lodge to the jurisdiction of a British colonial one. When the time approached for my Second Degree I was indirectly informed that they were not prepared to put me through the Second Degree. When I say indirectly, instead of telling me, the Lodge, which I'd visited several times, told the Australian Grand Lodge who told my Lodge who wrote to me via my father. The reason was that I had been associating with what were considered undesirable elements in the island – namely people who weren't white. So for the first time I realized that all the business about the brotherhood of man and brotherly love and all that applied largely to white Anglo-Saxon Protestants. And with the help of a Jehovah's Witness on the island who was brilliant in digging up references from the Bible, I composed a bitter letter of complaint about the behaviour of the Lodge, which I sent to the secretary of the Grand Lodge of New South Wales, quoting various references in the Bible about the brotherhood of man which had come up in various sections of the ritual. He didn't answer my letter. He told my father that the best thing to do was to wait until I came back to Australia and they'd continue with the process of making me a Master Mason there. His only excuse for the behaviour of the Fiji Lodge was to say that customs varied from country to country and I shouldn't be too harsh on local customs. I returned to Australia, took the second degree, third degree, became a Master Mason, continued to go to Lodge with my father, more as a social thing than anything else. But I eventually found it more and more boring, particularly because there was so much memorization. I thought that if I really wanted to tax my brain with remembering things, I could remember things of more use to me – like learning another language or something, instead of running through this endless ritual. And apart from the fact that one month it would be first degree, one month second degree, one month third degree, the *repetition* became boring. The food afterwards was lousy and I began to see little or no use in it intellectually.

'I continued as a Mason, but very intermittently. I went to live in Britain then in India. I didn't visit Lodges in India. I returned to Australia after about eight weeks as virtually a non-practising Mason, and I fell ill with a tropical fever, and was in hospital. This was in the early days of transistor radios, and the hospital had no radio sets or anything like that. One of our brother Masons owned a radio shop and he had a lot of transistors. My father asked him as a brother Mason, could he lend me a radio for my spell in hospital, and he said no. He said I might break it or something. That was just the final straw. It seems a trivial thing but I thought if he couldn't even lend me a radio, what the hell was the whole Brotherhood of Masonry about? And I just lapsed and let my subscriptions run out, and all that sort of thing. But, because it's once a Mason always a Mason, I could, no doubt, by reinstating my standing with the Lodge in Sydney, visit Lodges here and continue to be a Mason if I wanted to.'

CHAPTER 15

Jobs For the Brethren?

The traditional outsider's view of Freemasonry as a self-help organization is certainly an important facet of the Brotherhood in real life not, as many masonic apologists maintain, only in the imaginations of the 'profane'. Although a new initiate to Freemasonry declares on his honour that he offers himself as a candidate 'uninfluenced by mercenary or other unworthy motives', there can be no doubt that the majority of businessmen who become Masons do so because they believe it will assist them in business – as indeed it frequently does. Those who suggest that no selfish motive is ever present in the mind of the prospective Mason speak conscious humbug. One only has to speak to a handful of Freemasons and ex-Masons to realize how widespread the desire to 'get on' is in those who turn to the Brotherhood. This is not to denigrate the often very real desire for the legitimate privileges of Masonry – brotherhood, morality and charity – of many members. Many Freemasons, in addition to admitting that they joined primarily in the hope of having the edge in business and at job interviews, have told me they also think of Masonry as an insurance policy. If they become ill, they have the Royal Masonic Hospital. If they die, they feel confident that their wives and children will be taken care of financially. One man, the proprietor of a butcher's shop, a bakery and a launderette in a humble part of Cambridge, told me that he looked upon Masonic dues in precisely the same way as he did his National Insurance contributions, and as the union fees he had paid before becoming self-employed.

The exploitation of masonic membership, which, it must be said, most outsiders who are not directly affected by it accept as a part of the British way of life, comes into its own in the business world. Whether on the level of local trade or national commerce and industry, the Brotherhood plays a varying, often considerable, part in the awarding of contracts and in promotion.

On the local level, there is much cross-fertilization between Masonry and other groups of business people such as Round Table, Lions Clubs, and Rotary Clubs as well as Chambers of Commerce. Most of the male members of these organizations – and Chambers of Commerce at least contain an increasing number of women – are Freemasons as well. Men in business on their own account – for example, accountants, architects, builders, estate agents, restaurateurs, taxi firm proprietors, travel agents and shop keepers of all kinds – are strongly represented in Lodges up and down the country.

Commercial travellers frequently become Freemasons in order to be able to visit Lodges all over the country and to cultivate potential clients within the unique secret atmosphere of the Temple or the post-ritual dinner. There are no fewer than five Lodges named Commercial Travellers Lodge: in Darlington, Liverpool, London, Newcastle, and Preston.*

Ron Price, an insurance agent and a former Master Mason and Junior Deacon of a Lodge in Worcestershire, told me, 'Membership of Freemasonry is used considerably in the field of industry and commerce – because of the sign

*Nos 5089, 2631, 2795, 3700 and 3493 respectively.

one can give which is unnoticeable by anyone else. You can make it known to the other person that you are what they call on the square, and if the other person is on the square he will recognize the sign, and that can influence either your being able to make a sale or, if you are applying for a job, it can make the difference between whether you get the job or not.'

The sign by which a Mason may secretly make himself known to others in the room involves a particular arrangement of the feet. This arrangement is outlined in the ceremony of initiation to the First Degree. The Worshipful Master tells the Candidate, 'I shall, therefore, proceed to entrust you with the secrets of this degree, or those marks by which we are known to each other, and distinguished from the rest of the world . . . You are therefore expected to stand perfectly erect, your feet formed in a square, your body being thus considered an emblem of your mind, and your feet of the rectitude of your actions.' This is one of several bodily arrangements by which a Brother proclaims his affiliation to unknown brethren. If he is in a position to shake hands with the person to whom he wishes to identify himself, recognition becomes much easier. There are three basic handshakes in daily use, one for each of the first three degrees. The Entered Apprentice applies distinct pressure with his right thumb on the knuckle of the other man's forefinger. The Fellow Craft does the same thing with the second knuckle. The Master Mason applies distinct pressure with his right thumb between the knuckles of the other's middle and third finger.

Price went on, 'I have got business from two people as a result of being a Mason – not because I asked or made myself known particularly. Once it was actually in Lodge after dinner. I was sitting next to a man and he said, "Well, what is your business?" and I told him and he said, "Well, you can come along and have a chat with me," and I went along and had a chat and did some business. But after I came out of Freemasonry he didn't want to know. I had another case where I didn't really intend to convey that I was a Mason in any way but I obviously did so quite inadvertently because it was the natural way for me to shake hands. And as a result of that I got that particular client, but it faded when I resigned.'

A Grimsby restaurant owner told me that his one motive in joining Freemasonry was to 'ease the passage' of licence renewals. He said that before he became a Mason he had to contend with objections from the police and others, mainly individuals acting on behalf of his rivals. After becoming a Brother there were no further police objections because the majority of senior officers belonged to his Lodge, and such objections as were raised by others were from then on ignored by the local justices – because they, too, were members of the Lodge. He said, 'We help each other. Why not? It's what it's all about innit? I mean, you come to me, you scratch my back and I'll scratch yours. I'd be a bloody masochist if I didn't take advantage like everyone else, wouldn't I? We're all human.'

A Past Master of Eden Park Lodge No 5379 in Croydon told me he had worked for many years as a consultant for Taylor Woodrow, the construction, home building and property development group of companies. He said, 'Looking back, although I didn't think anything about it at the time, I suppose it was wrong. But quite a few times I know I got contracts because I gave a masonic grip. The whole board of directors of Taylor Woodrow were Freemasons then. I don't know about now.

'You'll find that nine out of ten architects are Masons – and there is no getting away from it, I would put in a tender and when I did so, I'd shake the architect by the hand. "Oh," he'd say, "you're a Mason. The contract is yours."

'Looking back on it now I can see that it was a bit too "wheels within wheels" to be right. I probably shouldn't have done it, but that's the way Masonry works. If there's a contract going from an architect, the chances are he's a Mason, so the chances are a Mason will get it.'

John Poulson, the notoriously corrupt architect whose activities in bribing local government officers, councillors, Civil Servants, officials of nationalized industries and others created a scandal which has been described by more than one commentator as the British Watergate, was an avid Freemason. Nothing surprising in itself, perhaps, but Poulson did use Masonry as a back door to obtaining business. In *Web of Corruption*, the definitive story of Poulson and his infamous PR man T. Dan Smith, the authors state:

If the Church was one of the focal points in Poulson's life, the Freemason's Lodge was another. In business much of what he did was behind closed doors, and he was naturally attracted to the secret society of Freemasonry, which practised morality, charity and obedience to the law and yet offered its members enormous political and business advantages. In the Middle Ages, you had to be a cathedral builder to become a Freemason but, in Poulson's Pontefract, the rule had been stood on its head, and an architect really needed to be a Freemason to design a block of flats. Poulson joined two lodges, De Lacy, code number Pontefract 4643, and Tateshall, code number 7647.* Together these lodges had recruited most of the town's business and professional people.

Poulson, say the authors, 'liked the ritual of Freemasonry, the rites and trappings and chivalric brotherhoods. He became master of both his Lodges and capped his underground career by being elected Provincial Grand Deacon of Yorkshire.' He exploited Masonry to the full in

*This is a typographical error in *Web of Corruption*. Tateshall Lodge, which meets at the Masonic Hall, Carleton Close, Pontefract, is numbered 7645.

advancing his professional interests and establishing contacts in all fields of potential advantage.

Banking is another stronghold of Freemasonry in the world of business. I have met bank employees at all levels from clerks in small local branches to directors of national clearing banks. It is generally accepted that promotion, although far from impossible for the non-Mason, less so now that so many women are entering banking, is nevertheless much more likely for the man who joins a Lodge early in his career. This is especially true of promotion to branch manager level and higher, where very few women or non-Masons reach even today. The Bank of England is rife with Masons and has its own Lodge.

I have been told by several informants how details of their bank accounts have been obtained by parties with no right to the information by way of masonic contacts in banks. The high proportion of bank managers and bank staff who are Freemasons can make the acquisition of this kind of confidential information relatively easy for a Mason, having as he does the right of access to every Lodge in the country. One man wanted to discover how much his twenty-nine-year-old daughter had in her two bank accounts, and to whom she had written cheques over the past year. He paid several visits to the Lodges in the town, about thirty miles away, where his daughter lived. Eventually he found a brother Mason who worked in a bank. It was an easy task for this Mason to telephone – through the legitimate inter-bank enquiry system – the branch where the other Mason's daughter had her accounts. When he obtained the information, the bank employee passed it to the father, doubtless convinced it was for good reasons as the request had come from a fellow Freemason. Indeed, the father himself believed it was for good reasons because he suspected that his daughter was involved with a man who was draining her of all she had. In fact, the daughter had a steady and long-term relationship with a man four years her junior who was studying for a PhD in London. They intended to marry when he got his doctorate. Meanwhile the woman was supporting him. This arrangement infuriated the father, whose view of life dated from the sterner 1920s. He traced the fiancé through the cheque records illicitly obtained from the bank, and wrecked the relationship by revealing to the man that his daughter had been pregnant by someone else when she met him, and had later, without his knowledge, had an abortion. This information had also been gleaned from clues obtained from cleared cheques from the masonic contacts in the bank.

In industry, Masonry is far stronger among white-collar workers and management up to the highest echelons, although once men on the shop floor attain the position of foremen or its equivalent, there is usually distinct advantage in joining the appropriate Lodge. The nationalized industries are rife with Freemasonry, especially the British Steel Corporation, the National Coal Board, British Rail, the Post Office, the regional gas and electricity boards and the Central Electricity Generating Board, the Atomic Energy Authority and London Transport. Mr Raymond B. Mole (Past Assistant Grand Director of Ceremonies, 1977), chief executive of the Royal Masonic Hospital at Hammersmith, told journalist Robert Eagle, 'You often find that when a man with London Transport gets promotion and a bit of gold braid on his uniform, he then starts thinking of becoming a Mason.'

Eagle's investigation was centred on Masonry in the medical profession, which is prevalent, especially among general practitioners and the more senior hospital doctors. Hospital Lodges prove useful meeting places for medical staff and administrators. Most main hospitals, including all the London teaching hospitals, have their own Lodges. According to Sir Edward Tuckwell, former Serjeant-

Surgeon to the Queen, and Lord Porritt, Chairman of the African Medical and Research Foundation, both Freemasons and both consultants to the Royal Masonic Hospital, the Lodges of the teaching hospitals draw their members from hospital staff and GPs connected with the hospital in question. Tuckwell and Porritt are members of the Lodges attached to the teaching hospitals where they trained and later worked – Porritt at St Mary's, Paddington (St Mary's Lodge No 63), which has about about forty active members out of a total of 300, half of them general practitioners; and Tuckwell at St Bartholomew's (Rahere Lodge No 2546), with about thirty active brethren. Other London hospital Lodges include King's College (No 2973); London Hospital, Whitechapel (No 2845); St Thomas's (No 142) and Moorfields (No 4949).

Many of the most senior members of the profession are Freemasons, especially those actively involved with the Royal College of Physicians and the Royal College of Surgeons, which has benefited from a massive £600,000 trust fund set up by the Brotherhood for medical research. Masonry does seem to have had an influence over certain appointments. Tuckwell emphatically denied that membership of the Brotherhood ever helped any doctor's career, telling Eagle that there was not the slightest truth in the rumour '. . . whereas Lord Porritt more circumspectly said that "it would be hard to deny that some people have been helped"'.

Although the governing bodies of most major hospitals are formed largely of Freemasons, the one overriding consideration in medicine, at least in the non-administrative areas, seems to be placing the best person in the job, whether Mason or otherwise. This is perhaps best illustrated by the staffing of the Brotherhood's own hospital. The Royal Masonic Hospital is not staffed exclusively by Freemasons, although most of its consultants are Brothers.

Chief executive of the hospital Raymond Mole says that Masonry is not a criterion for appointment. The only qualification demanded is that a Royal Masonic consultant be a consultant at a teaching hospital. Robert Eagle again:

> ... registrars at the hospital are not usually Masons ... one of the few women doctors to work at the Royal Masonic Hospital told me that during the several years she held the job she heard very little mention of the subject.
> 'Obviously no one asked me to join; but I had no idea whether even my closest colleague there was a Mason.' As she subsequently became a consultant at the hospital she does not seem to have been the victim of Masonic misogyny either.

Freemasonry plays a significant but declining role in the field of education. It is common for junior and secondary school headmasters and college lecturers to be Brothers. There are as many as 170 Old Boys Lodges in England and Wales, most of which have current teaching staff among their members.

The ambulance and fire services are strongly represented in Masonry, and there is a higher proportion of prison officers than police officers in the Brotherhood. Unlike the police, though, there is little fraternization between the higher and lower ranks in the service. The senior officers of prisons have their Lodges, the 'screws' theirs, and rare the twain shall meet. One premier London Lodge has in a matter of a few years completely changed its character due to an influx of prison officers from Wormwood Scrubs Prison. Lodge La Tolerance No 538, consecrated in 1847, until recently considered something of an élite Lodge, was in need of new members. One of the brethren knew a senior officer at the Scrubs who was interested in joining the Brotherhood, and it was agreed that he should be considered. The prison officer was interviewed and accepted into the Lodge. Such was the interest among the new initiate's colleagues that one by one the number of prison officers in Lodge La Tolerance increased. As more and more joined, so more and more older members left because they were unhappy with the changing character of the Lodge. Lodge No 538 is now dominated by prison officers from the Scrubs, where it is strongest in D Wing, the lifers' section. Although I have heard no allegations that promotion at the Scrubs is difficult for non-Masons, claims throughout the service of masonic favouritism are more common than in the police.

It is not possible in the space available to give more than a general survey of the part played by the Brotherhood in the field of business and work. The specific allegations investigated produce a picture of undeniable masonic influence over appointments, contracts and promotions in many areas, but also of widespread suspicion of masonic collusion where none exists. Certain strongly masonic areas of life not covered in this chapter are looked at in some detail elsewhere in the book.

CHAPTER 16

The Dissidents

One of my major sources of information was a former Grand Inspector Inquisitor Commander of the Thirty-First Degree of the Ancient and Accepted Rite who had withdrawn from Masonry in 1968 for religious reasons. As with so many other people in the labyrinthine world of Freemasonry, I was led to him by way of a series of contacts. He agreed through a third party to be interviewed by me concerning his conviction that no active Christian could in all conscience remain a Freemason.

When I met him I learned that he was a judge, and a particularly quick-tempered one. Although I had heard of him, I had hitherto known little about him.

We spent a long time talking about Masonry and religion, but after a while I began to ask him about the Ancient and Accepted Rite of the Thirty-Third Degree. He was, after all, only the fourth initiate to the Rite who had agreed to see me. He answered quickly. 'No, I dare not go into that,' he said. 'We'd better stick with religion.' It seemed a perfectly normal answer – I had received many such replies over the months of my investigation. It *sounded* like the usual rebuff. But I thought immediately afterwards how strange it was that he had used the words '*dare* not'. Most people said, 'I'd *better* not', or 'I'd *rather* not'. I remarked on his use of the word. He said, 'Anyone in public life has to be cautious.'

'Cautious,' I repeated. 'That's a masonic word of recognition.'

'You've obviously delved into the ritual, so you know,' he said. 'But I mean cautious in the sense everybody understands it.'

'What must you be cautious about?'

'Mr Knight, I don't like this line of questioning. I agreed to speak to you in general terms about why my commitment to Jesus is incompatible with the masonic religion. I do not wish to be drawn into discussion of matters covered by whatever undertakings I have . . . taken.'

'By undertakings, do you mean masonic oaths?'

He paused. 'Yes, I do. I prefer the word obligation to oath. It's not the same.'

I remember thinking as I turned the conversation back on to the track I wanted it to follow that it would be interesting later on to return to this question of the distinction between an obligation and an oath. I never did.

'*Why* do you have to be cautious, careful?' I said. 'You're not a Mason any more. I've got copies of all the rituals of the 4th to 33rd degree. There is no obligation which could possibly be interpreted to forbid you from telling me what you meant when you used the word "dare" in an ordinary conversation.'

'This isn't about my religious convictions, is it?'

'Many of your former masonic colleagues are very powerful people in this country. Do you think there would be some kind of reprisal if you gave away any secrets?'

'Not of the kind you write about in your book about Jack the Ripper.' He laughed. A bit hollowly, I thought.

'Well, not murder, no, I wouldn't have thought so.' I, too, laughed. I felt oddly embarrassed. 'But there is *some* kind of reprisal to be feared then? Something more . . . subtle?'

He began to look angry. He had made a slip. 'That was a

figure of sp— I was making a joke. A very bad joke.'

'But you said—'

'I know, I know! And I do not believe for one moment that what you suggest in your book has happened in real life – then or ever.'

I could see the rattled ex-Mason automatically slipping back into the practice of a lifetime. *Sometimes you shall divert a discourse, and manage it prudently for the honour of the worshipful fraternity.* I would not be diverted into defending the evidence and arguments in my first book. I felt I was close to something. I pressed on.

'Leaving murder aside, can I ask you . . .' And then it hit me. 'Can I ask you, *as a Christian*, have you ever seen at first hand any sort of reprisals carried out by Freemasons using masonic influence against any non-Freemason or anti-Freemason?'

All at once, he seemed to relax, or to somehow collapse into a smaller man as he let all the anger go out of him. 'As a Christian . . .' He paused thoughtfully, and I noticed how very many times he blinked his eyes during this hiatus. I wondered at one point if he was praying for guidance. He drew a long, slow, deep breath. 'As a Christian, I have to tell you that I have never in my whole life witnessed or heard about a single act of hostility by a Freemason or group of Freemasons *that was sanctioned by Grand Lodge or Supreme Council.*' He looked at me significantly as he laid stress on that qualifying clause. 'There,' he said. 'I have said nothing which betrays my obligations.'

'I have heard from quite a lot of contacts about organized action by groups of Freemasons that have resulted in the financial or social ruin of certain people,' I said.

'So have I,' he said, still looking me straight in the eye as if telling me this was important. '*So have I, Mr Knight.*'

'Have you any direct knowledge of such happenings?'

'Not of such happenings *which had the backing of official Freemasonry.*'

'But of action which was *un*official? In other words, Masons abusing the Craft for their own ends?'

'You know the answer to that, from the way I have said what I have said.'

'I have also heard about people who have "crossed" certain Masons and finished up in prison . . .'

He stopped me in mid-sentence by placing a finger on his lips.

'If I told you everything I know about Freemasonry being betrayed by its members, it would surprise even you,' he said. 'It would make your hair stand on end. I can't tell you any more.' Then, as if it was an afterthought, but I don't believe it was, he said, 'Give me your phone number. You might hear from someone in a few days.'

I gave him the number. 'Who?' I said.

The finger went back to his lips and he went to fetch my coat.

'God bless,' he said as I left, and I ran pell-mell to a sandwich bar in nearby Chancery Lane to scribble down the notes on which this account of our meeting has been based.

Four days later I received a phone call from a man who told me he had seen my advertisement for people with information about Freemasonry in an old copy of the *New Statesman.** He said he had read my *Jack the Ripper: The Final Solution* and would very much like to meet me. I tried, as I tried with all my callers, to get him to say something concrete on the phone, but he would not even tell me whether or not he was a Mason. I had already

*This advertisment had appeared for four weeks in the summer of 1981, some nine months earlier.

received a dozen or so similar calls, some of which had proved useful, some wild goose chases. But the researcher's world is the natural habitat of wild geese and red herrings, and one accepts the necessity of chasing them. Despite his unwillingness to talk – perhaps, in a way, because of it – I arranged to meet him the following Saturday in the vestibule of the Café Royal. From there we would go to his club. He said his name was Christopher. Whether this was his Christian name or his surname I didn't know.

When I arrived, he was sitting in the armchair to the right of the fireplace just inside the entrance, smoking a small cigar in a holder and reading that day's *Times*. He was tall, more than six feet, slim and aged about fifty. Everything about him spoke of affluence, except his plain National Health Service glasses. We went to his club, which he pledged me not to name as it could be used to identify him. It turned out that Christopher was one of his three Christian names and that he was a very senior Civil Servant in Whitehall. He had contacted me, he said, not as a result of seeing the *New Statesman* advertisement – although he had seen it when it appeared – but at the request of my cautious Christian judge. He asked me what I wanted to know. I said I took it that he was a Freemason. He nodded and took some papers out of his slimline brief-case. He wanted me to be in no doubt as to his bona fides.

After examining the papers I told him I was interested to know what a person might have to fear from a group of influential Freemasons if circumstances made him, for instance, a threat to them in the business world; or if he discovered they were using Masonry for corrupt purposes; or had fallen a victim of their misuse of Freemasonry and would not heed warnings not to oppose them.

'It is not difficult to ruin a man,' he said. 'And I will tell you how it is done time and again. There are more than half a million brethren under the jurisdiction of Grand Lodge.

Standards have been falling for twenty or thirty years. It is too easy to enter the Craft, so many men of dubious morals have joined. The secrecy and power attract such people, and when they come the decent leave. The numbers of people who would never have been considered for membership in the fifties are getting larger all the time. If only five per cent of Freemasons use – *abuse* – the Craft for selfish or corrupt ends it means there are 25,000 of them. The figure is much closer to twelve or thirteen per cent now.'

It transpired that Christopher was one of a small and unpopular group within Masonry who some time in the early seventies had decided that either they had to get out of the Brotherhood or they had to do something 'to stop the rot' which the blinkered officers of Great Queen Street refused to admit was there. His reason for talking to me was to assure me that the Brotherhood was an essentially good body of men devoted to all that was best in the British social system and which promoted brotherly love and contributed to the wellbeing of the country and to the relief of suffering. He wanted this put firmly across to the public, and his group wanted pressure brought to bear on those in positions of responsibility within the Brotherhood to put Freemasonry's house in order – to institute proper policing, to close down Lodges used for shady dealings and to root out corrupt brethren and expel them. The group – it had no name – also wanted the whole business of masonic secrecy looked into by Grand Lodge, most of them believing that secrecy was more harmful than helpful to Masonry.

Christopher explained that Masonry's nationwide organization of men from most walks of life provided one of the most efficient private intelligence networks imaginable. Private information on anybody in the country could normally be accessed very rapidly through endless permutations of masonic contacts – police, magistrates, solicitors, bank managers, Post Office staff ('very useful in supplying copies of a man's mail'), doctors, government employees, bosses of firms and nationalized industries etc., etc. A dossier of personal data could be built up on anybody very quickly. When the major facts of an individual's life were known, areas of vulnerability would become apparent. Perhaps he is in financial difficulties; perhaps he has some social vice – if married he might 'retain a mistress' or have a proclivity for visiting prostitutes; perhaps there is something in his past he wishes keep buried, some guilty secret, a criminal offence (easily obtainable through Freemason police of doubtful virtue), or other blemish on his character: all these and more could be discovered via the wide-ranging masonic network of 600,000 contacts, a great many of whom were disposed to do favours for one another because that had been their prime motive for joining. Even decent Masons could often be 'conned' into providing information on the basis that 'Brother Smith needs this to help the person involved'. The adversary would even sometimes be described as a fellow Mason to the Brother from whom information was sought – perhaps someone with access to his bank manager or employer. The 'good' Mason would not go to the lengths of checking with Freemasons Hall whether or not this was so. If the 'target' was presented as a Brother in distress by a fellow Mason, especially a fellow Lodge member, that would be enough for any upright member of the Craft.*

Sometimes this information-gathering process – often

---

*I discovered from other sources that this system has been long established within Masonry for the 'legitimate' purpose of bringing succour to a distressed Brother Mason or to the family of a departed Mason. It is common for details of a Freemason's debts, for instance, to be passed to his Lodge by his masonic bank manager. This 'invasion of privacy' is for no more sinister reason than for his brethren to club together and pay off his debts. This occurs most often after the death of a Mason, but by no means always. And this, apparently, is just one example of the many methods by which Freemasons obtain information *about each other* for genuine purposes.

involving a long chain of masonic contacts all over the country and possibly abroad – would be unnecessary. Enough would be known in advance about the adversary to initiate any desired action against him.

I asked how this 'action' might be taken.

'Solicitors are very good at it,' said Christopher. 'Get your man involved in something legal – it need not be serious – and you have him.' Solicitors, I was told, are 'past masters' at causing endless delays, generating useless paperwork, ignoring instructions, running up immense bills, misleading clients into taking decisions damaging to themselves.

Masonic police can harass, arrest on false charges, and plant evidence. 'A businessman in a small community or a person in public office arrested for dealing in child pornography, for indecent exposure, or for trafficking in drugs is at the end of the line,' said Christopher. 'He will never work again. Some people have committed suicide after experiences of that kind.'

Masons can bring about the situation where credit companies and banks withdraw credit facilities from individual clients and tradesmen, said my informant. Banks can foreclose. People who rely on the telephone for their work can be cut off for long periods. Masonic employees of local authorities can arrange for a person's drains to be inspected and extensive damage to be reported, thus burdening the person with huge repair bills; workmen carrying out the job can 'find' – in reality *cause* – further damage. Again with regard to legal matters, a fair hearing is hard to get when a man in ordinary circumstances is in financial difficulties. If he is trying to fight a group of unprincipled Freemasons skilled in using the 'network' it will be impossible because masonic Department of Health and Social Security and Law Society officials (see pp 189-90) can delay applications for Legal Aid endlessly.

'Employers, if they are Freemasons or not, can be given private information about a man who has made himself an enemy of Masonry. At worst he will be dismissed (if the information is true) or consistently passed over for promotion.'

Christopher added, 'Masonic doctors can also be used. But for some reason doctors seem to be the least corruptible men. There are only two occurrences of false medical certificates issued by company doctors to ruin the chances of an individual getting a particular job which I know about. It's not a problem that need greatly worry us like the rest.'

He continued for about half an hour to list examples of the ways in which corrupt members of the Brotherhood could defeat opposition, repeating every few minutes that these kinds of circumstances involved a minority of the brethren and that most would be utterly appalled at even the suggestion that such things were happening, let alone countenance them. That they were happening at all reflected the deterioration of the Craft inasmuch as its entry requirements were no longer stringent enough. Those in power in Freemasons Hall knew something of what went on, but they felt defeated by it and preferred to look the other way rather than take steps to eradicate it. If Christopher and his group failed to force the issue into the open, he said, the organization would become so morally polluted that it would simply cease to exist. But he was not solely concerned with the Brotherhood. It was the victims of those who used Masonry as a source of personal power who had to be helped as well.

'Only the fighters have any hope of beating the system once it's at work against them,' he told me. 'Most people, fighters or not, are beaten in the end, though. It's . . . you see, I . . . you finish up not knowing who you can trust. You can get no help because your story sounds so paranoid that you are thought a crank, one of those nuts who think the whole world is a conspiracy against *them*. It is a strange phenomenon. By setting up a situation that most people will think of as fantasy, these people can poison every part of a person's life. If they give in they go under. If they don't give in it's only putting off the day because if they fight, so much unhappiness will be brought to the people around them that there will likely come a time when even their families turn against them out of desperation. When that happens and they are without friends wherever they look, they become easy meat. The newspapers will not touch them.

'There is no defence against an evil which only the victims and the perpetrators know exists.'

PART FOUR

The Law

CHAPTER 17

The System

A large number of people who have contacted me in the past seven years have been concerned that Freemasons in the judiciary and legal profession exercise a pernicious influence over the administration of justice. Allegations of collusion between judges and lawyers, on behalf of their brethren in the dock, have been rife. The impartiality of Freemason judges has been called into question. There have been claims of huge masonic conspiracies between rival firms of solicitors and suggestions that Freemasonry is such a Grey Eminence that proceedings in open court are merely outward show, while everything is decided in advance, long before cases involving Masons reach court. I have heard many claims of civil battles lost and won on the basis of masonic signs made in court. Even the odd murderer is said to have got himself off by pulling the trick at an opportune moment.

But are any of these fears grounded in truth?

The legal system of England and Wales has certainly been a bastion of Freemasonry for generations. For a first opinion on whether this poses any kind of threat I approached the head of the judiciary, the Lord High Chancellor of Great Britain.

One of the most powerful men in the country, the Lord Chancellor is responsible for the appointment of High

Court judges, Recorders, Circuit judges and magistrates, as well as having a host of other duties. In his office come together the three powers of government – judicial, legislative and executive – which in all other individual constitutional positions except that of the Sovereign are kept separate as a safeguard against tyranny. As head of the judiciary he is the most powerful man in the first of the three spheres of power; as President of the House of Lords he exercises legislative power; and as a member of the Cabinet he exercises executive power. At the time of writing, this position – eighth in order of precedence after the Sovereign – is occupied by the Rt Hon Lord Hailsham of St Marylebone. So fervent is Hailsham's faith in the incorruptibility of the legal system over which he presides that when I tackled him on the subject he swept aside the widespread concern that a Freemason judge might be tempted to show favour to members of the Brotherhood who appear before him. Freemasonry is irrelevant in the administration of justice in England, says Hailsham. He told me he was not a Mason and declared that my research was 'worthless activity' and my book 'a valueless project'.

Lord Gardiner, Labour's Lord Chancellor in the four years prior to Hailsham's first appointment to the office in 1970, was a senior Mason. Lord Elwyn-Jones, Lord Chancellor in the Labour years between 1974 and 1979, when Hailsham was reappointed on the advice of Margaret Thatcher, was not a Freemason.

After the Lord Chancellor, the highest judicial appointments are to the Supreme Court of Judicature. These are:

Lord Chief Justice: Head of the Court of Appeal (Criminal Division); Head of the Queen's Bench Division of the High Court; Member of the House of Lords. Current incumbent: Lord Lane of St Ippollitts in the County of Hertfordshire (Life Peer, born 1918).

Master of the Rolls: Lord Chancellor's deputy. Head of the Court of Appeal (Civil Division). In charge of superintending the admission of solicitors to the Rolls of the Supreme Court. Current incumbent: the Rt Hon Sir John Donaldson, PC (born 1920).

President of the Family Division: Head of the High Court division which handles matters including matrimonial appeals from magistrates' courts (maintenance, separation orders, etc.), marriage of minors, divorce, and non-contentious probate. Current incumbent: the Rt Hon Sir John Lewis Arnold (born 1915).

Vice-Chancellor of the Chancery Division: Head, after the official President (the Lord Chancellor), of the High Court division dealing with matters that include private, public and charitable trusts, the administration of the estates of those who have died, dissolving and winding up companies and other company-related matters, mortgages and land charges, wards of court, revenue, bankruptcy, contractual disputes, and commercial partnership matters. Current incumbent: the Rt Hon Sir Robert Megarry (born 1910).

I wrote to all these men asking if they were members of the Brotherhood. My first letter to Lord Lane received no reply; my second was opened and returned to me without comment. Sir John Donaldson, before he succeeded Lord Denning, a non-Mason, as Master of the Rolls, told me, 'I do not really feel that the question of whether or not I am a Mason is a matter of public concern . . . It is a totally irrelevant consideration in our work.' Sir John's wife is tipped as the first woman Lord Mayor of London, an office that membership of the Brotherhood is usually helpful in obtaining. Sir John Arnold, who did not reply to two letters, is a Freemason of grand rank. He was an Assistant

Grand Registrar in 1970 and was promoted to Past Junior Grand Warden in 1973. Sir Robert Megarry did not reply to two letters. If he is a Freemason, and most people I have spoken to who know him think it unlikely, he is not of grand rank.

Lord Lane's predecessor as Lord Chief Justice, Lord Widgery, was an extremely enthusiastic Freemason of grand rank, holding office as Past Junior Grand Warden and Past Senior Grand Warden.

CHAPTER 18

The Two-Edged Sword

A former High Court judge who had been a member of the Brotherhood for more than fifty years told me, 'Yes, I knew which judges were and which judges were not Freemasons in my time. I am speaking of the High Court and Court of Appeal only – and of course the Law Lords. I know, I think, most of the judges who are Freemasons who currently sit in those courts. I am not at liberty to give you names, you understand. If they wish you to know they will tell you themselves. For myself, I can't see why you shouldn't know. Being a Freemason is the last thing I would wish to hide. I *can* tell you that there were many judges in my time who were members of the Craft. Probably fifteen years ago, sixty or seventy per cent of us were Masons. It's lower now – probably not much above fifty per cent – and that's not necessarily good.'

I asked if in his view Masonry exerted any influence over judges.

'Of course it does. Freemasonry cannot fail to influence a man. It has a very great influence for good.'

'And ill?'

'Only very occasionally.'

'Can you be more specific?'

'Yes I can. Freemasonry teaches a man to love his fellow men. Now, that might sound twee, but it isn't. It's perhaps more important than anything else in the world.'

'The good it brings or can bring is like the good that can come from Christianity, then? Or Buddhism?'

'Yes. But it's bigger than Christianity. Bigger than all religions because it embraces them all.'

'You said it occasionally has a bad influence.'

'Judges are men. Freemasons are men. Being a Christian doesn't make you like Christ, try as you might. The problem is in understanding what your religion, be it Christianity, Buddhism, Hindu or whatever you like, is all about, isn't it? It's a misunderstanding of the tenets of Freemasonry's aims, which can cause serious moral problems sometimes. But judges are less likely to misunderstand or misinterpret than most other people. The problem of the judge, and you realize this every day you sit, is that he's human.

'I have known two cases in my entire life at the Bar and on the Bench when Freemasonry influenced a judge in a way he should not, properly speaking, have been influenced. Bear in mind this is two cases out of perhaps twenty or thirty occasions when I have seen a man indicate by a movement or form of words that he was a Freemason.'

'That sort of thing does happen, then?'

'Of course it does. But we ignore it.'

'Most judges who are Freemasons say it doesn't happen.'

'It can't truly be said that people don't try these things because some people do. And who can blame them? I think part of Freemasonry's problem is that it tries to pretend that men in the Craft are above using it for their personal benefit. That's rubbish. Many wouldn't consider using it – most I would say. But thousands do every day, in all areas of life.'

'So some Freemasons who appear in court do try to use their membership to help them.'

'I've said so. Some, but in my experience not many.

Hundreds of Masons must pass through the courts without
anyone knowing if they are in the Craft or not.'

'How can a Freemason make it known that he is a Mason
without non-Masons in the court being aware that he is
doing or saying something strange?'

'I am not at liberty to tell you these things because they
are covered by our pledge of secrecy. There are certain
words, certain phrases, certain motions. If you weren't a
Freemason you wouldn't notice. They are not big gestures
or anything like that, or strange mumbo-jumbo words.'

'What happened on the two occasions when the judge
was swayed by the knowledge that the man before him was
a Freemason?'

'It happened years and years ago when I was defending
two brothers on charges of larceny. After re-examination of
the younger of the two, the judge started asking him some
particularly awkward questions which hadn't been raised by
the prosecution. My client began to stumble over his words
and contradicted himself on a fundamental point. The
judge – who I should point out was a bit eccentric anyway
and was retired prematurely – spotted it straight away and
said that what my client had just said meant he could not
have been speaking the truth before. Before he had finished
speaking, my client made a sign which told the judge he was
a Mason. Instead of ignoring it, he reacted.'

'How?'

'He looked surprised and very disconcerted.'

'What did he say?'

'Nothing. And he did not ask the questions which
should naturally have followed.'

'What happened?'

'In his summing-up to the jury, the judge turned the
incident back-to-front and referred to my client's sincerity.
He went as far as suggesting that the jury might well
consider that any apparent contradiction in his evidence

was due not to a wish to befog the truth but to a confusion arising from the strain of a long hearing and natural nervousness.'

'Couldn't that have been true?'

'My client was lying. I knew it and the judge must have known. Nobody can say that the judge's summing up does not influence a jury, and on all but the main charge the Freemason was acquitted. The brother, who had not been the prime mover, was found guilty on all charges. In sentencing them, the non-Mason received two years and the Mason a year – for the same crime.'

'The other case?'

'Was when I was on the Bench, but it wasn't a case of mine. The judge was a very eminent Freemason, now dead. A man said something which made it clear he too was a Freemason. The judge told me afterwards that he had imposed a much more severe sentence than he would otherwise have done for that offence.'

'Why?'

'Because, as he saw it, the crime was the more reprehensible because a Freemason had committed it, and the defendant had compounded this "betrayal" of Freemasonry by abusing the masonic bond of brotherhood that existed between himself and the judge.'

'Do you agree with the judge's action?'

'No, I do not. But it does show that Freemasonry among the judiciary can be a two-edged sword.'

CHAPTER 19

The Mason Poisoner

'Frederick Henry Seddon, you stand convicted of wilful murder. Have you anything to say for yourself why the Court should not give judgement of death according to law?'

'I have, sir.'

Reading from notes, the poisoner calmly spoke of his innocence of the murder of his middle-aged spinster lodger Eliza Barrow. Then, turning to the judge, Seddon made a masonic sign. 'I declare before the Great Architect of the Universe I am not guilty, my lord.'

The Hon Mr Justice Bucknill, PC, who was approaching his sixty-seventh birthday, was a senior Freemason. In all his thirty-seven years as barrister, Recorder, and finally Judge of the Queen's Bench Division of the High Court of Justice, he had never encountered anything like this. He was appalled. He had no alternative but to sentence this avaricious killer to death. And now, at the very last moment, that killer had revealed himself as a fellow Mason – one of those whom Bucknill had sworn on bended knee and on pain of being 'severed in two, my bowels burned to ashes', to assist in adversity and to 'cheerfully and liberally stretch forth the hand of kindness to save him from sinking . . .'

This incident at the Old Bailey on 12 March 1912 passed

quickly into legend. Like most legends, it has grown, changed, and become confused in the telling. There are now almost as many versions of it as there are people who quote it. I have heard versions set as early as the 1850s and as late as the 1940s. I have heard it applied to murderers as diverse as William Palmer, Crippen, Haigh, Christie, Armstrong and Buck Ruxton. In 1972 a man being interviewed about Freemasonry on television applied the story to Rouse, the blazing car murderer who was hanged in 1931. In this version it was embellished to the point where the prisoner in the dock produced his full masonic regalia and appealed to the judge to free him! The judge in the case has been variously named as Sir James Fitzjames Stephen, Lord Justice Avory and others. Most people who repeat the yarn do not identify the characters involved. To them it is the story of the masonic murderer who made secret signs to the masonic judge and as a result . . .

The dénouement is another variable. Countless people have told me that the murderer was saved from execution as a direct result of the judge learning he was a Freemason. Many more, mainly Masons, denounce this as a lie.

It is important that the truth of this most famous of all stories about Freemasonry perverting the cause of justice within a court of law should be understood at the outset.

When Bucknill realized that Seddon was a Mason he was speechless. He seemed completely dazed as the black cap was placed on his head and oblivious to the usher crying out the traditional, 'Oyez! Oyez! My lords, the King's justices do strictly charge and command all persons to keep silence while sentence of death is passing upon the prisoner at the bar, upon pain of imprisonment. God save the King!'

Even now Bucknill sat as if struck dumb for a full minute. When he had composed himself enough to speak, he said, 'Frederick Henry Seddon, you have been found guilty of the wilful murder of Eliza Mary Barrow. With that verdict I am bound to say I agree. I should be more than terribly pained if you thought that I, in my charge to the jury, had stated anything against you that was not supported by the evidence. But even if what you say is strictly correct, that there is no evidence that you ever were left at a material time alone in the room with the deceased person, there is still in my opinion ample evidence to show that you had the opportunity of putting poison into her food or in her medicine. You have a motive for this crime. That motive was greed of gold. Whether it was that you wanted to put an end to the annuities or not, I know not. You only can know. Whether it was to get the gold that was or was not – but which you thought was – in the cash box, I do not know. But I think I do know this: that you wanted to make a great pecuniary profit by felonious means. This murder has been described by yourself in the box as one which, if made out against you, was a barbarous one; a murder of design, a cruel murder. It is not for me to harrow your feelings.'

All through the admonition, the judge was visibly shaken. The prisoner meanwhile listened calmly to Bucknill's quiet, gentlemanly tones. 'I do believe he was the most peaceful man in the court,' wrote Filson Young, a journalist who was there.

'It does not affect me, I have a clear conscience,' said Seddon.

'I have very little more to say,' went on Bucknill, struggling with the powerful emotional conflict Seddon had brought about by that one reference to the Great Architect of the Universe, 'except to remind you that you have had a very fair and patient trial. Your learned counsel, who has given his undivided time to this case, has done everything that a counsel at the English Bar could do. The Attorney General [prosecuting] has conducted his case with remarkable fairness. The jury has shown patience and intelligence I have never seen exceeded by any jury with which I had to do.'

Every now and again, the judge's voice dropped to a whisper. It did so now. 'I, as minister of the Law, have now to pass upon you that sentence which the Law demands has to be passed, which is that you have forfeited your life in consequence of your great crime. Try and make peace with your Maker.'

'I am at peace.'

'From what you have said,' and the judge was now all but sobbing, 'you and I know we both belong to one Brotherhood, and it is all the more painful to me to have to say what I am saying. But our Brotherhoood does not encourage crime. On the contrary, it condemns it. I pray you again to make your peace with the Great Architect of the Universe. Mercy – pray for it, ask for it . . .'

He continued speaking for about half a minute before pausing and bracing himself. 'And now I have to pass sentence,' he said, looking across the hushed courtroom at his Brother with tears filling his eyes. Another long pause. 'The sentence of the court is that you be taken from hence to a lawful prison, and from thence to a place of execution, and that you be there hanged by the neck until you are dead. And that your body be buried within the precincts of the prison in which you shall have been confined after your conviction. And may the Lord have mercy on your soul.'

This, then, is the real story about the Freemason murderer and the Freemason judge. But getting the facts straight is only half the battle. Only by perceiving what was behind the facts can we decide if this so-called 'classic' case is even relevant. Freemasons will say that Bucknill's reaction to Seddon's appeal for help is proof positive that there is no masonic influence on the execution of justice. Anti-Masons will argue that Seddon made his appeal too late, that by the time he made clear the esoteric bond between himself and the judge he was beyond help because the jury had already declared its verdict. Thus, although Bucknill might have wanted desperately to 'save him from sinking', his hands were tied.

Both these arguments are specious: the Bucknill–Seddon case proves nothing. The reason for this is simple. Seddon was *not* trying to exploit the masonic bond between them to influence the judge's actions.

This must be clear to anyone who returns to the original transcript of the trial. First, if he had intended to influence the judge in his favour, he would have made his membership of the Brotherhood clear at an earlier stage – certainly before the verdict had been returned, and before the judge's summing-up, by which a jury might conceivably be swayed. And if he had expected his Masonry to help him, he would surely have communicated the fact that he was a Brother to the judge in a way which would not have been noticed by others. There are methods, as I found out for myself, for Masons to identify themselves to one another without incongruous signals and invoking aloud the Great Architect. No, it is clear that Seddon was not saying to Bucknill, 'I am a Freemason like you. Help me,' but that he was using the masonic term for God to reinforce the usual oath he had taken on entering the witness box to speak the truth, the whole truth and nothing but the truth. It came as a natural culmination of his carefully thought-out speech in his own defence:

. . . The prosecution has not traced anything to me in the shape of money, which is the great motive suggested by the prosecution in this case for my committing the diabolical crime of which I declare by the Great Architect of the Universe I am not guilty, my lord. Anything more I might have to say I do not suppose will be of any account, but still if it is the last words that I speak, I am not guilty of the crime of which I stand committed.

As he said, 'I declare . . .', he lifted up his hand to accompany the oath and to show it was his solemn word. Yes, it was a masonic sign. Yes, they were masonic words. But they were the natural words of a Freemason wishing to convey with all possible gravity that he was speaking the truth. That Seddon's action was perfectly natural and quite lacking in the sinister undertones ascribed to it by anti-Masons and others is shown by the openness with which it was performed. Because there was nothing hidden in the interaction between Seddon and Bucknill, it remains interesting to the student of Freemasonry only in the depth of brotherly feeling which was either inborn in Judge Bucknill or which Freemasonry had instilled in him. It tells us nothing of any alleged influence by Masonry in the courts.

CHAPTER 20

Barristers and Judges

Where Freemasonry does play a big part – and this is why so many judges are Masons – is in the process by which appointments to the Bench are made. I discovered this as a result of acting on the advice of a London Circuit judge who wrote to me:

Apart from the professional judiciary, I would think it just as important to ascertain the position in respect of the lay magistrates who decide the overwhelming number of cases, especially outside London . . . I would not hold out much hope of success, but it might be worth asking the Lord Chancellor's Department if any consideration is given to Masonry when applicants for the Magistracy are interviewed.

There would have been no hope of getting a straight answer to the question by a direct approach, but after some weeks I established contact with an acquaintance of an acquaintance of a contact of a trusted fellow writer. This man, as a senior official in the Lord Chancellor's Department, knew a great deal of the behind-the-scenes wheeling and dealing which culminates in the appointment of a judge, magistrate or other member of the judiciary.

Judges are appointed from the ranks of those barristers and solicitors who have been in practice for at least ten years. Although there is a growing tendency for solicitors to be given preferment to the judiciary, the great majority of judges are former barristers.

To understand why Freemasonry is so powerful in the law, it is helpful to be familiar with the distinct roles of the two branches of the legal profession.

The barrister is the only member of the profession who has the right of audience in any court in the country. Whereas solicitors may be heard only in Magistrates' Courts, County Courts and, in certain circumstances, Crown Courts, a barrister can present and argue a client's case in all these as well as in the High Court, the Court of Appeal, and the House of Lords. But unlike the solicitor, the barrister cannot deal with the client direct. Contact between client and barrister is supposed always to be through the solicitor, although this does not always work out in practice. The etiquette of the profession demands that the solicitor, not the client, instructs the barrister. Thus the barrister is dependent on the solicitor for his living.

In England, the rank of barrister-at-law is conferred exclusively by four unincorporated bodies in London, known collectively as the Honourable Societies of the Inns of Court. The four Inns, established between 1310 and 1357, are Lincoln's Inn, Gray's Inn, the Middle Temple and the Inner Temple. Prior to the establishment of the latter two Inns, the Temple, which lies between Fleet Street and the River Thames, was the headquarters of the Knights Templar, declared heretics by King Philip IV of France and wiped out during the early fourteenth century. There is a modern-day Order of Knights Templar within British Freemasonry which claims direct descent from the medieval order. From the beginning the men of law were linked with Freemasonry.

Each Inn has its own library, dining-hall and chapel. Thousands of barristers' chambers are crammed into the large, impressive eighteenth- and nineteenth-century houses. There are cobbled alleys, covered passages, Gothic arches and winding stairs. There are gardens, swards, opulent residences and courtyards, all turning their backs on the outside world and looking into their own small world, redolent of dusty ledgers, moth-eaten wigs, public school mores, black gowns, scarlet robes and all the ponderous unchanging majesty of the law of old England.

Each Inn is owned by its Honourable Society and is governed by its own senior members – barristers and judges – who are known as Benchers. The Benchers decide which students will be called to the Bar (that is, made barristers) and which will not. Their decision is final. As with so much else in British Law, ancient customs attend the passage of students to their final examinations and admission. Candidates must of course pass examinations, which are set by the Council for Legal Education. But in addition they must 'keep twelve terms', which in everyday language means that on a set number of occasions in each legal term (Hilary, Easter, Trinity and Michaelmas) for three years, candidates must dine at their Inn. If they do so without fail, pass their exams and pay their fees they will then be called, and the degree, or rank, of barrister-at-law will be bestowed upon them.

The Scottish equivalent of a barrister is an advocate, and the Scottish equivalent of the Inns of Court is the Faculty of Advocates in Edinburgh. King's Inn, Dublin, is the Irish counterpart of the English Inns.

In 1966 a Senate of the Inns of Court was set up as an overall governing body. Its first president was, not unexpectedly, a Freemason of grand rank: Mr Justice Widgery. Widgery had been Junior Grand Warden in the United Grand Lodge in 1961. In Masonry he went on to become Senior Grand Warden in 1972, and in the non-secret world to become the first Lord Chief Justice of England to have been a solicitor as well as a barrister.

The Senate itself was superseded in 1974 by a new body which combined the functions of the Senate with the General Council of the Bar. This was given the name of Senate of the Inns of Court and the Bar and to its ninety-four members including six Benchers from each Inn devolved the duty to oversee the conditions of admission, legal education and welfare, and the authority to discipline and disbar, which was previously vested in each Honourable Society. The presidents since 1974 have been Lord Justice Templeman, Lord Scarman, Lord Justice Waller, Lord Justice Ackner and Lord Justice Griffiths. Of these, Waller is a Freemason of grand rank; Templeman did not respond to letters of enquiry; Ackner, asked if he was a Mason, could 'give . . . no information at all concerning Freemasonry'; Griffiths, in reply to the same question, regretted that he was unable to enter into correspondence on the matter raised; and Scarman did not reply.

Gray's Inn has its own Craft Lodge – No 4938 – which has its own Royal Arch Chapter and which meets at Freemasons Hall on the third Monday of January, March and October (its yearly installation meeting) and on the first Monday of December.

Some specialized sections of the Bar have their own Lodges, such as the Chancery Bar Lodge (No 2456), constituted in 1892, whose membership comprises barristers dealing mainly in chancery matters and judges of the Chancery Division of the High Court. The Lodge meets in Lincoln's Inn Hall. Masonic barristers are among the hardest Masons of all to persuade to talk, or even admit to being part of the Brotherhood. Take, for example, the barrister with chambers in Gray's Inn who, unable in truth to deny his membership, told me, 'I don't know in what circumstances you may or may not have been told and I am not in a position to discuss the matter with you in any shape or form.' While the Bar remains a masonic stronghold, there is not such a high proportion of masonic barristers as masonic solicitors, who are looked at in Chapter 21.

One reason there was always less need for a barrister to join the Brotherhood is that barristers traditionally had the compensation of circuit life. One barrister told me: 'We are already a brotherhood in a sense. We are a small profession and are therefore very close to each other in any event, and don't really need the additional qualification of being Freemasons in order to be known among ourselves.' Despite this, Masonry remains strong. Why?

The Bar is a strange profession in many ways, not least because most of the very top people *do not want* preferment, thus creating great opportunities for second-raters. I was first given insight into this phenomenon by an experienced barrister, a non-Mason, who had excellent contacts in Masonry. He told me, 'A top silk can earn between a quarter and half a million pounds a year. He will not thank you if he is promoted to being a High Court judge, because his income will drop by ninety per cent.* And with the prestige and respect in which he is already held, the automatic knighthood that goes with an appointment to the High Court would be neither here nor there. This applies to half a dozen, perhaps a dozen of the really household names.

'And there has been considerable evidence, certainly since the war, that the appointments to the High Court bench have been – with a few notable exceptions – if not second eleven members, at least not the first rank of the first division.

'This was underlined with the appointment of Henry Fisher to the Queen's Bench Division of the High Court in

*The annual salary of a High Court judge in 1982-3 was £42,500.

1968. Fisher had been an absolute top practitioner in City matters – commercial law and the like. He accepted the appointment to the High Court Bench, then two years later made legal history by resigning to go back into commercial life. He couldn't return to the Bar of course, but he went into the City as a company director. In 1973 he became Vice-President of the Bar Association for Commerce, Finance and Industry, and he has conducted several important enquiries, notably into the operations of Lloyd's. It has been said by his friends, although he hasn't said it, that it was not just the loss of financial income that led him to resign, it was the horror at suddenly moving away from the most eminent businessmen in the country and their really intellectually stimulating problems, and just sitting there trying criminals and listening to old ladies who get hit by motor cycles and claim a couple of thousand pounds' damages. He didn't even have the patience to wait for promotion to the Court of Appeal as he was bound to get. And even if he *had* got to the Court of Appeal, only one case in twenty is of any intellectual stimulation.'

The top lawyers who don't want preferment are the specialists, those with outstanding ability and long experience in specialized branches of the law like patent law, Common Market law, restrictive practices, Revenue, Chancery, shipping, and so on. These are the first rank of specialists, and for the most part have no ambitions to become judges.

There are therefore never enough people of ability to fill all the posts such as circuit judges, stipendiary magistrates, chairmen of employment tribunals, National Health Service commissions, and so on. First, the pay is a fraction of what people of outstanding ability can command; secondly, they are often soul-destroying occupations. That of circuit judge was described to me thus:

Can you imagine sitting there for eleven months of the year listening to people repeating the same old excuses as to why they have committed crimes? And then you can't even make a decision for yourself – you sum up to the jury, then the jury makes the decision guilty or not guilty. Even when it comes to your discretion on passing sentence, it's all on a scale, and if you exceed the scale you're either going to be reversed by the Court of Appeal or the Home Secretary is going to say the judges are not doing what they're told.*

Oh, they give them a bit of prestige. They dress them up in colourful robes and call them, 'your Honour' and the like. One of the few reasons for a lawyer of real ability to want to become a circuit judge is the very attractive pension arrangements.

But of course, preferment becomes *extremely* attractive to people who do not have that level of personal ability that they are going to maintain their professional career up to retirement age. Because once you're a little bit over the top, you're fifty or fifty-five, if you haven't made it, or unless you are offering a specialist service, you are what is called a *general* practitioner. And all the general practitioners always have young and attractive men and women following behind them and they get pushed out as has-beens. Therefore there is *terrific* competition on the part of the second-rate barrister to get what I call 'minor' preferment. And these second-rate barristers are the people who are prepared to join a Bar Lodge of Freemasons.

There are of course circuit judges who are of the first order of ability. And among the London stipendiary magistrates there is a small number who have chosen that particular appointment in preference even to being a High Court judge or a circuit judge because they feel it more rewarding to work *in* the community. Equally, there are individual circuit judges who feel they can best serve society in that capacity. There are several outstanding examples in men who have specialist knowledge – particularly of family law. There are some extremely compassionate circuit judges in this field who feel they are more

*Under the separation of powers, of course, judges are not supposed to do what politicians tell them.

valuable dealing with divorce, custody and related matters in the County Courts than they would be higher up. There are also circuit judges of the first ability who have accepted what many regard as a second-rater's appointment because they resent the dogmatic or Establishment-mindedness, even the narrow-mindedness of the typical authoritarian circuit judge and want to dilute that quality.

Be this as it may, the vast majority of 'top' lawyers do not want preferment. They are, by the nature of brilliance, rare men of law in any case – probably not more than a hundred in number.

So what of the others, the second- and third-raters? Beneath the first rank of specialists there is another rank of specialists. These barristers are not highly specialized in that they are not dealing in extremely erudite and abstruse subjects which require a high level of qualification. They are in areas where, because of experience, they are able to practise in a limited field where there is a degree of mystique and expertise, where the longer they go on the more they are going to know, and where the youngster can never achieve the older man's knowledge by ability alone, only by passage of time. This second group of specialists can do moderately well by the standards of the legal profession – and can be reasonably confident that they can continue in practice beyond what barristers call the 'has-been age' in life because their knowledge will always be saleable.

The spectre of the 'has-been age' drives many barristers into Freemasonry. Those who most dread it are the general practitioners with no specialist knowledge. Some of this largest of all groups will do extremely well because they have a degree of success, one good case, and they become fashionable. But most, of course, don't become fashionable. Because they do not specialize in a particular field, they feel under constant threat by brilliant young people coming up behind them. If a young barrister is talented and gets the opportunity for experience, it will probably take him or her no more than five years to be as good in general practice as a man or woman twenty years older. As a barrister gets older, his cases do not get better. He is briefed in exactly the same kind of cases when he is sixty as when he was thirty.

It is at this level that barristers live in fear of not getting preferment. They realize that if they are not appointed to the Bench in their early fifties, they probably will not have a practice after they are fifty-five. The only way they can hope to maintain their earning capacity into their late sixties or early seventies is by being appointed to the circuit bench, the stipendiary magistracy, to a chairmanship of tribunals or such like.

These are the men who turn in large numbers to Freemasonry,* because initiation unlocks a door and allows them admission to the right place where they can be seen by the right people. There is a euphemism at the Bar for this 'right place'. If a barrister is seeking preferment and wishes to see and be seen by judges and executives and Civil Servants of the Lord Chancellor's Department, he must 'join the Bar Golfing Society'.

I was told by a leading QC who is a Freemason, 'There is a legitimate Bar Golfing Society, but most people who talk about being members of the Bar Golfing Society can't play golf at all. They are Masons. Why this childish code has come into being I do not know. They behave as if they are ashamed of being Freemasons. Using Masonry as a stepping stone to the Bench is not wrong. Why do people pretend they don't do it? It *would* be wrong if on becoming judges

---

*There is nowhere for women barristers in the same position to turn.

they were tempted to abuse it, but I don't believe for the most part they do.'

Although it is not essential for candidates for the judiciary to be QCs, it is a big move in the right direction, and there is no doubt at all according to sources both masonic and otherwise that joining the Brotherhood, while not a prerequisite, certainly helps in getting to be a QC. Of course, first-rate barristers will be successful in their applications whether they are Masons or not. In fact, the most successful practitioners have to become QCs or the amount of their work becomes impossible. A barrister in the Inner Temple told me; 'At the risk of over-simplification, it can be said that a QC does a smaller number of larger cases. If a successful barrister remains a junior barrister [a barrister who is not a QC, not necessarily very junior in years], his practice becomes so top heavy that he just cannot cope. You can't start refusing work otherwise your practice disappears. Indeed, you become a QC if only to protect your position.'

But these men rarely want preferment, as said before. It is the second-raters, those who want to become QCs in their late forties in the hope that it will help them to attain other appointments, who join the Bar Lodges.

My masonic contact among the senior executives of the Lord Chancellor's Department told me, 'When a barrister joins the right Bar Lodge he can be certain of getting on intimate terms with scores of influential judges, big names many of them, and with large numbers of my colleagues in the Lord Chancellor's Department. And this is right and correct, a right and proper method for men of integrity to come to the Bench. Being a judge is an important, exacting task. Strength of character, personal probity, courage, are all qualities a good judge should have in full measure. And compassion. Where better to find out if a man has these qualities than in Lodge? Can you tell me? This is why most judges are Freemasons. Because Freemasons make the best judges.'

I asked him in whose opinion it was that the best people to be judges were Masons. He replied, 'By those whose job it is to select and recommend. By those who are judged the best people to know.'

Which, of course, was a way of saying, 'Freemasons'.

I asked him about the Lord Chancellor's position in all this, about how Lord Hailsham's not being a member of the Brotherhood affected the procedure. Surprisingly, he had not known whether Hailsham was a Mason or not. But it seemed a matter of indifference to him. 'The Lord Chancellor is in a very peculiar position,' he said. 'Hailsham is good. Absolutely brilliant, whether he's a Mason or not. I hope you don't think I'm saying that *only* Freemasons make good judges. Of course, the Lord Chancellor has the final say in the appointment of puisne judges, but as he should and is only right, he takes note of the recommendations of existing judges and of the Department. I am sure Hailsham doesn't care whether a man's a Mason or not.'

The fact is, Hailsham as a non-Mason does not know who among the judges he appoints are Freemasons or otherwise. By his own admission, he does not think the issue worth considering. Without knowing it he is fed recommendations of Freemasons by Freemasons. Perhaps there is no great ill in this. Perhaps Masons *do* make the best judges, although men like Lord Denning and the few women judges such as the Hon Mrs Justice Heilbron in the Family Division of the High Court indicate the calibre of some of the non-Masons in the law.

There is surely something more admirable in a woman or man who has proven her or his ability and reached the Bench of the High Court without having to resort to the secret ladder of Freemasonry. In this sense, it could be argued with some force that it is non-Masons who make the best judges.

The best potential judges are, of course, to be found both within the Brotherhood and outside it, and the very best are going to be appointed regardless. But so long as the system that allows Freemasonry to be a factor in the appointment of judges persists, those of 'second division' ability within Masonry will always have the advantage over their equals outside the Brotherhood – and the majority of judges in this country will continue to be Freemasons.

Most of the non-Mason judges I spoke to knew nothing that pointed to any secret influence in the courts. But, many of them added, as outsiders they would be unlikely to know even if it existed unless it was blatant. Two non-Mason judges were particularly strong in denying the Brotherhood had influence. One, a London judge, told me, 'If the judiciary is at all under the influence of Freemasonry it is a very well kept secret as I have never heard the subject mentioned during eight years as a Metropolitan Stipendiary Magistrate and nine years as a Circuit Judge. To be truthful, the thought has never crossed my mind. In my seventeen and a half years' experience on the full-time bench I do not think the subject of Freemasonry has ever been discussed in front of me by my colleagues and I have never been aware of any influence it has had in their appointment, promotion, or their professional lives.'

The strongest statement disputing allegations of untoward influence in the courts I received from a non-masonic judge (I received some much stronger ones from Masons, as might be expected) was from Judge Rodney Percy of the North Eastern Circuit: 'Although I was in practice at the Newcastle Bar for thirty years from 1950 onwards, I never became aware that Freemasonry played any part in "influencing" any decisions made either in or between counsel themselves or counsel and judges. I am sure that I should have recognized and remembered such occasions, but I can recall none.'

A Hertfordshire judge whose father and father-in-law are both Freemasons, but who is not one himself, told me, 'I have not experienced anything in my profession as barrister or judge to indicate any sinister influence at work by Freemasons.' A judge currently serving on the North Eastern Circuit, which covers courts in Leeds, Newcastle-upon-Tyne, Sheffield, Teesside, York, Bradford, Huddersfield, Wakefield, Durham, Beverley, Doncaster and Hull, was representative of many non-Mason judges in his view: 'In the whole of the time I have been in the legal profession I have never been conscious of Freemasonry playing any part in any decision.'

There is, of course, a natural disinclination by anyone who has spent his life dispensing justice to the best of his ability to acknowledge the possibility that some of his colleagues, whoever they are, might not be doing the same. And a judge not being aware of a certain phenomenon does not necessarily mean it isn't there, as evidenced by the Kent judge who does not know 'any member of the judiciary to be a Freemason', although they are all around him. This judge, too, has 'no reason to think that Freemasonry plays any part in the administration of justice'.

One of the most eminent judges in the Queen's Bench Division of the High Court, who associates with masonic judges daily, has this to say: 'I am not a Freemason although I have had numerous opportunities of becoming one. I have a fundamental objection to any secret society, which has the power of influencing decisions affecting its members in a manner which would otherwise not have occurred, and/or to the disadvantage of non-members.'

Strong stuff, but to the chagrin of those seeking evidence

of the masonic influence in the courts, he adds, 'I have, of course, no evidence that Freemasons exercise such a power in that way.'

A former Lord Justice of Appeal stressed how general ignorance of the existence of masonic influence was no guarantee that it did not exist. 'I had chambers for many years in Lincoln's Inn,' he said. 'I was not aware of any masonic activity whatsoever. I then learned what a thriving centre of Masonry the Inn was. They kept the secret so well that I never knew there was any secret being kept. We mix with people all the time and still after many years know nothing about them. One heard of the occasional bad judgement – in civil cases – and as a barrister one saw them also. Later, many more bad judgements came one's way. I know personally of one judgement on the part of a judge in the Family Division of the High Court, who is a Freemason, that I can explain only in terms of this organization.'

This case was also brought to my notice independently by one of the main participants. The outline that follows is based on the documents of the case; interviews with the main participant; the former Lord Justice of Appeal who made behind-the-scenes enquiries after first hearing of the case, two barristers who were present during the proceedings, and other well-known and highly respected witnesses involved in the case; and upon my own observations during part of the hearings.

The first point to be stressed is the integrity and standing of the main participant, whom I shall call Randolph Hammond. Hammond had been unjustly deprived of all rights over his only child, a girl aged four. Custody of the child has been awarded to his wife, from whom he is legally separated, and access to his daughter has been made so inhumanly difficult for him by a judge that in practice he is never likely to see her again.

I shall call Hammond's wife Olivia, née Denbeigh. Her main witness was her father, a doctor, for our purposes to be called Roland Denbeigh. According to the evidence I have seen and heard it was Denbeigh who is to blame for breaking up Randolph and Olivia's marriage, and Denbeigh who instigated the custody action. Olivia herself has described her father to several people as being 'insanely' jealous and possessive of her, having broken up all her previous relationships, some with well-known and respected people who were willing to testify to the truth of Hammond's statements. But the judge in the case refused to hear the evidence of these vital witnesses. Olivia has spoken to many people over the years of her father's complete domination of her, of her inability to resist him and of her lifelong desire to 'escape' from him. He had only to forbid her to marry her previous lovers for her to comply helplessly with his demand. There is evidence that Denbeigh still has this sinister Svengali-like influence over Olivia, although she is well into her thirties. Now, Hammond fears, he is exerting that influence over his granddaughter as well.

During his cross-examination at the trial, it became apparent what a peculiar man Denbeigh was. At a crucial stage in the questioning it came out that he had subjected Olivia to internal examinations every day when she was pregnant, although a Harley Street specialist was in regular attendance. Skilful questioning was beginning to chip away at his upright, moral image and hint at the unnatural relationship he had with his daughter. This in turn showed what a morally and psychologically tainted atmosphere the child would be raised in if Olivia were to be awarded custody. Counsel for Hammond was getting close to showing that the father–daughter relationship was at least mentally incestuous, and was going on to find out the likelihood of there having been actual incest in the past.

Hammond was confident he was on the point of gaining custody of his child, that the judge could not fail to see what an undesirable and even sinister home his daughter would be raised in if custody were awarded to Olivia. But one of the barristers in court was by no means so sure. He told me afterwards, 'That whole case had a bloody strange feel to it. The whole atmosphere of it gave me a very bad gut feeling. All my instincts told me that Hammond was in the right but that he would go down, and that's what happened. The decision went the wrong way for no obvious reason I could gauge. But from the evidence in court and the papers of the case, Hammond was in the right.'

This barrister either did not see or thought nothing of a movement made by Denbeigh at what was for him the most perilous moment of his cross-examination. He suddenly placed his left arm stiff at his side, his finger tips pointing to the floor, and at the same time craned his head round over his right shoulder, his right hand above his eyes as if shading them. 'It was as if,' said Hammond later, 'he was watching an aeroplane in the back corner of the court.' At the time it happened, Hammond thought nothing of it other than as evidence of the old man's strangeness. Only later, thinking back over the judge's inexplicable behaviour immediately afterwards, did he recall Denbeigh's action. Asked by a friend to describe the action, Hammond imitated it and was astonished to be told that it was a Freemasonic signal. As soon as the judge saw the signal, he jumped forward in his seat and ordered counsel to cease his questioning of Denbeigh, utterly mystifying Hammond.

From that moment Hammond's case was doomed. Counsel was blocked at every step in his questioning and, as stated, was refused permission to call necessary witnesses.

Before the first mention of Masonry to him by the friend he told about the sign, Hammond knew virtually nothing of the Brotherhood. Later, when he aped Denbeigh's courtroom antic for my benefit, I was able to tell him that he was making the masonic sign of Grief and Distress, which is associated with the fourth of the Five Points of Fellowship, sacred to the Brotherhood: 'When adversity has visited our Brother, and his calamities call for our aid, we should cheerfully and liberally stretch forth the hand of kindness, to save him from sinking, and to relieve his necessities.'

In other words, Denbeigh was appealing to the judge to save him from the disastrous cross-examination and to make certain that custody was awarded to Olivia. When Hammond told me the name of the judge I was able to tell him that he was indeed an advanced Freemason. The name of that judge appears nowhere in this book, but will I hope later feature prominently in the report of whatever official enquiry is set up to examine this case.

The other barrister I spoke to signed this statement:

I had known [Randolph Hammond] for about six months when he asked me to come in and listen to his case, which I agreed to do. I attended court during most of the action and took notes. I tried to remain objective throughout.

I have no hesitation in stating that in my view the judge showed strong bias from the start. [Hammond's counsel] outlined his case, made his points, successfully took apart the testimony of [Olivia Hammond's] witnesses, placed certain cases with clear judgements before the court but was never heard in any real sense. The judge's findings in his judgement are totally contradicted by the evidence of many examples.

[Mr Hammond's] suggestions concerning the masonic aspects of his action are matters which warrant consideration. I have no knowledge of Masonry but having sat through the action feel that something very funny was going on.

The former Lord Justice of Appeal was in no doubt, finally, that the judgement was 'so bad, so wrong' that Freemasonry, not Right, was the ruling factor in this case. But he could only give an opinion, he said. He could produce no *evidence* to an enquiry that this was so, and he doubted if it were capable of proof.

I was reminded about the story of the judge who told a prisoner still protesting his innocence after sentence, 'These are not Courts of Justice, they are Courts of Law.'

An enquiry into this case at the earliest possible time is clearly essential.

There are occasions, of course, when the masonic boot is on the other foot. One masonic judge, for instance, stopped a case mid-way, turned to the jury and told them that the defendant had just indicated to him that he was a Freemason. As the judge, too, was a Mason he felt it would be proper to withdraw from the case, and did so.

One of my 'moles' in the higher echelons of West Midlands Police, a Freemason, insisted, however, that the masonic link between judges and police officers was 'most damaging to society and to Masonry'. He added, 'The connection between us – the police – and the judiciary is very wrong. I'm not against judges being Masons. It's this unseen intimacy between the groups that is bad.

'I really don't like the way the organization [Freemasonry] is going, particularly with the judges and an overwhelming majority of the magistracy being Freemasons. I have seen policemen indicate to judges that they are Masons. They usually do it by making a deliberate mistake when taking the oath – "I swear by the Great Archit— oh, I'm sorry, I swear by Almighty God . . ." Every Freemason in court then knows he's a Brother.'

I asked him what a police officer could possibly hope to achieve by this.

'Oh, I've seen it so often,' he said. 'If the policeman has a sticky case where he's been under heavy pressure, it certainly won't do him any harm for the judge to know he's a fellow Mason. He will hold back on the criticism he might have of the officer's handling of the case, for instance. He will also take the word of the police officer as gospel, where he would not necessarily do so if neither of them were Masons.'

'And you've seen this happen?' I asked.

'As recently as last Thursday, yes.'

'How often does it happen?'

'I don't really know these days. I don't go to court very often now. I used to see it a lot when I did. I was listening in at Birmingham Crown Court on another matter and I saw it happen. I had a quiet smirk to myself actually. There was no need for it because it was no open-and-shut thing. This rather nattily dressed Detective Superintendent did it in court. There was not a lot of benefit in it, if that's what you're thinking. It's just that I can't see that this famous impartiality of judges can exist under these circumstances.'

If the perversion of justice by masonic judges were at all frequent, I am confident that my research would have produced direct evidence of it. There have, as we have seen, been cases of obvious masonic abuse, several reported to me by men of integrity and standing in the law. There are instances where Freemason judges are influenced by their loyalty to the Brotherhood to act in a way they otherwise would not, either to the detriment or benefit of the defendant. Such cases, in whichever direction the judge is influenced to bend or stretch the law, are nothing less than dereliction of duty. They are by their very nature dis-honourable and always detrimental to society. But it can safely be stated that such incidents are rare exceptions in the higher courts, although those courts are presided over by a majority of Freemasons.

It is only common sense that if there was a single

Freemason judge in England who regularly tried to influence juries in favour of masonic prisoners, who showed favour to masonic litigants, or who regularly passed the lowest permissible sentence on his masonic brethren, he would have been exposed long ago, given the large number of assiduous journalists, honest and otherwise, this country boasts.

CHAPTER 21

Solicitors

Masonry is very powerful among solicitors in England and Wales. According to a survey in which I questioned all the solicitors in twenty selected towns, and a cross-section of London solicitors, it is less prevalent in the capital than it is in the provinces. This assessment of the situation from a Cambridgeshire lawyer who, although not a Mason, knows a great many Freemasons and receives regular unofficial briefings from members of the Brotherhood, rings true:

In London there are plenty of other things to do. Life is much more impersonal and Freemasonry is not necessarily going to do a solicitor a great deal of good. What is more, good solicitors are so thin on the ground that if you are really good, you don't need to be a Freemason to get your clients. And if you're not any good, being a Freemason is not going to impress your client.

Solicitors, especially those outside London, have a particular incentive for becoming Freemasons. By the rules of their profession they are forbidden to advertise. They are therefore reliant upon passing trade, which is often sparse, and recommendation, which is hard to get. I have interviewed countless solicitors who joined Freemasonry purely to get on close terms with the businessmen and worthies of their community, and to gain personal contact with police, JPs, magistrate's clerks and any local or visiting members of the judiciary – men they could rely upon either to put business their way or whose good offices would be professionally valuable.

One young ex-Home Counties solicitor told me that after he began to practise in his town he was regularly advised by local Freemasons to join the Brotherhood. He resisted because of his religious convictions – he was a practising Christian – and because he was repelled by the idea of being unable to succeed on his own merits alone. But business was so bad that he eventually relented to the continuing pressure of his colleagues in the firm and to their promises that by becoming a Mason he would get all the clients he needed. He said: 'I was initiated and within days clients began to contact me out of the blue. Within a few weeks I had more than I could cope with. That went on for some months, but it troubled me, and I left Masonry before being made up to the second degree. Most of my clients melted away as fast as they had appeared. They were all Masons. So I moved to London. You don't need Masonry or advertising if you're good here – there's more litigation than all the London solicitors can deal with.'

The governing body of the 40,735 solicitors in England and Wales is the Law Society, which has its headquarters at 113 Chancery Lane, London WC2. The Society controls the admission of solicitors and the education for trainee solicitors. Although no solicitor may practise without certification by the Law Society, membership of the Society is not compulsory. At the end of March 1982, 33,226 practising solicitors were members of the Society and 7,509 were not.

The Law Society is one of the most masonic institutions in the world. This has proved an almost insurmountable obstacle to certain 'profane' individuals involved either willingly or unwillingly in litigation with Masons, because it is the Law Society whose job it is – with the Department of Health and Social Security – to decide who will be awarded legal aid and who will not. It also dictates the conditions on which legal aid is granted in each separate case. The difficulty is compounded if the subject of any proposed action by an applicant for legal aid is not only a Mason but a solicitor as well. There are cases where the decision whether or not an individual should be granted financial aid in order to pursue his case or defend himself against a case being brought against him has been in the hands of close colleagues of the applicant's counsel.

A great many of the sixty-odd members of the Law Society Council as well as a high proportion of the Society's staff and committees – one estimate puts it as high as ninety per cent of all male staff above the age of thirty – are ardent Freemasons.

I have thousands of papers on one case alone, a case so well documented it can be followed in minute detail. It involves one of the many masonic members of the Law Society Council, who had personally committed an act of gross negligence which caused one of his clients to lose a £100,000 inheritance. Deliberate action on the part of several other firms of masonic solicitors – some of the biggest names in the legal profession – acting in collusion with the original solicitor and with each other to cover up the negligence, brought the client to the edge of financial ruin. Having mortgaged his home, spent £15,000 in legal fees to lawyers who deliberately ignored his instructions, wasted valuable time and generated hundreds and hundreds of expensive, unnecessary documents, he was forced to apply to the Law Society, of which his chief opponent was an influential member, for legal aid. Finally, in 1982, after fighting masonic manipulation of the legal aid system for more than a year, and only after a direct appeal to a senior and non-masonic official in the Department of Health and Social Security, which works in tandem with the Law

Society on legal aid applications, he was granted a legal
aid certificate – but on extremely onerous conditions. As
this case is still not closed, and far from lost following
recent unexpected developments in the client's favour, no
further details can be disclosed as yet.

The term 'masonic firm' is used more often in the law than
in any other profession. This is because there is a greater
preponderance of companies which are exclusively run by
members of the Brotherhood in this area of society than
elsewhere. It refers to those firms of solicitors whose senior
partners are, without exception and as part of a deliberate
policy, Freemasons. In such firms, and this is equally true in
London as in the provinces, most of the junior partners will
also be 'on the Square'. Some masonic firms will not allow
the possibility of a non-masonic partner. In these cases only
existing brethren will be taken on. In some larger masonic
firms there will be one, perhaps two, of the junior partners
who are not Masons. These non-Masons generally never
even suspect the secret allegiance of their fellow partners.
At a certain stage in their career they might receive an
approach from one of the Brothers within the firm – not a
blunt invitation to join, but a subtle implantation of an
idea, a curtain twitched gently aside. Usually if this is
passed over nothing further will occur. If it is recognized
and rebuffed, the non-Mason will probably be actively
looking for a partnership elsewhere shortly afterwards, as
work becomes unaccountably more demanding and as he
finds he no longer seems to measure up to the standard
expected of him. Most will not realize that it is the
standard which has moved in relation to them rather than
vice versa. This does not often occur as the senior men in
masonic firms 'have been taught to be cautious', and do not
make overtures to outsiders without having first estab-

lished that the odds are in favour of a sympathetic response.

Many of the largest and most prestigious firms of solicitors in London are masonic firms. During my research for my book *Jack the Ripper: The Final Solution*, I was introduced to Ben K——, an elderly Royal Arch Freemason who had been a partner of one of these firms for more than thirty years. An avid and jocular Mason, Ben told me often how appalled he was by the frequent misuse of masonic influence, especially in his own profession. He gave me a lot of help in my researches in the early seventies and we have kept in touch since. In 1980, the year before I was commissioned to write *The Brotherhood*, he mentioned a case which had been brought to his attention by one of his friends at another top London (masonic) firm. This friend was likewise infuriated by the corruption of Masonry's precepts. The case involved blatant misuse of Freemasonry to conceal criminal conduct on the part of a senior partner in another, even more prestigious, masonic firm. At that time I was in the middle of my second novel and was convalescing from a major operation, so I did not follow it up.

In June 1981 I saw Ben again, and asked if he could get me further details. Meanwhile, I went to see the main casualty of the alleged masonic conspiracy. He was visibly shocked at how much I knew of his case. He was also a very frightened man, and told me that he was thinking of joining the Brotherhood himself for his own protection. As a result of harrowing personal experience, he had come to hate the power of Freemasonry, but believed that becoming part of it was his only hope of survival in the highly masonic world of the law. Whether or not he was right in this, it does indicate the tremendous power certain cliques of Masons can exert. It was clear that he wanted very much to speak about his experiences, that his conscience told him he should. But in the end his own sense of self-preservation triumphed and he told me regretfully that he could not help me to publicize the evils which had nearly ruined him.

All was not lost. Ben, my Royal Arch companion, phoned me late in July and said he had 'a little something' for me. We met in the Freemasons Arms in Long Acre that evening. His 'little something' was a bundle of photocopies tied up in red tape: the complete file on the case.

The story begins in 1980 at the offices of one of the most celebrated firms of solicitors in London. A fashionable yet long established company, it counts several well-known members of the nobility among its clients. Only one partner of this firm whom I shall call Gamma Delta LLB, was not a Freemason. Delta, who had been with the company for seven years, handled general litigation.

One of his senior colleagues had to take an unexpected period of leave. Delta was asked to handle the Mason's work during his absence. As he worked through the documents, familiarizing himself with the various cases, Delta became increasingly puzzled. Finally, to his horror, it dawned on him that his absent partner was engaged in corruption on a large scale. The papers made it clear that the solicitor, acting in case after case on behalf of clients seeking compensation from insurance companies, was in fact in league with the insurance companies. He would settle out of court for sums much lower than he and the insurers knew could be obtained, and he would then receive a rake-off from the insurance companies. Delta at first found it impossible to believe. 'I had no idea such things could happen,' he told another of my informants, a client of his colleague and a victim of his deliberate malpractice.

Stunned by what he had found, Delta at first did not know what he should do. At last, having checked and rechecked the papers to make certain there was no other explanation, he approached the senior partner of the firm and showed him what he had found. The senior partner immediately called a partners' meeting - and Delta was sacked on the spot. There was no explanation given, merely that his services had been dispensed with, and within two days he was on the street. Why the partners had not been as horrified as he by the conduct of his criminal colleague he could not imagine. It was only then, when he approached a barrister friend who was a Mason, that he learned that the company he had worked for had, without his ever giving it a moment's consideration, been a masonic firm. He had had the temerity to attempt to expose not a crooked and negligent lawyer, but a crooked and negligent *Freemason* lawyer. Having been found out, that Freemason was in distress. And his colleagues were all of that mould of Mason which takes it as read that, no matter what qualifying clauses appear in Masonic ritual, a fellow Mason must be extricated from distress at all costs. There was also, of course, the consideration that if the case came into the open, the inevitable publicity would harm the whole company.

The manner in which Delta was dismissed was designed to give him no credence should he talk about the documents he found. When an instant dismissal of that kind occurs in the legal profession, there is usually only one inference: the person sacked has had his hand in the till.

Delta's first move was to approach another of the leading firms in London, another 'big name' company much involved in the world of international finance. The company agreed to act for Delta in his claim against his erstwhile employers for compensation for termination of partnership. But according to an informant within this second company, which also turned out to be a masonic firm, the senior partner of the first company contacted his masonic colleagues at the top level of the second firm, and this firm (this is also documented) dropped Delta like a hot

potato. Not only did they drop him after they had agreed
to act, they actually then agreed to defend the first firm in
any case brought against them by Delta!

Eventually, though, Delta found a solicitor who was not
a Mason and, evidently fearing adverse publicity, the
original firm settled out of court, paying Delta £50,000
compensation.

But even after he got his money, and set himself up in his
own practice elsewhere in the country, Delta was still aware
of the potential power of Masonry to ruin him, and decided
that the only safe place was within.

This 'if you can't beat 'em . . .' attitude is prevalent,
especially among tradesmen and the proprietors of small
businesses in all parts of the country.

PART FIVE

Powers Temporal and Spiritual

CHAPTER 22

Government

Almost every local authority in the country has its own Freemasonic Lodge, the temple often situated actually within the Town or County Hall. These local government Lodges are known variously as 'A Borough Lodge', 'B County Lodge, 'C Town Hall Lodge' or 'D Council Lodge', depending where they are. In London alone there are no fewer than twenty-four Lodges which from their names in the Masonic Year Book can be identified as being based on local authorities.* There are at least as many again in Greater London whose identity is cloaked under a classical or other obscuring title like 'Harmony'.

In addition to these there are the Lodges based upon the City of London Corporation, with which I deal in Chapter 24, and the Greater London Council Lodge No 2603 for officers and members of the GLC, originally consecrated as the London County Council Lodge in 1896.

In the provinces, virtually every County Council, district council and parish council has its own Lodge.

*The boroughs of Acton, Bethnal Green, Camberwell, Finchley, Finsbury, Greenwich, Hackney, Islington, Newham, St Pancras, Shoreditch, Stepney, Woolwich; Barnet London Borough Council; City of London; City of Westminster; Greater London Council; Guildhall; Holborn Boro' Council; Lambeth Boro' Council; St Marylebone Borough Council; Tower Hamlets; Wandsworth Borough Council; Westminster City Council.

One thing is clear: the vast majority of councillors and officials join these Lodges, rather than a Lodge based on a geographical area or on an institution or profession, because they believe it increases their influence over local affairs.

How realistic is this belief, strongly denied by some but generally acknowledged by the more honest of local authority Masons, especially after one or two whiskies?

The basis for what criticism there has been of the concept of local authority Lodges is that they undermine the process of democracy.

For democracy to work at its best there has to be a party system, preferably with at least two strong parties politically at odds. The British system of democracy avoids widespread corruption in government by a series of checks and balances. One of the most important of these is an official Opposition party. The Opposition has a duty to oppose the majority party that forms the government. Only by the criticism and constant watchfulness of an Opposition can a government be kept up to the mark. The bad points of the ruling party are by this means constantly shown to the public, and if its strengths do not outweigh its weaknesses the government will eventually, in theory, fall.

This efficient system of keeping government inefficiency and corruption to a minimum can scarcely be threatened when it comes to central government, where there are so many checks and balances and where both Press and public are vigilant in the extreme. But on a local level journalists are usually in their teens or early twenties and do not have the experience or wherewithal to keep such a critical eye on the processes of democracy, and the majority of residents do not take much interest in their local authority beyond its decisions about the annual rate increase.

The parliamentary system works as well in the local council chamber as it does in the Commons – except, say the critics, where Freemasonry rears its head in the shape of a Town Hall Lodge.

Within the Lodge three things which are generally considered undesirable can happen:

(1) There is fraternization between council officers and elected members, who in the public interest should keep each other at arm's length.
(2) Party differences are broken down and men who have a duty fiercely to oppose each other in the council chamber and in all their actions on behalf of the electorate are brought together in intimate harmony.
(3) There is undesirable contact with local businessmen – builders, architects, etc. – who often join such Lodges blatantly to curry favour and exploit the masonic bond to canvass for local authority contracts.

None of these objections would be valid, perhaps, if all Freemasons scrupulously avoided discussing business, politics or religion with each other within the Temple. But of course Freemasons are human, and no matter what claims are made that such talk never goes on at masonic gatherings, there is ample evidence that it does. Additionally, there is no bar against talking business, religion or politics at the customary drinking session up which follows the ceremonies in the Temple.

The critics say that Lodges where leading members of the majority party swear an oath of allegiance to leading members of the Opposition party, and vice versa, destroy the two-party system. From there on, especially when council officers belong to the Lodge as well, democracy is finished. Whatever debate occurs in public is a façade that covers the disturbing truth that everything has been decided in advance.

Are the critics right? In 1974 Prime Minister Harold Wilson presented to Parliament the findings of his committee on local government rules of conduct. The committee had been set up in the wake of the Poulson scandal and amid growing public concern about corruption in local government. Under the chairmanship of Lord Redcliffe-Maud, the committee had produced a seventy-two-page report that analysed the problems and ended by recommending a National Code of Local Government Conduct.

On the question of fraternization between council officers and elected members, the code had this advice for councillors:

(i) Both councillors and officers are servants of the public, and they are indispensable to one another. But their responsibilities are distinct. Councillors are responsible to the electorate and serve only so long as their term of office lasts. Officers are responsible to the council and are permanently appointed. An officer's job is to give advice to councillors and to carry out the council's work under the direction and control of councillors.

(ii) Mutual respect between councillors and officers is essential to good local government. *Close personal familiarity between individual councillor and officer can damage this relationship and prove embarrassing to other councillors and officers.* [My italics.]

(iii) If you are called upon to take part in appointing an officer, the only question you should consider is which candidate would best serve the whole council. You should not let your personal or political preferences influence your judgement. You should not canvass the support of colleagues for any candidate and you should resist any attempt by others to canvass yours.

Elsewhere the report deals with proper declaration of interests by councillors. Numerous minor cases of failure to declare pecuniary interests can be cited: where, for instance, a councillor discussed and voted on the arrears of rent by Council tenants without admitting that he was himself a Council tenant in arrears with his rent; or where a councillor voted on the question of his own expenses.

Failure to declare pecuniary interest is illegal. But failure to declare non-pecuniary interest is not against the law and is therefore hard to combat. Even so, a councillor can be influenced in his decisions by his connection with an organization or a person just as strongly as he can by financial considerations.

A councillor should never take part in debate or voting on such matters as a relative or friend seeking planning permission, rehousing, or employment with the council or where any other conflict of interest exists.

The report goes on:

There are other interests which are less easily defined but where the same principles of disclosure, and usually, of non-participation, should apply. Trusteeship in a charitable body, membership of a religious denomination, a trade union, a professional association or *a society such as Freemasonry* [my italics], or even ordinary friendship, can all create situations where it is to the member's credit, and for the health of local government, if he is quite open about them.

The committee did not think that these matters needed to be covered by standing orders because what was involved was a principle rather than a procedure. And the principle should be for councillors *to treat non-pecuniary interests on the same lines as pecuniary interests* – which means very seriously indeed.

In its final recommendations, the committee again refers to kinship, friendship, membership of an association or society (Freemasonry, etc.) and other bodies and states where such membership 'can sometimes influence your judgement or give the impression [it] might do so'.

So it is acknowledged that the dangers are real enough.

But has Freemasonry ever actually undermined local democracy to any extent worth worrying about?

One does not have to look too far for the strongest evidence that it has.

In its report to the Royal Commission on Standards of Conduct in Public Life, chaired by the Rt Hon Lord Salmon between 1974 and 1976, the Society of Labour Lawyers makes this statement:

We regret the timidity of the Redcliffe-Maud Committee in their recommendations relating to the disclosure of interest. We think it essential that there should no loopholes; oral and public disclosure of all direct and indirect interests, financial and otherwise, must be made (for example) by local councillors at every meeting of council or committee in addition to a comprehensive written record; this obligation should not be avoided by a councillor absenting himself from a meeting. In case of absence his interest must be declared at the meeting at the instance of the councillor concerned by the chairman or clerk. We say 'financial or otherwise' because it is well within the experience of our members that secret decisions or understandings are reached in places which would not exist if generally known. In particular, we refer to 'town hall Lodges' which, we know, existed at each and every one of the local authorities concerned in recent criminal proceedings and almost all of the defendants were members. These Lodges take into membership leading councillors across the political divide together with a limited number of senior officers, to the prejudice of the justification of the two-party system – that of public dispute and decision – and to the prejudice of the proper relationship between councillor and officer. It is no part of our message to decry the traditions and charitable good work of the masonic movement; we imagine that the national leaders would be as distressed as anyone if they knew of the extent to which the town hall Lodges were used, at the very least, to ease communication of matters which would never have been communicated at all in the full glare of publicity. Membership of such groups as these must be subject to disclosure and if this should offend the rules and practices of an organization of the nature of Freemasons, the remedy is to dissolve Lodges based upon restricted membership of those in a local field of public life. If those concerned complain that it limits their opportunity to engage in the honourable and altruistic activities of their movement, their desires can, no doubt, fructify in the company of like-minded persons elsewhere than in or about the town hall.

The authorities referred to as being involved in criminal proceedings and all having a masonic thread running through the corruption were, among others, Bradford, Birmingham, Newcastle and Wandsworth.

The town hall Lodge at Wandsworth in south-west London was consecrated in 1903 as Wandsworth Borough Council Lodge No 2979. Its members are not only current officers and members of the council (now the London Borough of Wandsworth) but also past members and officers and others associated with local government. A number of builders, architects, civil engineers and such like belonged to the Lodge in the 1960s when masonic corruption starting there spread outwards until it engulfed and ruined national figures like former Home Secretary Reginald Maudling, himself a Freemason. As former Wandsworth Town Clerk Barry Payton told me: 'The real seriousness of the Wandsworth affair was the incestuous relationship between the two opposing leaders, Sidney Sporle and Ronald Ash. Sporle was the Labour leader. He had no visible means of support, he didn't have a job, but he nevertheless lived at a fair old rate, always having rolls of five-pound notes in his pocket. Although his home life was not in any great style, he really enjoyed entertaining and going out and being the grandiose host. He got his income through his association with certain dubious activities. Ash, the Conservative leader, was the proprietor of Lewis of Balham, a builders' merchants.'

One example of the oddity of the relationship between

Sporle and Ash was in relation to an organization called the South London Housing Consortium. This had been formed by a group of south London local authorities who were engaged in a lot of building work at that time. The object of forming the consortium was to enable the authorities to buy building materials in bulk direct from the manufacturers, thus making big savings and also being sure of obtaining materials when they were required. For a reason that has never been discovered the consortium employed Lewis of Balham as an intermediary. This negated the reason for forming a consortium in the first place: there is small point in a consortium if a middle man is used. It is interesting to speculate that if Lewis of Balham earned only one per cent for acting as intermediary, which is an improbably low rate of commission, this previously modest business would, on a turnover of £10 million, have made £100,000. And that sort of money in the late sixties was a very great sum indeed.

In the municipal election in 1968 Labour was defeated in Wandsworth and Ash became the Leader of the Council. Shortly afterwards, the new Tory controllers of the council had their first meetings to appoint committees and nominate members to outside bodies. The Conservatives' first group meeting was to consider whom to nominate as the council's representatives on the South London Housing Consortium. Ash fought tooth and nail to nominate the Labour leader, Sidney Sporle. Finally, Ash forced the issue by threatening to resign if he didn't get his way, and his members reluctantly voted for Sporle. It was not known to them that the two 'opponents' were close friends, and that their friendship had sprung from the deep ties of being Brother Masons in the same Lodge.

Sporle, now dead, was a corrupt man who used the Lodge at Wandsworth unashamedly for setting up crooked deals. Among seven charges of corruption for which he was later jailed for six years, Sporle was found guilty of taking a job from T. Dan Smith, PR man and fellow conspirator of architect John Poulson. It is generally thought that Smith, who did so much to further the interests of Poulson (himself known to have exploited his masonic membership at every opportunity), was also a member of the Brotherhood. According to what he told me, and I have no reason to disbelieve him, he is not and never has been a Freemason, however. This is what he said when we met for a cup of tea at the Charing Cross Hotel: 'People have always assumed that I am a Mason, so gradually I found the way they shook hands and the way they made the next move – and because I virtually detested them (for no reason other than that I hate that kind of organization) I always used to give them the handshake back. Still do. I met a journalist last week from the *Daily Mirror*. He gave me a Freemasonic handshake and I gave him one, and he said, "Oh, you're on the Square." He said, "As you're on the Square, why didn't you pass the money to Ted Short* *that* way?"

'I said, "Well, how do you do it that way?" He said, "Very simply. *You just pass it through the organization.*"'

There are clues that there is a well-established system within Freemasonry for passing money untraceably from one Mason to another. No fewer than seven informants within the Brotherhood as well as T. Dan Smith on the outside have told me of the system. If such a system does exist, it is probably connected with the method by which the vast sums of money collected in charity by individual

---

*Edward Short, MP for Newcastle Central, was an old friend of Smith's and a Freemason. He accepted £500 from Smith 'for the work you have done on behalf of the firm'. The DPP later considered prosecuting Short for accepting a bribe but decided there was no case to answer. Eleven years after the event, when it all came out, Short, by then deputy Prime Minister and Leader of the House, astonished Parliament by not resigning despite dissatisfaction with his explanation.

Lodges each year is transmitted to Grand Lodge. Until further clues come to light, however, I am unable to say more than this. It seems highly unlikely that the officers at Great Queen Street are in on the secret – unless, of course, they have some legitimate purpose for operating such a system, and this can be used by corrupt members without the knowledge of the hierarchy or the Charity trustees.

At any one time there seems to be only about thirty to sixty Freemasons in Parliament, and there is no real discernible influence by Freemasonry on voting in the Commons: even if there were a large number of masonic MPs, debates so rarely touch issues masonic that any kind of cross-party collusion by members of the Brotherhood is inconceivable. There are far greater and more important vested interests than Freemasonry at Westminster.

The majority of MPs who are Masons – witness Cecil Parkinson, Paymaster General and Chairman of the Conservative Party* – have no time to attend Lodge meetings. Those who do have the time tend to pursue their Masonry on a local level with no connection with Parliament. So far as I have been able to discover there is no House of Commons or parliamentary Lodge. Members of Margaret Thatcher's post-Falklands Cabinet* who have told me they are not members of the Brotherhood include Lord Hailsham (see pp 153–4 above), the Lord Chancellor; Sir Geoffrey Howe, Chancellor of the Exchequer; James Prior, Secretary of State for Northern Ireland; John Nott, Secretary of State for Defence; George Younger, Secretary of State for Scotland; John Biffen, Secretary of State for Trade; David Howell, Secretary of State for Transport; Leon Brittan, Chief Secretary to the Treasury; and

*Again reshuffled by Thatcher in June 1983.

Norman Tebbit, Secretary of State for Employment. Lord Carrington, Foreign Secretary before the Falklands crisis, told me he is not and never has been a Freemason. Those who ignored my letters include Home Secretary William Whitelaw, almost certainly a Mason, Sir Keith Joseph, Francis Pym, Peter Walker and Michael Heseltine. Neither Humphrey Atkins, Lord Privy Seal, nor Patrick Jenkin, Industry Secretary, wished to comment.

In the Labour, Liberal and Social Democratic parties, no senior member owns to being a Freemason now or in the past. And even Tony Benn, whom one would expect to make political capital from anything getting close to masonic influence in Parliament, has 'never heard Freemasonry mentioned'. None of the main parties has any particular policy on Freemasonry, although a Labour Party assistant information officer did say the party regarded the Brotherhood 'as a secret and select club and object to the way it undermines the National Health Service by providing private hospital beds', a reference to the Royal Masonic Hospital at Hammersmith, West London. The officer then took the sting out of her bold accusation by saying, 'The problem is that we do not know enough about it to be critical.' Even the Communist Party can muster insufficient enthusiasm to talk about the subject, and simply dislike it because in their view it reinforces the class structure.

Two men in particular seemed to have achieved high office in the Labour Party directly through membership of the Brotherhood: Attlee, Prime Minister from 1945 to 1951, and Arthur Greenwood, Deputy Leader of the party from 1935. On 22 November 1935 a masonic Lodge whose members included Transport House officials and several Labour MPs held one of its regular meetings. The party meeting to select a new Leader was fixed for 26 November. Three men were in the running. Even though Attlee was a Mason, it was Greenwood, a member of the Transport

House Lodge, who was, according to Hugh Dalton, Labour Chancellor of the Exchequer between 1945 and 1947, 'the Masons' Candidate'. In his book *The Fateful Years* Dalton wrote:

Most members of the Lodge were closer friends of Greenwood than they were of the other two candidates, Attlee and Morrison. On the first ballot the result was Attlee 58, Morrison 44, Greenwood 33. As had been decided in advance, the bottom candidate, Greenwood, dropped out. On the second ballot, all but four of Greenwood's supporters voted for Attlee, giving him a victory over Morrison of 88 to 48.

First, of course, this is not an example of Freemasonry at work in Parliament but inside an individual party, which is quite different. Secondly, considering the facts coolly, it is hard to see much that is sinister in them. Freemasons getting together in secret to decide whom they as a group want to have as leader seems no different from the Tribunites, the Manifesto Group or any other sub group within a party doing the same thing. Were there a secret non-party band of Freemasons influencing matters behind the scenes and manipulating this Mason into power in this party and that Mason into power in that party, the matter would be somewhat different.

There have been several attempts in Parliament to initiate official enquiries into the effects of Freemasonry on society. Every one of them has failed.

On 11 April 1951, Fred Longden, MP for the Small Heath district of Birmingham, stood up in the Commons and asked Prime Minister Clement Attlee whether 'in the interests of all sides' he would move for the appointment of a Royal Commission to enquire into the effects of Freemasonry on the political, religious, social and administrative life of the country.

Foreign Secretary Herbert Morrison, a non-Mason, said, 'I have been asked to reply. No, sir. This is not a matter for which the government are responsible, and my right honourable Friend the Prime Minister does not think that an enquiry of this kind would be appropriate.'

To this, Longden said, 'As I have received a large number of letters on this question might it not be good for Freemasons themselves if, apart altogether from their rites and ceremonies, the suspicions and accusations concerning their influence on personal appointments and interference with our constitutional institutions were brought to the light of day?'

'I understand the point made by my honourable friend,' said Morrison, 'but I really think we have enough troubles without starting any more.'

Masonic MP for Kidderminster Gerald (later Sir Gerald) Nabarro sprang to his feet and said, 'Would not such an enquiry be an infringement of human liberties?', and the House passed on to the car mileage allowance of threepence-ha'penny per mile for army chaplains, the cheese ration, and to a question about a speech given in South Shields by the Home Secretary in which he had said, 'We cannot control General MacArthur because we do not pay him.'

Whitehall and the Civil Service generally is the side of central government where Freemasonry plays a part. Membership of the Brotherhood can be an important factor in promotion, especially to the ranks of the powerful Permanent Secretaries. In some ministries, Defence for example, it can be a distinct disadvantage not to be a Mason. Several people have recounted how when they were interviewed for senior positions at the Ministry of Defence, they were suddenly, in the middle, asked how they interpreted a certain biblical quotation. One of my informants, a non-Mason, could not remember the exact quotation. Both the others, one a Mason, did remember. The two quotations were not quite accurate, but amended as Masons amend them for use in their ceremonies. The Mason identified himself as such and was appointed. The two non-Masons, not knowing what to make of a request to interpret a biblical reference, were not. This might all, of course, be coincidence. We do not know how able the individuals were and how well or ill they suited the posts for which they were applying. What is certain is that the Civil Service has real and continuing power in the administration of this country, in that it remains while governments come and go; and that power is largely in the hands of members of the Brotherhood. This area of masonic influence warrants a book in itself, and will, I hope, command an entire section in future editions, when more detailed research is completed.

CHAPTER 23

The Highest in the Land

On 5 December 1952 His Royal Highness the Duke of Edinburgh, consort of the new Queen Elizabeth II, as yet uncrowned, was initiated into the secrets of Freemasonry by the Worshipful Master of Navy Lodge No 2612. He joined against his will. His uncle, Earl Mountbatten of Burma, was – in the words of an impeccable source close to the Royal Family – 'fiercely opposed' to Freemasonry, and had strongly advised Philip to have nothing to do with it. But in 1947 when Philip became engaged to Princess Elizabeth, his future father-in-law King George VI had made it plain that he expected any husband of his daughter to maintain the tradition of royal patronage of Free-masonry. George was an ardent Mason and finally extracted a promise from Philip to join the Brotherhood. George died before Philip was able to fulfil the promise, but despite his own reservations (he regarded the whole thing as a silly joke) and his uncle's hostility, he felt bound to honour his promise to the dead King.

But having been initiated to Freemasonry as an Entered Apprentice, Philip felt honour was satisfied and he was free to act as he chose – which was to forget the whole business as quickly as possible. and while still nominally a member of the Brotherhood, the Duke has taken no active part for thirty years and has refused all invitations to climb the masonic ladder and achieve grand rank.

His determination to rise no higher in the masonic hierarchy has meant that, in masonic terms, Philip is inferior in rank to thousands of commoners. This has caused much irritation in the sealed rooms of Great Queen Street, and annoyed the masonic elders considerably in the 1960s when a successor to the Earl of Scarborough, who had taken office as Grand Master the year before Philip was initiated, was being discussed. The monarch's husband, the Freemason of the highest standing in the non-masonic world, was considered the natural successor. But Philip would not have it.

Finally, in 1966, after much speculation both within Masonry and outside, the new Grand Master was named – in the William Hickey column of the *Daily Express*. He was to be the thirty-year-old Duke of Kent, the Queen's cousin, who was a major in the Royal Scots Greys stationed at Hounslow. The Duke, who was initiated into Masonry in 1964, would be following in the footsteps of his father who had been Grand Master between 1939 and 1942, when he was killed in action. Hickey's prediction came to pass and the Duke was installed as Grand Master by the Earl of Scarborough at the greatest masonic spectacular of all time – the 250th anniversary celebrations at the Royal Albert Hall in June 1967 when Masons from all over the world attended in full regalia and Arab Mason walked with Israeli Mason only ten days after the Six Day War.

Philip's apathy and Mountbatten's antipathy have had their effect on Prince Charles, the heir to the throne. Mountbatten, as Charles' favourite uncle, made a lasting impression on the future King and Charles remains adamant, despite rumours to the contrary, that he does not wish to become a Freemason. A greater influence in this direction than either his father or his uncle, however, has been his grandmother, Queen Elizabeth the Queen Mother, who had much of the responsibility for Charles' upbringing when his parents were travelling. The Queen Mother, despite – perhaps because of – being the wife of a devoted Freemason, does not approve of the Brotherhood. She is a committed Bible-believing Christian and, largely due to her influence, Prince Charles too is a committed (as opposed to nominal) Christian.

Great pressure was brought to bear on Charles when he was in his early and mid-twenties to follow family tradition and become a Freemason. It was assumed by high Masons that when Charles reached his twenty-first birthday in 1969, he would be initiated and take over from the Duke of Kent. He refused to be pressed into doing so, and when approached he gave an emphatic 'No', adding, 'I do not want to join any secret society.' When he was twenty-five the *Sunday Mirror* published an article by Audrey Whiting, described in her byline as 'an authoritative writer on Royal affairs'. She said that the pressure brought to bear on Charles to become a Mason had been 'considerable'. She continued:

If he persists [in refusing] he will become in due time the first monarch in centuries who has not been the titular head of Freemasonry in Britain . . . Freemasonry will survive and flourish, as it does today, without a monarch as its titular head – but the Prince's refusal to adopt the traditional role in [the] ranks of Masonry as heir to the Throne was and is a great blow to a body of men who are above all traditionalists.

But by this time there was talk that Charles 'was not strictly against Freemasonry', but that he simply had no wish to become involved. According to Whiting, he wanted to prove himself as a man 'who can meet and beat all the tests which could face a fighting man and an adventurer'.

A senior court official told me: 'The answer is that without benefit, if you can call it that, of wartime experience, Charles is determined to be as good as his father – and perhaps even better.'

The question remains: Will Charles, in the end, conform to tradition?

Despite rumours that the Prince had suggested that 'if' he joined the Brotherhood, it would be as an initiate to the Royal Air Force Lodge No 7335, there is still no indication that Charles has changed his attitude.

I failed miserably to ascertain more clearly Charles's current thinking on the subject. The Court is brimming with Freemasons and my own enquiries never got past Charles's masonic private secretary, the Hon Edward Adeane. Adeane, son of Lt-Col the Rt Hon Lord (Michael) Adeane, former private secretary to the Queen and Freemason of Grand Rank, refused to ask the Prince if he would be prepared to say why he had decided to go against tradition. He told me: 'The basis for the suggestion that His Royal Highness has any view on the matter at all depends purely on speculative statements in the press, and the Prince of Wales does not comment on other people's speculation.'

The first part of this statement was really not true for anyone who had contacts within the Grand Lodge, the Palace or at Windsor. The suggestion that the Prince had views on the matter was *not* a matter of speculation. However, I wrote back asking if I might rephrase my question in the light of Adeane's statement: 'Rather than asking why the Prince has taken a stand, which I now realize to be in doubt, can I ask the Prince what his thinking is on the subject of Freemasonry, not necessarily whether he intends joining the movement or not, but simply his thoughts on the organization?' I received a two-line reply. The first line thanked me for my letter. The second said: 'I am afraid that I cannot assist you in this matter.'

It is an interesting anomaly that the Queen, as a woman, is banned from entering a masonic temple – yet she is Grand Patroness of the movement. Her two younger sons are already marked down by the elders of Great Queen Street as possible future Grand Masters, should they not go the way of their brother Charles. Prince Michael of Kent is already a Brother of Grand Rank, having been Senior Grand Warden in 1979.

CHAPTER 24

The City of London

As darkness closed in on the City of London in the late afternoon of 16 February 1982, a number of influential men converged on the ancient Guildhall, seat of the City's medieval-style government. They came in taxis, in chauffeur-driven limousines, and on foot. They came from all parts of the City – and beyond. Between them they represented a wide spectrum of wealth and power. Their decisions, in the worlds of high finance, the law, industry, international trade and commerce and politics, affected the lives of thousands.

Each of the men, beneath his outer garments, wore a dark lounge suit, and most of them carried small oblong cases, some inscribed in gold leaf with the owner's initials. These cases contained the regalia the men would put on when they reached their destination. The men came from different directions and entered the Guildhall by various entrances. Some came across Guildhall Yard, some along Aldermanbury, some by way of Masons Avenue. Once inside the Hall, each turned his steps towards the Crypt, which was cordoned off so that no intruder could make his way down the stair and report the goings-on to any 'Gentile'. A Tyler, or Outer Guard, was posted at the door to block the path of any stranger who might slip past the Guildhall commissionaire.

At precisely 5.15 P.M. the participants in the drama which was to be acted out had gathered in the Crypt, which had been transformed into a Masonic Temple. The brethren of Guildhall Lodge No 3116 took their places. Outgoing Worshipful Master Brother Frank Nathaniel Steiner, MA, knocked once with his gavel. The sound echoed around the East Crypt with its low vaulted ceiling and clustered pillars of Purbeck marble. The coat of arms of Sir Bernard Waley-Cohen, a member and former Worshipful Master of the Lodge, had pride of place at one of the six intersections of the vaulting, because he had been Lord Mayor when the Crypt was restored in 1961. Other coats of arms included those of Edward the Confessor, Henry IV, in whose reign the Crypt was built, and Queen Elizabeth II. A masonic prince among royal princes.

Two knocks, like echoes of the first, followed in quick succession from the Senior Warden and the Junior Warden.

'Brethren,' said Worshipful Brother Steiner solemnly, 'assist me to open the Lodge . . .' Addressing the Junior Warden, Steiner continued, '. . . what is the first care of every Mason?'

'To see that the Lodge is properly tyled.'

'Direct that duty to be done.'

The installation ceremony of Worshipful Brother Charles Richard Coward, JP, as Worshipful Master of the Lodge for 1982-3 had begun.

The Guildhall Lodge was consecrated at the Mansion House, the official residence of the Lord Mayor of London, on Tuesday, 14 November 1905. Since then, no fewer than sixty-two Lord Mayors have been Masters of the Lodge, whose membership comprises both elected members of the Corporation of London and its salaried officers.

The Worshipful Master of the Lodge both in 1981-2 and 1982-3 was not the Lord Mayor, because neither was a

Freemason. So Steiner, Common Councilman for Bread Street Ward and Deputy Grand Registrar of the United Grand Lodge, was elected in place of Col Sir Ronald Gardner-Thorpe, and Coward in what would have been the natural place of the Lord Mayor, the Rt Hon Sir Christopher Leaver, had he been of the Brotherhood.

The Lodge was opened in the First Degree. The ritual dismissal of the Entered Apprentices was intoned. The Lodge was opened in the Second Degree. Worshipful Brother Coward, Senior Grand Deacon of the United Grand Lodge, stood waiting to be presented to the Installing Master. He wore a lambskin apron lined with garter-blue, ornamented with gold and blue strings and bearing the emblem of his rank. A four-inch-wide band of garter-blue ribbon embroidered with a design combining an ear of corn and a sprig of acacia lay on his shoulders and formed a V on his breast.

Among the brethren in the temple were Anthony Stuart Joliffe, Alderman and Sheriff of the City of London, director of numerous companies including SAS Catering Ltd, Nikko Hillier International Trading Co Ltd, Capital for Industry Ltd, Marlborough Property Holdings (Developments) Ltd, and Albany Commercial and Industrial Developments Ltd. Joliffe, Senior Warden of the Lodge for the current year, has been vice president of the European League for Economic Co-operation, Hon Treasurer of Britain in Europe Residual Fund, and a trustee of the Police Foundation, and he has held many other influential positions.

Also in the Crypt that night was the Lodge Chaplain, Christopher Selwyn Priestley Rawson, chairman and managing director of Christopher Rawson Ltd, an underwriting Member of Lloyd's, and an honorary member of the Metal Exchange. As a Freemason of London Grand

Rank, he wore a collar of garter-blue ribbon with narrow edging.

Installing Master Steiner proceeded with the ceremonial listing of qualities which Worshipful Brother Coward would need as Master: to be of good report, well skilled in Masonry, exemplary in conduct, steady and firm in principle. The secretary of the Lodge then addressed the Master Elect and recited a fifteen-point summary of the Ancient Charges and Regulations.

Steiner then asked Coward, 'Do you submit to and promise to support these Charges and Regulations as Masters have done in all ages?' Coward replied by placing his right hand on his left breast with the thumb squared upwards. This, the 'sign of fidelity', meant 'I do', and the ceremony continued as he swore on the Bible faithfully to discharge the duties of Master and to abide by Masonry's 'Landmarks'.

The ritual went on and on. When all but Installed Masters had been dismissed from the Crypt, the 'secrets of the Chair' were communicated to Worshipful Brother Coward. Bent on both knees, he took a second oath, with his hands resting on the Bible. There had been no penalty attached to the first obligation. But now Coward faced having his 'right hand struck off and slung over my left shoulder, there to wither and decay', if he betrayed his oath. After more ceremony he was told the secret sign of the Installed Master (a beckoning movement made three times with the right hand); the secret grip (whereby two Installed Masters place their left hands on each other's left shoulder while keeping their arms straight); the secret word (Giblum, meaning Excellent Mason); and finally the sign of Salutation ('Bowing and saluting with the right hand from the forehead three times, stepping backwards with the right foot').

At the end of this long ceremony, with all those of lower degree recalled from the Crypt, Worshipful Brother Coward, now Master of the Lodge, invested the officers of the Lodge for 1982–3 as follows:

IMMEDIATE PAST MASTER: W. Bro. Frank N. Steiner, MA, Deputy Grand Registrar of the United Grand Lodge 1981–2; Common Councilman, Bread Street Ward.

SENIOR WARDEN: Bro. Alderman and Sheriff Anthony S. Joliffe, Fellow of the Institute of Chartered Accountants; Justice of the Peace; Alderman for Candlewick Ward.

JUNIOR WARDEN: Bro. Rev Basil A. Watson, OBE, MA, RN.

CHAPLAIN: W. Bro. Alderman Christopher Rawson, Former City Sheriff; Common Councilman (Bread Street) 1963–72; Alderman (Lime Street); Associate of Textile Industries; Associate of the Institute of Marine Engineers.

TREASURER: W. Bro. Frank N. Steiner, MA.

SECRETARY: W. Bro. Deputy H. Derek Balls, Justice of the Peace; Deputy (Cripplegate Without).

DIRECTOR OF CEREMONIES: W. Bro. Sir John Newson-Smith, Bt, MA, former Lord Mayor of London; Deputy Lieutenant, City of London, 1947; Member of HM Commission of Lieutenancy for the City of London; Deputy Chairman, London United Investments Ltd.

SENIOR DEACON: W. Bro. Michael H. Hinton.

JUNIOR DEACON: Bro. David M. Shalit, Common Councilman (Farringdon Within).

CHARITY STEWARD: W. Bro. Richard Theodore Beck, Fellow of the Royal Institute of British Architects; Fellow of the Society of Antiquaries; Fellow of the Royal Society of Arts; Member of the Royal Town Planning Institute; Deputy (Farringdon Within); Sheriff of the

City of London 1969–70; Prestonian Lecturer (*the* annual masonic lecture delivered at Freemasons Hall, London), 1975.

ALMONER: W. Bro. Matthew Henry Oram, TD, MA, Common Councilman (Cordwainer).

ASSISTANT DIRECTOR OF CEREMONIES: W. Bro. Colin Frederick Walter Dyer, ERD, Past Assistant Grand Director of Ceremonies and Past Junior Grand Deacon of the United Grand Lodge; Common Councilman (Aldgate); Prestonian Lecturer 1973.

INNER GUARD: W. Bro. Gerald Maurice Stitcher, CBE; Past Grand Standard Bearer of the United Grand Lodge; Common Councilman (Farringdon Without).

STEWARD: Bro. Deputy Arthur Brian Wilson; Deputy (Aldersgate).

Between them, these men play vital roles in all aspects of the running of the City – including police, housing, education, social services, town planning and the courts of law.

As Senior Warden of the Guildhall Lodge, Anthony Joliffe was the front runner for Master of the Lodge in 1983–4. This was no accident as he was to be and became Lord Mayor during the same period.

Ancient institutions survive and hold sway in the City of London more than anywhere else in Britain. Although the City is one of the most important financial and business centres in the world, medieval custom and tradition are apparent everywhere. Even the Bank of England, the nationalized central bank which holds our gold reserves, conducts the government's monetary policy, regulates lending and finances the national debt, retains its 'Old Lady of Threadneedle Street' image, its messengers or waiters wearing pink waistcoats and top hats as they go about their time-honoured business. Once a year the Worshipful Company of Butchers presents the Lord Mayor with a boar's head on a silver platter, exactly as it did in the fourteenth century. The Port of London Authority's garden in Seething Lane is leased to the Corporation as a public amenity for an annual rent of a nosegay. Every October at the Royal Courts of Justice the Corporation's legal officer – the Comptroller and City Solicitor – pays the Queen's Remembrancer a hatchet, a bill hook, six horses and sixty-one nails – the so-called Quit Rents for two of the City's holdings, the Forge in St Clement Danes and the Moors in Shropshire. 'The City's institutions are as varied as they are ancient,' wrote the late Blake Ehrlich.

Five 'wise men' set the world price of bullion in the opulent Gold Room of N. M. Rothschild and Sons,* St Swithin's Lane, at 10.30 each morning, but, before these gentlemen are out of bed, the gentlemen from the Fishmongers Guild, their boots silvered with fish scales, are exercising their immemorial functions down by the river at Billingsgate, London's fish market. On the other side of the City, predawn buyers eye hook-hung carcasses at Smithfield, the world's largest dressed-meat market. Nearby nurses begin to prepare patients for surgery at St Bartholomew's ('Bart's), London's first hospital (founded 1123) and the place where, in the 17th century, William Harvey first demonstrated the circulation of the blood. Closer to St Paul's Cathedral, the vans begin to deliver prisoners whose cases will be heard that day at Old Bailey, as the Central Criminal Court is known, where most of Britain's sensational murder trials have been held.

These daily occurrences, the mundane modern mingled inextricably with the flavour of the Middle Ages, are what lend the City its unique life.

Only the sovereign takes precedence over the Lord Mayor within the City's square mile. Even the Prime

*The Rothschilds have been Freemasons for generations.

Minister – *even* Margaret Thatcher – will walk behind the Mayor in official processions through the City.

The City is not entirely an island in the river of time. It is rather a place where two historical clocks are running: one which for the past thousand years has been going so slowly that its hands have picked up the ceremonial dust of the centuries, of which very little has been lost; the other which operates with the impeccable efficiency of quartz crystal. It is the continuing belief in the importance of ancient tradition which is largely responsible for the undying strength of Freemasonry: for Freemasonry underpins all the great and influential institutions of the Square Mile. According to confidential statistics from Great Queen Street, there are 1,677 Lodges in London. Hundreds of these are in the City. Between the hours of eight in the morning and six at night when the City's residential population of about 4,000 swells to 345,000 with the influx of commuters, the Square Mile has the highest density of Freemasons anywhere in Britain.

The Royal Exchange, the Corn Exchange, the Baltic Exchange, the Metal Exchange, the Bank of England, the merchant banks, the insurance companies, the mercantile houses, the Old Bailey, the Inns of Court, the Guildhall, the schools and colleges, the ancient markets, all of them have Freemasons in significant positions. Among the institutions with their own Lodges are the Baltic Exchange (Baltic Lodge No 3006 which has its own temple actually in the Exchange in St Mary Axe); the Bank of England (Bank of England Lodge No 263); and Lloyd's (Black Horse of Lombard Street Lodge No 4155).

Like any local authority – and like central government itself – the City Corporation is formed of a council of elected representatives (the Aldermen, Deputies and Common

Council) and of salaried permanent officers whose job it is to advise the council and execute its decisions. For administrative purposes the City is divided into twenty-five wards. Ten of these wards have their own Lodges.* Five of the six Common Councilmen representing Aldersgate Ward – Arthur Brian Wilson (Deputy), Hyman Liss, Edwin Stephen Wilson, Bernard Joseph Brown, JP, and Peter George Robert Sayles – are Freemasons. Only Michael John Cassidy is, at the time of writing, not a member of the Brotherhood. Every ward, without exception, has at least one Freemason among its representatives.

One Common Councilman who openly admits he is a Freemason spoke to me about the commonly held belief that there is an immense Freemasonic influence on affairs in the City. He asked me not to identify him as it would put him in 'bad odour' with his brethren.

'I have never noticed any direct masonic influence. It's always *there*, one accepts that, always just beneath the surface as it were, but I would say the City is run more on an Old Boys network than on a Freemasonry network, just as somewhere you meet people and get to know them and presumably get chummy with them. I wouldn't have thought there's much influence. You see, we read about that scandal in Italy – P2 wasn't it? – I can't believe it's true. I don't think Freemasonry had anything to do with it.' (See Chapter 26, below.)

I asked if he knew how many of his fellow Common Councilmen were Freemasons.

'No, but I'd have thought the majority. Certainly if you

---

*Aldgate Ward Lodge No 3939; Billingsgate Lodge No 3443 (mainly for those associated with Billingsgate Fish Market); Bishopsgate Lodge No 2396; Cordwainer Ward Lodge No 2241; Cornhill Lodge No 1803; Cripplegate Lodge No 1613; Farringdon Without Lodge No 1745; Langbourn Lodge No 6795; Portsoken Lodge No 5088; and Tower Lodge No 5159.

count out the Roman Catholics and the women I should think the great majority. Probably some of the younger ones aren't. It's rather an old man's game, let's face it. Youngsters don't really want to get involved in these sort of things. They've got more interesting things to do. I should have thought two-thirds of the older ones are Masons. By older, I mean those past fifty. I certainly know personally a lot who are. A lot in the Lodge I'm in are on the Common Council.'

'*Do all Freemasons vote together?*'

'If the strength of the vote I've often got when I've put up is any indication, I'd have thought that none of them voted for me. I don't think there's anything in that suggestion. I've had some very bad votes when I've put up for things and I'm quite a prominent member, and if Freemasonry had done me any good I'd certainly have got a great many more votes than I got.'

Frederick Clearey, CBE, Deputy of Coleman Street Ward, told me, 'I have been a member of only one Lodge, Old Owens No 4440, my school Lodge, but I think Freemasonry engenders a very fine spirit, cementing members of the Lodge with the school. I believe too many people feel that Freemasonry is some secret society where members rush about making signs and getting business from each other which, of course, is utterly untrue. In my experience it has generated an enormous amount of friendship, goodwill and charity, which is what Freemasonry is about.'

All the main salaried officers of the Corporation are Masons. Indeed, it is virtually impossible to reach a high position in Guildhall without being an active Brother, as three senior officers currently serving and two past officers have informed me. The subject of Masonry is spoken about openly in interviews for high posts. At the time of writing, the Town Clerk, the Chamberlain, the City Marshal, the

Hall Keeper, the City Solicitor, the City Architect and the City Engineer are all members of the Brotherhood.

One of the first steps I took in looking into the extent of Freemasonry within the Corporation of London was to write to every male member of the Common Council including all Deputies, Aldermen and Sheriffs, setting out the purpose of my book and asking each recipient if he would be prepared to tell me if he was, or ever had been, a Freemason. I telephoned the general enquiry office at the Guildhall and explained I was writing to each member in connection with a book which included a section on the City – studiously avoiding any reference to Masonry. I asked if I might deliver the letters by hand, rather than separately post 153 letters to the same address. The lady I spoke to assured me I could, that it would cause no problems whatever, and, after checking with her superior, she said that when I arrived at the Guildhall I should ask for a particular official. I followed these instructions and later that day a commissionaire showed me into the appropriate office.

The official remained seated, looked up as if irritated that I should have disturbed the sanctity of his glass-sided booth overlooking Guildhall Yard, and said nothing.

'Hello,' I said, in my friendly way.

'Yes?' he said curtly. 'What is it?' Even then I thought he might ask me to take a seat, but I was disappointed.

'I wonder if you'll help,' I began. 'I'm writing a book which will have a section devoted to the City of London and a lady in your enquiry office said I could deliver these letters to the members of the Common Council by hand to you.'

'Oh, no,' he said, looking dismissively back at the papers on his desk. 'We can't accept them.' It was apparent that he regarded that as the final word in the matter and that he expected me to withdraw.

I sat down and, hail-fellow-well-met, asked him how one went about writing to the members.

'I can't help you,' he said.

'Presumably, if I posted all these to the Guildhall, they would arrive in a bundle like this and be distributed to the people concerned?'

'Presumably.' Still he didn't look up.

'I can't see the difference between the GPO delivering them in a bundle and me delivering them in a bundle. Do you have a Post Room to which I could deliver them . . . ?'

'That's impossible. If I accept your letters, I'll have to accept everyone's.'

'But the Post Room . . . ?' No, I knew I was flogging a dead horse. On impulse, as I rose to leave, I thrust my hand into his and gave him the handshake of the Master Mason, applying distinct pressure with my thumb between his second and third joints.

His attitude changed completely.

Now he was giving me all his attention. 'I'm sorry,' he said, with a sheepish sort of grin, and got up from his chair. He came round to my side of the desk and said, 'I think the best thing you can do is go upstairs to the enquiry office, tell them I sent you and say you'd like a list of the addresses of all members of the Council. That will be much the quickest way of contacting them all.'

Now very solicitous and quite the genial host, he accompanied me to the door, repeated the directions, shook my hand again and wished me well. I followed his advice and it proved sound.

Brother official had helped another member of the Brotherhood – or thought he had.

The influential Livery Companies are almost entirely peopled by Freemasons. Like the Brotherhood, the Livery

Companies – the name derives from the ceremonial dress of members – have developed from the medieval craftsmen's guilds and from religious or social fraternities. Some companies are involved in education and some are influential in the operation of their trade. There are close links between the guilds and livery companies and the Corporation: the City and Guilds of London Institute, set up in 1878 to promote education in technical subjects and set examinations, is a joint venture. And the Lord Mayor of London is selected each year from two of the city's twenty-six aldermen who are nominated by the 15,000 liverymen. To qualify for membership of one of the livery companies, a man must be a Freeman of the City, an honour generally awarded by Freemasons to Freemasons, although there are many notable exceptions. A number of Livery Companies have their own Lodges* and the City Livery Club has its own temple. A masonic alderman told me: 'There are so many competing bodies, especially in the City. What with Livery Companies, Rotary, Chamber of Commerce, Ward clubs, there are so *many* competing clubs. I would have thought that most people in the City attach much more importance to their Livery than they do to their Freemasonry – although of course the majority of Livery Club members are Freemasons as well.'

The Corporation of the City of London is so strongly masonic that many connected with it, some Masons included, think of it as virtually an arm of Grand Lodge. But it must not be forgotten that the City is first and foremost a financial centre. And money to a successful financier – Freemason or not – speaks louder than anything. When it comes to a choice between serving

---

*Basketmakers Lodge No 5639; Blacksmiths Lodge No 7175; Cutlers Lodge No 2730; Farriers Lodge No 6305; Feltmakers Lodge No 3839; Paviors Lodge No 5646; Plaisterers Lodge No 7390; Needlemakers Lodge No 4343, etc., etc.

Mammon and serving the Brotherhood, all but a few Freemasons in the City act upon the masonic principle enshrined in the fifth paragraph of *The Universal Book of Craft Masonry*, which declares, 'Freemasonry distinctly teaches that a man's first duty is to *himself*...'

CHAPTER 25

The Devil in Disguise?

Enemies of the Brotherhood have been denouncing its rituals as devil worship for more than 250 years. One of my purposes was to discover if these denunciations were true or false. Another was to try to resolve, by taking an entirely new approach, the continuing problem of whether or not Masonry was compatible with Christianity.

For the average reader, the difficulty of overcoming any religious objections to Freemasonry is increased rather than lessened by the very abundance of printed matter on the subject. Much of the vast literature of Masonry is devoted to religious issues. The problem is further aggravated by the extreme unreliability of a large portion of this bibliography, wherein scurrilous tirade frequently masquerades as learned treatise.

Almost everything written so far on Freemasonry and religion has fallen into one of two categories: arguments attacking Masonry by non- or anti-Masons, and arguments defending Masonry by committed Masons. There is virtually nothing from neutral outsiders. This, then, would be my approach: as a neutral investigator holding no brief for Christianity and no automatic aversion to devil worship. For the purposes of the investigation, I would suspend moral judgement, admit no good, bad, right or wrong because these could only confuse the issue further. The questions were: Is Freemasonry compatible with

Christianity? and, Is masonic ritual, or any element of it, diabolism? By sticking to these and looking unemotionally at facts, both questions were surely capable of a yes or no answer. The reader could then make his or her own moral judgements.

Another part of my 'new approach' was to avoid the sophisticated theological arguments which have inevitably entered – in fact dominated – the debate. In fact the answers can be arrived at simply and on strictly logical grounds. One does not have to be a theologian – nor even a Freemason or a Christian – to recognize that Christians and Freemasons would have to worship the same God for the two to be compatible. The question simply, then, is do they? If Freemasonry were found, despite its protestations to the contrary, to be a quasi-religion and to have a different god from the Christian god, then the two would naturally be incompatible.

It has been said that these issues are of no concern to Freemasons, but hundreds of members of the Brotherhood have spoken to me of the turmoil they experience in attempting to reconcile their religious views with the demands of masonic ritual. It is of obvious importance to a section of those interested in Freemasonry, whether they be initiates or among the ranks of the 'profane', to attempt to find some answers which can be understood without profound religious knowledge.

First, then, is Freemasonry a religion?

The Rev Saul Amias takes the official masonic line in saying that Freemasonry is neither a religion nor a substitute for religion.

'There are Christians, there are Moslems, there are members of every religion in Freemasonry,' he told me. 'Catholics are not allowed by their own church to become Masons, although some do come in. There's nothing incompatible with my religion as a Jew, as an orthodox

Jew, in Freemasonry, nothing at all. It is not a religion.'

Other Masons told me that Freemasonry is no more a religion than are Rotary Clubs or tennis clubs. Amias agreed with this.

'But,' I objected, 'the Rotary Club and the tennis club do not meet in such solemn environs. You have a masonic *temple*. You have an *altar*. You *kneel* before your *deity*, the Great Architect. You swear oaths on your *Volume of Sacred Law* – the Bible, the Koran, whatever is deemed most appropriate. All these are surely religious trappings?'

He replied, 'Agreed. But these are to *enhance* the individual Mason's belief in his God. *Vouchsafe Thine Aid, Almighty Father, Supreme Governor of the Universe, to our present convention, and grant that this candidate for Freemasonry may so be endowed* . . . and so on. This is a prayer to the *Almighty* that is said by the chaplain, in the case of my Lodge, by myself. A prayer to Almighty God in whom Jews and Christians believe. This is to enhance it, to encourage it. But we do not pray and worship to a masonic God. There is no idol.'

A former Freemason, City of London merchant banker Andrew Arbuthnot, was also able to speak on the question with the knowledge of an initiate. He told me: 'If you take a purely objective view of religions in the plural, one has to accept that Freemasonry is a religion. It induces a sense of brotherhood and togetherness by means of a secret society, which always gives that sense, but it leads people towards the thought of a Supreme Being, to the transcendental. It is at least as much a religion as the average, dry Church of England conventional matins service.'

When Walton Hannah's *Darkness Visible* appeared in 1952, it caused a sensation. This book alone deals conclusively with the matter of whether or not Masonry is a religion as well as reproducing word for word the entire ritual of Freemasonry in the three Craft degrees and concluding that Masonry and Christianity are not compatible. Following its publication, an Anglican vicar who, unlike Hannah, was a Freemason, wrote a book under the pseudonym Vindex, which was entitled *Light Invisible*. This was subtitled: *The Freemason's Answer to Darkness Visible*, and sought to disprove Hannah's assertion that Masonry and Christianity were incompatible. Where the book is valuable, however, is in confirming that Masonry does in fact regard itself as a religion, whatever it might tell outsiders:

We now come to the core of the matter. What *is* the religion of Freemasonry?

It is the oldest of all religious systems, dating from time immemorial [my italics]. It is not in itself a separate religion, and has never claimed to be one, but it embodies in itself the fundamental truths and ancient mysteries on which every religion is based. Taunts that it worships a 'common denominator' God are rather wide of the mark if the phrase indicates any inadequacy or limitation in nature or title of the God we worship, for we worship and believe as a first principle in the fullness of the Godhead of which other religions see only in part.

This 'Total God' which Freemasonry claims for itself is not presented to potential initiates as such. Thousands of practising Christians in Britain today worship the Freemasonic God believing it to be precisely the same as the Christian God, *if they will it*. This is perhaps the most prevalent misunderstanding by the average Freemason of his own Brotherhood.

Candidates for initiation are told that one of the basic qualifications for membership is belief in a Supreme Being of some kind - Jehovah, Allah, the Holy Trinity of Christianity, it does not matter. So long as this belief is present, then whichever divine creator an individual Freemason wishes to follow can be accommodated under the masonic umbrella term for all Supreme Beings (the impossibility of more than one Supreme Being is ignored), that of Great Architect of the Universe,* or sometimes the Grand Geometrician, who created everything with one sweep of His divine compasses. As Vindex puts it in his general downgrading of all the Faiths as mere parts of the Masonic Whole:

As Masons, we believe in God, the Father, Almighty. As Christian Masons we may believe in a symbolical triune essence, and that Jesus Christ is His Son, Our Lord. As Moslem Masons we are equally entitled to believe that Mahomet is His prophet. With these subsidiary and secondary beliefs Masonry has nothing to do, giving her members a perfect liberty to interpret the Godhead as they please.

This is what Freemasons are taught, and this is what the majority of Freemasons believe. Even if it were true, there is enough in this statement to show that Masonry and Christianity are mutually exclusive. Because in this official view propounded by Vindex for public digestion, the very essence of Christianity is obliterated. In Masonry, we learn, Christ is not God but man – in Vindex's estimation the man who showed 'more than any other man who ever lived' what God is like. He later adds: 'I for one can never understand how anyone who takes an exclusive view of Christ as the only complete revelation of God's truth can become a Freemason without suffering from spiritual schizophrenia.'

There are many people who would agree with this non-exclusivity of Christ's teaching. But Christianity does not agree with it. The definition of a Christian is one who believes in Christ's teachings. And Christ taught, rightly or wrongly, '. . . no one cometh unto the Father, but by me'.

Therefore Vindex, although an Anglican cleric, was not a

---

*Denoted in printed masonic rituals as TGAOTU.

Christian. And the Freemasonic God he describes is not a Christian one.

Earlier I used the words 'even if it were true' when referring to the statement made by Vindex and by Freemasonry of the nature of the Masonic God. I did this because the assurance given to candidates that the name Great Architect of the Universe can be applied to whatever Supreme Being they choose is worse than misleading: it is a blatant lie.

In fact the Masonic God – cloaked under the description Great Architect – has a specific name and a particular nature, which has nothing to do with Christ, Vishnu, Buddha, Mohammed or any other being recognized by the great faiths of the modern world.

Two-thirds of Freemasons never realize the untruth of the line they are fed as to the identity of the Great Architect, because it is deliberately kept hidden from them. It is no overstatement to say that most Freemasons, even those without strong religious convictions, would never have joined the Brotherhood if they had not been victims of this subtle trick.

The true name, although not the nature, of the Masonic God is revealed only to those Third Degree Masons who elect to be 'exalted' to the Holy Royal Arch. The Royal Arch is often thought of as the Fourth Degree (but as explained in Chapter 5, the Fourth Degree is that of Secret Master), by others as a 'side degree'. In fact the Royal Arch is an extension of the Third Degree, and represents the completion of the 'ordeal' of the Master Mason. Only about one-fifth of all Master Masons are exalted. But even these, who are taught the 'ineffable name' of the masonic God, do not appreciate its true nature. This is basically because of deliberate obfuscation of the truth by some of those who know, and a general acceptance that everything is as they are told by most members of the Brotherhood.

In the ritual of exaltation, the name of the Great Architect of the Universe is revealed as JAH-BUL-ON – not a general umbrella term open to any interpretation an individual Freemason might choose, but a precise designation that describes a specific supernatural being – a compound deity composed of three separate personalities fused in one. Each syllable of the 'ineffable name' represents one personality of this Trinity:

JAH = Jahweh, the God of the Hebrews.
BUL = Baal, the ancient Canaanite fertility god associated with 'licentious rites of imitative magic'.
ON = Osiris, the Ancient Egyptian god of the underworld.

Baal, of course, was the 'false god' with whom Jahweh competed for the allegiance of the Israelites in the Old Testament. But more recently, within a hundred years of the creation of the Freemason's God, the sixteenth-century demonologist John Weir identified Baal as a devil. This grotesque manifestation of evil had the body of a spider and three heads – those of a man, a toad and a cat. A description of Baal to be found in de Plancy's *Dictionary of Witchcraft* is particularly apposite when considered in the light of the secretive and deceptive nature of Freemasonry: his voice was raucous, and he taught his followers guile, cunning and the ability to become invisible.

In 1873, the renowned masonic author and historian General Albert Pike, later to become Grand Commander of the Southern Jurisdiction of the Supreme Council (of the 33rd Degree) at Charleston, USA, wrote of his reaction on learning of Jah-Bul-On. He was disquieted and disgusted by the name, and went on: 'No man or body of men can make me accept as a sacred word, as a symbol of the infinite and eternal Godhead, a mongrel word, in part composed of the name of an accursed and beastly heathen god, whose name has been for more than two thousand years an appellation of the Devil.'

I have spoken to no less than fifty-seven long-standing Royal Arch Freemasons who have been happy to talk to me, to help me in my ambition to give Freemasonry 'a fair crack of the whip'. Most of them spoke quite freely, explaining without hesitation their views, reactions and answers to the criticisms and queries I raised. However, all but four lost their self-assurance and composure when I said, 'What about Jah-Bul-On?' Some, although they had previously told me they had been exalted to the Royal Arch, and therefore must have not only received the lecture on the name but also studied the passages and enacted the ritual relating to Jah-Bul-On, said they had never heard of it. In most cases the interviewees very rapidly brought the meeting to a close when I asked the question. Others laughed unconvincingly and extricated themselves from having to reply by jauntily saying such words as, 'Oh, that old chestnut', and passing quickly on to some other subject, normally going on the offensive with something like, 'Why are you so interested in Freemasonry in particular? Why don't you look into Christianity or something? Why do people always pick on Freemasonry?' – thereby diverting the conversation from the course I had plotted. If I insisted on returning to Jah-Bul-On, almost invariably the interview would be unceremoniously terminated. Others said that although they had heard of the word, they did not know what it meant. To them it meant God, and previously erudite Freemasons, with a precise knowledge of every other aspect of Masonry we had discussed, suddenly became vague and claimed ignorance of this most central of all Freemasonic subjects. While professing an almost total lack of knowledge of Jah-Bul-On, several dismissed it as of no real importance.

Charles Stratton, one Royal Arch Freemason for whom I have the utmost admiration, told me this of Jah-Bul-On: 'No one ever has time to think about its meaning, you're too busy trying to remember your words. As far as I know it's just another name for Jehovah.'

Acute silences, chiefly of embarrassment, followed my question on many occasions, as happened when I spoke to a most co-operative officer both of Grand Lodge and Grand Chapter.

We had been discussing whether or not Freemasonry was a religion, and I had run through my customary list of religious terms used in Freemasonry. Then I added, 'One comes across the phrase, "the *sacred* tenets of Free-masonry". This seems to imply that Masonry thinks of itself as a religion.'

The Grand Officer replied, 'No, I haven't said that . . . the *sacred* tenets?'

'Yes.'

'Well, the word sacred means holy.'

'Yes. Then there's the "Holy" Royal Arch.'

He paused. When he began to speak again it was much more slowly.

'Yes. The Holy Royal Arch. They are all expressions of . . . religion in its fullest sense, not in a masonic sense. I cannot stress too strongly the fact that there is no masonic religion, no masonic god, deity or someone or something to which a Freemason must swear loyalty. No.'

'What about Jah-Bul-On?'

He was obviously taken off-guard. He said nothing for nearly ten seconds and looked most discomfited. At length, proceeding with the extreme caution of a man feeling his way through a thicket of thorns, he said: 'These are . . . Hebrew words which are . . . murdered from their original. And *Jah* is the Hebrew word for God, so it's God again. You come back to God, the *real* God. But these – ha!

[he chuckled] – these are ways in which we express our *loyalty* to God.'

'It's interesting you should choose only to define the first syllable, which is of course the most acceptable to those with religious convictions. But what about the other parts of that word which are, are they not, Baal and Osiris?'

Another long pause. 'I don't know them. That's the higher echelons of Freemasonry.'

'That's in the Royal Arch, isn't it?'

'I don't do Royal Arch. I do Chapter, but not Royal Arch.'

This was the first lie he had told me, and I could see it was unpleasant for him.*

I continued: 'It is established that Jahbulon is a composite name for God, made up of Jah—'

'What's Bul-On?'

'Bul is Baal and On is Osiris, the Ancient Egyptian god of the dead.'

'Well . . .'

'Pike was outraged when he heard that name for the first time and saw it associated with Freemasonry, which of course was so dear to him. He said that nothing would induce him to accept as the name of God a word which is in part the name of a pagan god and for more than two thousand years an appellation of the devil.'

'I agree on that, but I . . . I . . . I don't know about it. It's not that I don't want to. I don't know about it so I really can't comment. You'll have to ask someone who knows.'

'Does it worry you?'

'In one of the higher degrees they use Jesus Christ.'

'Yes, there are several masonic orders which are exclusively Christian – the Knights Templar, the Ancient

*See Mackey's *Revised Encyclopaedia of Freemasonry*, Volume I, p 191.

and Accepted Rite, the Societas Rosicruciana, the Knights of Malta, the Order of Eri. But does the name Jah-Bul-On worry you?'

'Many Masons wouldn't subscribe to those Christian degrees.'

The implication was clear: if Christ was an acceptable part of Freemasonry even to a non-Christian, why not the devil as well? Unacceptable though he might be to most initiates, he has his place.

The Church of England has been a stronghold of Freemasonry for more than two hundred years. Traditionally, joining the Brotherhood and advancing within it has always been the key to preferment in the Church. This situation has altered in the past twenty years and today there are fewer Masons within the Church than ever before. Even so, the Church is still rife with members of the Brotherhood. This is why, despite overwhelming evidence of Masonry's incompatibility with Christianity and the shattering revelation as to the nature of the Masonic God, no amount of pressure from inside or outside the Church has so far succeeded in forcing an enquiry into the subject.

Thirty years ago a thirty-eight-year-old Anglican clergyman, the Rev Walton Hannah, gave up his living in Sussex to devote himself to studying and writing about Freemasonry. In January 1951, Hannah launched his attack on clergymen Freemasons in an article in *Theology*. The article created a fissure through which poured the pent-up anxieties and suspicion of non-masonic Anglicans, which had been rumbling beneath the surface for years. The controversy spread far beyond the pages of theological journals as spin-off 'shock-horror-sensation' pieces appeared in the popular press. The furore led to a debate in the

Church Assembly and it began to look as if the whole subject of Freemasonry in the Church might be brought before the Convocation of Canterbury. But as the Archbishop of Canterbury himself (Fisher) was a powerful Freemason, the Brotherhood had little trouble in blocking the attempt, and it was ruled out of order on a technicality.

Hannah later published his condemnation of Freemasonry and his arguments against its compatibility with Christianity in his book *Darkness Visible*, in which he pointed out that every Christian Church that had studied Freemasonry has declared that it was incompatible with Christianity. These condemnations ranged from the famous papal pronouncements, the first of which was in 1738, to an instruction of General Booth, founder of the Salvation Army, that 'no language of mine could be too strong in condemning an Officer's affiliation with any Society which shuts Him outside its Temples'. The Greek Orthodox Church, pointing out that Lutheran, Methodist and Presbyterian communities had also declared Masonry incompatible with Christianity, condemned the movement formally in 1933 in part and significantly because 'it constitutes a mystagogical system which reminds us of the ancient heathen mystery-religions and cults – from which it descends and is their continuation and regeneration'.

Dr H. S. Box, author of *The Nature of Freemasonry*, attempted to raise the issue of Freemasonry in the Canterbury Convocation of the Church of England in 1951. 'Due largely,' Hannah says, 'to the persuasive influence of the Masonic Bishop of Reading, Dr A. Groom Parham, this was never debated.' There was, though, a debate in the Church Assembly in 1952. Hannah records that the 'critics of Masonry were frankly out-manoeuvred by the unexpectedness and speed with which Masons acted': the motion for an enquiry was overwhelmingly rejected. The Church of England has still never considered the matter officially.

Hannah's conclusion, echoed today by several deeply concerned Church of England clergy and bishops in private conversation, is that 'the Church . . . dares not offend or provoke thousands of influential and often financially substantial laymen by enquiring into the religious implications of Freemasonry'.

The present Archbishop of Canterbury, Dr Robert Runcie, is not a Freemason and a recent survey suggests that many fewer bishops are Freemasons today than in the 1950s, when it would have been hard to find half a dozen bishops who were not Masons.

One great difficulty, today as in the 1950s, is for non-Masonic clergy and laity – and indeed the general reader – to obtain reliable information about the religious implications of Freemasonry. The vast – though often inaccessible – masonic literature is contradictory and full of gaps. It is all but impossible to know which books and what parts of them reflect the inmost beliefs of the masonic leadership.

To take one striking example: in the first three degrees – the 'blue' Craft Masonry conducted in Lodges – the initiate is introduced right away to 'The Great Architect of the Universe' as the masonic deity. He will doubtless assume according to his upbringing that this is merely a quaint way of referring to Jahweh, Allah, or the triune God of Christianity. If he should wonder why this title is a masonic secret and why masonic texts therefore cryptically refer to the 'GAOTU' instead of simply to God with a capital 'G', he will probably see no more than a little harmless clandestinity, maybe guessing (incorrectly) that it is a time-honoured vagary deriving from the days of 'operative' masons.

The average Christian man who has not studied the theological implications of the oaths, rituals and lectures usually experiences a certain initial moral and religious disquiet about what he has done in joining. Many have admitted to being somewhat ashamed by the initiation ceremony they have undergone. But all this is allayed by the reassurance that so many of the eminent and reputable have for centuries done the same and that the masonic system somehow enjoys an immunity in these matters sanctioned by tradition. As already stated, it is only when a Master Mason is 'exalted' to the Royal Arch and becomes a member of a Royal Arch Chapter, that the real name of the 'GAOTU' – Jahbulon – is communicated to him. Even then, carried so far by his experience of the first three Craft degrees, and being used by that time to the ambivalence surrounding all masonic ritual and symbolism arising from the fact that the one masonic dogma is that there are no immutable truths, most fail to appreciate that they have been deliberately misled into thinking 'GAOTU' is the one God of the great monotheistic religions. No one will enlighten the duped Royal Arch Masons for no one has the authority to do more than sketch his own personal interpretation of what the attributes of Jahbulon may be.

Those that have a feeling for the occult – the true adepts – recognize each other: they appreciate the real significance behind the deliberate masonic ambiguities. They develop a confidence in drawing their own deductions, making their own interpretations of symbolism and ritual. Such people come slowly to be accepted into the inner sanctum of the Brotherhood. But even among themselves – to judge by what senior masonic defectors have reported, and by the rare esoteric literature solely for advanced Masons – there is no mention of anything openly suggestive of satanism. There is no need: long practice of the masonic system ensures that the understanding is on another level. In just the same way, in worldly matters, all Masons at their initiation are required to 'declare on your honour that – uninfluenced by mercenary or other unworthy motive, you freely and voluntarily offer yourself . . . for the mysteries and privileges of Freemasonry'. Most candidates fully understand that this is humbug: they know full well that many join primarily or at least partly in the hope that membership will forward their worldly ambitions. But they give their word – and so, right from the beginning, they enter into the double-speak of Masonry. A double-speak some learn to talk like a guided missile homing on its target. It is a double-speak the student of Masonry must learn to recognize and not allow to confuse him.

Against all this, the Church of England's Society for the Propagation of Christian Knowledge (SPCK), for example, even today carries no literature examining Freemasonry and discussing whether a Christian should be a Mason. Hannah states that the SPCK issued a directive to their bookshops that his book *Darkness Visible*, probably still the most accurate and scholarly general work on the matter, should not be stocked. The Archbishop of Canterbury is the President of the SPCK. The Archbishop of Canterbury responsible for banning Hannah's book was Dr Geoffrey Fisher – a Freemason of long standing.

There is no doubt that Freemasonry is extremely anxious to have – or to appear to have – good relations with all Christian Churches and, knowing that no serious masonic scholar and no Christian theologian has been prepared to argue compatibility, the Movement remains silent. There is evidence of very considerable efforts being made by Masons – including pressures on publishers, distributors and libraries – to suppress works critical of the Brotherhood.* Hannah related how a mysterious gentleman invited him to the foyer of the Savoy Hotel where he offered the author £1,000 in notes for not publishing *Darkness Visible* or any other attack on Masonry. It should be stated that there is no evidence of this particular incident except Hannah's word.

Hannah ends his review of the attitudes of the Christian Churches towards Freemasonry by remarking: 'There is fear on both sides, hence the search for truth is stifled, and the religious bigamy continues. Only Rome can afford to smile at the situation, and continue to win converts.' For once, Hannah – who became a Roman Catholic after the Church of England had failed to examine Masonry and pronounce upon it – was wrong.

The Church of Rome, traditional arch-enemy of Freemasonry, is even more the object of masonic attention than the Church of England.

Roman Catholics of the older generation remember pamphlets published by the Catholic Truth Society (the Roman Church's equivalent of the SPCK) about the incompatibility of Freemasonry and Catholicism at every church bookstall. They understood that a long line of Popes had declared Freemasonry illicit and that Catholics who were Freemasons were automatically excommunicated by the mere fact of membership.

The situation today has mysteriously changed. Like the SPCK, the CTS has ceased publishing any guidance on

*This even extends to the Brotherhood's own publications. When the British Library applied in the normal way to Freemasons Hall for two copies of the *Masonic Year Book* for the Reading Room in 1981, it was informed that it would not be permitted to have copies of the directory then or in the future. No explanation was given. See also pp 9–12 on the prepubliction adventures of *The Brotherhood*.

Freemasonry. Priests, although perhaps better trained today than ever before, are commonly ignorant about the subject and are themselves unaware of their Church's present position.

I have discovered that there is a deliberate policy in operation within the English hierarchy of the Roman Catholic Church to keep its members in ignorance of the true standing of the Church on the question of Freemasonry. This policy is intended to cover up a huge mistake made by the English Catholic Bishops in 1974 which led to Catholics in Britain being informed that after two hundred years of implacable opposition from Rome, the Holy See had changed its mind and that with the permission of their local Bishop Catholics could now become Freemasons. As well as covering up what I can now reveal as this blunder on the part of the English hierarchy, the wall-of-silence policy conceals, perhaps inadvertently, a more sinister situation in Rome, where I have evidence that the Vatican itself is infiltrated by Freemasons.

In 1982 I asked a trusted friend, a Roman Catholic and like myself an author and journalist, to raise the matter of the widespread ignorance of Catholics with the present Archbishop of Westminster, Cardinal Basil Hume. The Archbishop's response was: 'I think it would be wise to wait for the publication of the new Canon Law before taking any public stance on the questions of Freemasons.' His General Secretary, Monsignor Norris, wrote in amplification: '. . . we have been informed that Free-masonry in this country has no connection with Freemasonry of an unpleasant kind on the Continent'. He went on to add that a Catholic's Bishop could give permission for a man to join the Brotherhood if 'convinced [membership] will have no bad effect on the person's Catholicity'.

Only now, after independent investigation by my Roman Catholic friend and myself, and contact with the Roman Church's hierarchy in Rome, can this statement be revealed as inaccurate. Norris's comment that '. . . we have been informed . . .' begs the question – *who* convinced the English hierarchy that English Freemasonry is fundamentally different? What happened to the Canon Law automatically excommunicating Freemasons? The story is a strange one.

By the 1880s eight Popes had already condemned Freemasonry when Freemasons urged that these condemnations had been based on erroneous information and were excessively severe. This led Pope Leo XIII to issue his famous encyclical *Humanum Genus* in 1884. Leo XIII classed Freemasonry as a grouping of secret societies in the 'kingdom of Satan' and, like the Greek Orthodox Church half a century later, stated that it wished 'to bring back after eighteen centuries the manners and customs of the pagans'. He qualified Masonry as subversive of Church and state, condemned it for its rejection of Christian revelation, and for its religious indifferentism – the idea that all religions are equally valid. He warned against the effectiveness of masonic organization, its use of figurehead leaders, and its subtle use of 'double-speak'. He urged the bishops to whom the Encyclical was addressed 'first of all to tear away the mask of Freemasonry, and let it be seen for what it really is'.

There were further condemnations in 1894 and 1902. Then the Canon Law promulgated in 1917 provided in Canon 2335 that '*ipso facto* excommunication' is incurred by 'those who enrol in the masonic sect or in other associations of the same sort which plot against the Church or the legitimate civil authorities'. One reason for the unusual frequency of these papal condemnations is that Freemasonry has always had sympathizers, even members, clerical as well as lay, in the Roman Catholic Church.

From the 1920s Freemasons increasingly urged that British Freemasonry (and indeed other Freemasonry which did not accept the avowed atheism of the French and certain other 'Grand Orients' which had cost them recognition by the British Grand Lodges) was different from what the Popes had had in mind and so was unjustly condemned: they insisted that this British-type Freemasonry did not plot against either Church or state. The Vatican paid no attention, but three Jesuits with masonic contacts (Gruber, Bertheloot and Riquet) successively urged study of the possibility for a rapprochement.

Then came Vatican II and the great impetus this gave to the ecumenical movement – the reconciliation of all Christians. Senior members of the Brotherhood saw an opportunity to exploit this enthusiasm and used its ecclesiastical contacts to renew its call for an end to Catholic hostility. In America, France and Germany, notably, there were a number of small indications that the Catholic attitude to Masonry was softening. These were enough for Harry Carr,* one of those leading Freemasons who, like Dr Theophilus Desaguliers in the eighteenth century, exercise immense influence from a discreet position some rungs below the top of the Grand Lodge ladder. Carr spoke of the possibility of reconciliation to the London Grand Lodge Association in February 1968.

As related in his book *The Freemason at Work*, a questioner asked Carr how there could be any such move while 'defamatory and inaccurate' anti-masonic literature was on sale at Westminster Cathedral bookstall. Carr

*Past Junior Grand Deacon; Past Master of Quatuor Coronati Lodge No 2076 and of four other Lodges – 2265, 2429, 6226 and 7464; Hon. Member of six Lodges – 236, 2429, 2911, 3931, 7998 and 8227; Hon. Member of eight Lodges in France, the USA and Canada.

wrote to Cardinal Heenan, then Archbishop of West-minster, who undertook to have the offending literature, if indeed inaccurate, withdrawn. It was. Heenan saw Carr on 18 March 1968.

Carr stressed the old distinction between British and atheistic Continental Freemasonry and said that both as a Jew and a Mason he hoped the time had come for a reconciliation. According to Carr, this led Heenan to offer himself as 'intermediary' between English Free-masonry and the Vatican. Carr says he saw Heenan again on the eve of the Cardinal's departure for Rome. There was talk of a revision of Canon 2335 and of meetings between the Brotherhood and the Holy See.

On the surface nothing happened for nearly three years until the spring of 1971 when the Jesuit Father Giovanni Caprile, a leading and very hostile Catholic expert on Freemasonry, changed tack and wrote a number of conciliatory articles in the quasi-official *Civilta Cattolica*. It was widely believed that Caprile's new line was backed by none other than Cardinal Villot, then Vatican Secretary of State. The story is that Villot, dubbed a 'progressive', used Father Caprile's articles to overcome the resistance to any change in the Church's teaching on Masonry by Cardinal Franjo Seper, Prefect of the Sacred Congregation for the Doctrine of Faith.

Against this background Carr saw Heenan a third time on 26 April 1971 and Heenan related how the Holy See had granted dispensations to two English Masons to remain members of the Brotherhood after their reception into the Roman Catholic Church.

On 12 June 1973 Heenan felt able to warn his priests that a change in Rome's policy towards Masonry was imminent. He was right. After years of procrastination Cardinal Seper felt obliged on 19 July 1974 to authorize the Sacred Congregation for the Doctrine of the Faith to write a confidential letter to certain Episcopal Conferences, the English among them, commenting on the interpretation to be given to Canon 2335.

Seper said no more than he had to: someone had pointed out that, as there was no comma in the definitive Latin text of Canon 2335, it was not clear whether *all* Freemasons were automatically excommunicated, or *only* those Freemasons whose particular group plots against Church or legitimate civil authorities. Wherever a Canon provides for penalties, Seper was obliged to point out, the most restrictive interpretation had to be given in the case of ambiguity. Therefore, the Canon reserved automatic excommunication only for the plotters.

Of itself the cautious letter signalled no change in the Church's attitude to the Brotherhood. But Caprile in *Civilta Cattolica* published what was allegedly an 'authorized commentary' suggesting that the Church now officially accepted that there were masonic associations which did not conspire against Church or state, that the Church now intended to leave it to local Episcopal Conferences to decide whether their local Masons were in this category – and if they were, there need be no ban on Masonry.

The English bishops accepted this view and issued a statement of general guidance which reads in part:

Times change. The Holy See has reviewed the Church's present relationship with Freemasonry . . . the Congregation has ruled that Canon 2335 no longer automatically bars a Catholic from membership of Masonic groups . . . And so a Catholic who joins the Freemasons is excommunicated only if the policy and actions of the Freemasons in his area are known to be hostile to the Church.

The Catholic News Service announced that the effect of this guidance 'is to move from a ban on Catholics belonging to the Masonic Movement to a cautious procedure whereby such membership may in some cases be sought'.

For Carr and for Masonry this was the definitive breakthrough: the reconciliation so long sought by the Masons had been achieved. As Carr puts it, 'There must be hundreds of dedicated Masons all over the world who have played some part in the achievement of this long desired end. We have seen masonic history in the making . . . the sad story which began in 1738 is happily ended.' Masons hastened to spread the word that Catholics could at last be Freemasons without incurring their Church's displeasure.

Inside sources have informed me that behind all this disarray in the Vatican there may well have been a small number of masonic prelates – specifically an Archbishop who in July 1975 was dismissed from his post when 'unquestionable proof' of his being a Freemason was submitted to the Pope. *Prima facie* evidence of a few such cases does certainly exist, but as Paul VI, fearing scandal, ordered no enquiry to establish the truth, rumour has taken over and spurious lists of high-ranking 'masonic prelates' have been passed around, making the facts more than ever difficult to establish.

Everywhere there was confusion. In Brazil, on Christmas Day 1975, at the request of the Masonic Lodge Liberty, Cardinal Abelard Brandao Vilela, Primate of Brazil, celebrated Mass to commemorate the Lodge's fortieth anniversary. For his attitude towards the Brotherhood the Cardinal next year received the title 'Great Benefactor' of the Lodge.

All this happened under Pope Paul VI who, whatever

his other virtues, is widely considered to have been a weak man unable to face scandal if need be to keep masonic influence out of the Vatican and national Episcopal conferences.

With the advent of Pope John Paul II it soon became clear that Harry Carr had been over-sanguine in suggesting that the story was at an end. On 17 February 1981 the Sacred Congregation for the Doctrine of the Faith issued a 'declaration' stating that the 1974 letter had given rise to 'erroneous and tendentious' interpretations. It insisted: '. . . canonical discipline regarding Freemasonry remains in force and has not been modified in any way, consequently neither excommunication nor the other penalties envisaged have been abrogated'.

The 1974 letter had merely drawn attention to the fact that the Church's penal laws must always be interpreted restrictively. In evident reproof of the English bishops, the Congregation declared that it had *not* intended Episcopal Conferences to issue public pronouncements of a general character on the nature of masonic associations 'which would change the position of the Church in regard to Freemasonry'.

The 1981 declaration pulls the rug from under the new understanding of the relationship between the Roman Catholic Church and Masonry. Yet it has had virtually no publicity and the myth that canon law on the subject was changed in 1974 persists.

Roman Catholics seeking a true answer to the question of the Church's position on Freemasonry can find it only in the pages of this book. A high Vatican official, well qualified to explain the present position of the Holy See, said I should make four points:

First: the purpose of the Vatican letter of 19 July 1974 was simply to point out that only the restrictive interpretation of

Canon 2335 should be applied: in other words only those Freemasons whose organization plots against the (Roman Catholic) Church, or the legitimate civil authorities are automatically excommunicated, a matter which it is of course extremely difficult to determine in the case of a secret society where the thinking of its clandestine leading members is not known to the ordinary membership.

Secondly: the Church wishes to reduce wherever possible the offences that incur automatic excommunication. Consequently the new Canon Law now before the Pope may very well end automatic excommunication for Freemasons even under the restrictive interpretation of the present Canon 2335.

Thirdly, and most important: *it does not follow that because some action may no longer attract automatic excommunication it becomes licit.* If something is contrary to Divine Law it is illicit even though the Church may apply no extraordinary sanctions. The Vatican draws particular attention to the findings of the German bishops as recently as May 1980. After prolonged study in co-operation with German Freemasonry of only the first three 'Craft' degrees, the German bishops concluded that 'Masonry has not changed' and can in no way be reconciled with Christianity. The position of the Catholic Church is thus that, as Freemasonry is essentially similar in Britain and Germany, the German bishops' conclusions that Freemasonry is contrary to Divine Law *applies to British as much as to German Freemasonry.*

Fourthly: there are moral as well as theological and political issues. It is unChristian to join any secret organization which systematically benefits its own members to the detriment of the legitimate interests of non-members. Insofar as Freemasonry is guilty of this, Roman Catholics obviously should not join it.

The Vatican's position is thus plain enough for anyone able to travel to Rome and obtain an audience with an eminent official. As most Catholic clergy and laity are not in a position to do this, it is curious that the English hierarchy have left English Catholics in ignorance. It is impossible to guess how long they would have remained ignorant had not New English Library decided to commission this investigation into Freemasonry.

An eminent prelate in Rome, who enthusiastically welcomed the prospect of this book and described the project as 'work of great importance', disclosed how the English Roman Catholic hierarchy, far from hastening to 'tear away the mask from Freemasonry' as urged by Pope Leo XIII, is in practice out on a limb in its toleration of Freemasonry and its unwillingness to give any guidance to Catholics, even to its own priests. He explained, 'The English bishops are anxious to give an English face to Catholicism. So, because Freemasonry is so English, they feel they must come to terms with it. The bishops wish for silence.'

Effectively, then, the true position of the Roman Catholic Church is not unlike that of the Church of England. Faced with the prestige, influence, and pre-valence of Freemasonry in British society, both are similarly paralysed. The Vatican contact said, 'The Catholic hierarchy are well aware too of the pressures on the Roman Catholic laity in many walks of life to join Freemasonry if their worldly interests are not to be too gravely prejudiced in an increasingly masonic world. If the English Bishops do not consider they should demand that the faithful make the sacrifice required by the official Vatican position, it is hardly surprising that Freemasonry among Catholics is on the increase. It is certainly no longer safe to assume that Roman Catholic professional men are not Freemasons.'

The people and places in the following episode have been given obvious pseudonyms to make identification impos-sible and so to protect my informant, an Anglican vicar. For more than five months after I first heard of this man's plight, he was guarded about what was happening to him. Eventually, though, he decided that the disturbing events which took place in and around his parish during 1981 should be widely known – if only to warn other clergymen of the trouble in which they might become embroiled if they did not handle their local Freemasons skilfully. At this time the vicar requested that I did not disclose his name. Less than two days later, after much contemplation and soul-searching, he decided that he must stand up and be counted even if it meant placing himself in jeopardy again. But his fear overcame him once again and the pseudonyms were inserted into his story.

The Parish Church of Epsilon lies between the Berkshire villages of Zeta and Theta. From the porch there is a beautiful view of the Kappa valley and the highway beyond. For the Vicar of Epsilon, however, all beauty ends when he enters his church. He strongly suspects, from his experiences since taking up the living in 1980 and from his own observations and research, that the building called Epsilon Parish Church is not a church at all, but a pagan temple. It is full of masonic symbols. The Rev Lamda Mu says he came close to being driven out of his parish and his livelihood after opposing plans, on Christian grounds, for a service in the church for members of the two local masonic Lodges. When I met the Rev Mu he told me, 'In May 1981 I knew almost nothing about Freemasonry, but I have since come to understand the spiritual implications of this whole secret society, religion, or whatever you may care to call it.'

On 5 May 1982, before deciding finally that it would be too dangerous to be named, he wrote to me, 'Apart from my testimony, there are two principal reasons why I have decided to contribute to your work on Freemasonry.' He asked that I list these reasons in full in his own words:

(1)   A number of people for one reason or another in contributing to this book were unwilling to give their names and I am
told that some of the evidence had to be disguised. This in
fact would make it possible for people to criticize the book
as sheer fabrication. I was impressed by the author's motives
in preparing this book on Freemasonry as he wanted to
examine the subject from all points of view so that the reader
might be able to make his own judgement on Freemasonry. I
have learned that Freemasonry is very big indeed and I am
only describing *my* contact with Freemasonry.

(2)   I am contributing as a member of the established Church,
that has had strong contacts with Masonry for a very long
time. In this day and age it is fashionable to criticize the
establishment, and my very real fear is that should anything
vaguely comparable happen in this country with regard to
Freemasonry as happened with the P2 Lodge in Italy [see
Chapter 26], it could not only seriously undermine but possibly destroy confidence in authority and the use of authority
in this land. I therefore wish to dissociate myself from all
those who desire to use criticism of Masonry for their own
ends.

Mu wished it to be said that he bore Masons no
animosity or ill-will. He said that in whatever contacts he
had had over the events so far, the Freemasons themselves
had been courteous and polite. 'I must also add that there
are a number of Masons in my parishes, some of them are
very close friends of mine, and some of them played a very
active part in saving one of my churches from certain
closure.'

This is the Rev Mu's story.

'I remember as a small boy that my mother announced
after seeing a postcard that somebody had gone to the
"Grand Lodge Above". She then showed me my father's
masonic apron. In 1967 at theological college, there was a
discussion about Freemasonry among some of the
students. I had no idea what Freemasonry was. I was given
a book on heresies by one of the students which contained

eight pages on Freemasonry. I read it and this in fact has coloured all my thinking on Masonry. I felt, as a Christian believing in Jesus Christ, I could not become a Mason as this would mean denying Jesus Christ as the Saviour of the world.

'Before I became Vicar of [Epsilon] in Berkshire in 1980, I was told that the Freemasons had an annual service once a year in [Epsilon] Church. I raised this with the Bishop, who advised me to allow the Masons to have their service but ask to see the order of service beforehand and to insist on every prayer being said "in the name of our Lord Jesus Christ". In May 1981, I received a letter from the [Theta] Lodge requesting a service in [Epsilon] Church. The letter gave no indication as to what exactly the Masons wanted and I was concerned that I would be involved in all sorts of bizarre rituals. I later discovered that they had only wanted Prayer Book Evensong. The surprise for me on the letter was a masonic symbol, *which I recognized immediately as being like a sign in [Epsilon] Church.* I had to reply to the letter fairly quickly, but I had no idea what to do. The one person I felt I could talk to about this was away on holiday. I did not know who were Masons and who were not. I did not know what the feelings of the local clergy were on Masonry, and I was not absolutely certain if even the Bishop was a Mason. (As it turned out he most certainly was not.) I remembered hearing something of a clergyman who was driven from this country to Canada or somewhere because he opposed Masonry. I later discovered that this was Walton Hannah. I had no wish to follow him but I was extremely reluctant to be involved in any way with a society that wanted a service in church but wanted the Founder of the church excluded. It took me four or five days to summon up enough courage to reply to the Masons. I said that all my knowledge of Masonry was second hand, I knew very little about Masonry, except that Masons had services which did not allow the name of Jesus Christ to be used, and for that reason I was not happy about them having a service. I did not flatly refuse to give them a service, but made the same conditions as those suggested by the Bishop, only adding that *I* should preach the sermon. Had I known then the kind of hymns Masons sing, I would have wanted to see those in advance as well.

'Over a period of time, I became aware of a gathering storm, and I began in desperation to search for books about Masonry. I found one which only confirmed my views and made me even more aware of the true nature of Freemasonry. Also I began to find out who were Masons in all three of my parishes, and this provided me with many surprises. I sensed a major storm was brewing and I felt totally ill equipped to face what was about to happen. I had become aware that a number of Popes had condemned Masonry and I discovered a number of books on the subject at Douai Abbey. I had practically no time to read them before I was given six days' notice that the only subject on the agenda for the next Parish Church Council meeting at [Epsilon] was the Annual Freemasons' Service. In that brief period of time I tried to prepare as convincing a case as possible as to why I knew a Christian could not be a Mason. I used some information from the recent *Credo* television programme, and I even quoted from the 39 Articles the relevant articles which should convince any Anglican that he cannot be an Anglican and a Mason. I was not allowed to explain anything about the rituals of Masonry as the meeting suddenly exploded in uproar. Some of the members were very angry with me and felt that I had insulted their relatives dead and living. In the end the PCC passed a resolution asking me to consider writing to the Masons inviting them back again. If I did not do this, I was told that they would all resign, and one person warned me that I might become "a Vicar without a Parish". They then decided to have a further meeting two weeks later.

'What surprised me most of all was that they could not accept or could not hear me say that Masonry was contrary to the first three of the Ten Commandments and denied Christ. They said that as many clergy were Masons, including bishops, there was nothing wrong with it. I do not recount all this in order to criticize the way the PCC reacted. I felt that for many decades the PCC had been badly let down by the clergy who have been Masons and believed that it was compatible with their allegiance to Christ. It grieves me to think of those times and the only reason why I relate all this is hopefully to spare some other vicar and PCC the kind of experience we all suffered at that time. The next morning, I wrote to the Bishop and said that I had no intention of sending any letter to the Masons. One of my churchwardens came to see me. He was greatly distressed by all that had happened and asked me to reconsider writing to the Masons and he told me how upset many people were, and that unless I wrote a letter they would all resign. I wrote a further letter to the Bishop suggesting how I proposed to resolve the crisis. The Bishop replied with a very tough letter condemning Masonry in no uncertain terms. He supported my actions, adding that had he been in my position he would have done as I did. The letter displayed his deep loyalty to Christ. Nevertheless at the next meeting, I did produce a letter which was not accepted. I produced another letter, in which I regretted the upset I had caused everyone and that I had not realized that all they wanted was Evensong. I also said that I thought that they had wanted a masonic service. Even with the letter that I finally sent to the Masons I had to omit the one and only reference I made to Jesus Christ. One of my churchwardens worked overtime to restore peace and harmony, and he succeeded.

'I felt very puzzled by all that had happened. I could not understand why the PCC acted in the way it had. Why had they been so angry and upset? What puzzled me most of all was that none of them were Masons! There had to be a reason behind it all and I just did not know the reason. The Bishop came to see me. At first I was worried as he had told me before I became a vicar that he would support me in my parishes but if he felt that I was wrong over something he would tell me privately. I need not have worried, his real concern was how I had taken everything, and he only came to support me and my wife. In retrospect I feel she suffered most of all through the crisis. We had a long and happy time with the Bishop over a meal discussing all that had happened; he also told me to expect further consequences of my actions. I did not understand at the time what he meant, and to a certain extent, I still do not understand. I had only just weathered a major crisis. Without the firm support of the Bishop, it is unlikely that I would still be Vicar of [Epsilon]. I was still very puzzled by all that had happened and I just did not appreciate the spiritual implications of Freemasonry.

'If ever I faced another crisis over Freemasonry, I felt that I had to know what Freemasonry was. I came up against another problem: nearly all the books that I had borrowed on Freemasonry had been out of print for many years. It took many months even to obtain one or two of the books. Someone lent to me a copy of Richard Carlile's *Manual of Freemasonry*. This was the first masonic book I ever saw that gave full details of the rituals of Masonry. Although produced early in the last century, it remains a very important document on Freemasonry. I also wrote to London Weekend Television in the hope of obtaining a copy of the German Bishops' Report on Freemasonry from James Rushbrooke, a scholar who had appeared on the *Credo* programme. On the same day, I received not only James Rushbrooke's translation of the Report, but also another translation from some other source. Not only that but the Rev John Lawrence, who had also been involved in the *Credo* programme, contacted me, and not long afterwards, I was also visited by James Rushbrooke. James impressed upon me how large a thing Masonry was and considered that I had acted bravely in taking the action I did, ". . . because you know they will put your name down on their list of clergymen who are actively opposed to Freemasonry".

'There were two other things that happened. One was that the local Masons went to another church and the preacher at the service made some unpleasant comments about my attitude towards Freemasonry. The Vicar of the parish came and apologized to me afterwards. I felt very sorry for him and tried to ease his conscience, but I also pointed out that I as a Christian could not accept Masonry. The other incident was that a member of one of my parishes, a Mason, asked to see me. I had made a point of seeing the churchgoing Masons and I thought I had reassured them that I had no intention of driving Masons out of church. The minute you drive any sinner out of church you go against the principle that the church exists to reform penitent sinners through our Lord Jesus Christ. Freemasonry does not operate on that principle and therefore I explained that I was against the *system* but not the people involved in it. This parishioner was still worried and confused by my actions. We had a very long conversation in which I began to have the feeling that Masonry really did have a false spirit behind it. The fellowship of Masonry was a counterfeit of the fellowship of the Holy Spirit. I was taken by surprise for a moment when he told me that if I wanted to join a Lodge, I would be made very welcome!

'I have only told you the bare bones of what happened. I have deliberately avoided as far as possible giving theological opinions about Masonry or indeed details about the rituals of Masonry as there is plenty of information available to anyone who wishes to find it. The books on Masonry are endless. During the following months, I learnt more and more about Masonry and discovered many more symbols of Masonry in [Epsilon] Church to the extent that now I really wonder if it is a church at all.

'I have also learned that the last family owner of [Epsilon] Court had been a top Mason. I found this out from an old masonic book which listed two pages of his many masonic connections. I have also become alarmed by the deep occult connections there are in Masonry.'

The one fortunate discovery Mu has made, he told me, was the testimony of former Masons who have renounced the Brotherhood and turned 'wholeheartedly to Christ'.

In May 1981 – a month of controversial masonic activity in a number of disparate areas – another clergyman was sacked from his church and ordered to leave the manse. He later claimed before an industrial tribunal that the Presbyterian Church of Wales had dismissed him purely because he had preached against Freemasonry. The Rev William Colin Davies of Whitchurch, Cardiff, requested through his lawyer that there should be no member of the Brotherhood on the tribunal, which was agreed.

The minister's duties called for him to preach thirty-six Sundays of the year at his own church and twelve Sundays in other churches without a regular minister. In August

1979 Davies wrote to the Church's rota secretary stating that he did not wish to be seen to be helping in the teachings of tenets of Freemasonry, which he believed to be 'a challenge to the discipleship of Jesus Christ'. He enclosed a cheque for £108.00 to cover his absence from certain churches where he felt his presence had been both unexpected and unwanted because of his views on Freemasonry. When I spoke to him about his case in May 1982, Davies said that the Presbyterian Church of Wales was particularly strongly influenced by members of the Brotherhood among its own members and administration. He explained, 'I became a minister in 1974 and Cardiff was my first pastorate. I had two churches. In one of them I encountered some Freemasons. I did not know then what I know now. I researched into Masonry and found it entirely incompatible with faith in Jesus Christ. I spoke privately to some men in the church, and without making it a bee in my bonnet I did some comparisons between Freemasonry and Christianity during the course of some sermons. I compared, for example, the meaning of faith in Christianity and the masonic meaning of faith.

'In February 1980 I discovered a booklet called *Christ, the Christian and Freemasonry* which I circulated among the members of the church.

'By this time I had been reported to the local church governing body – the presbytery – and a committee of seven men came to see me. I know now that some of them were Freemasons. They accused me of being an evangelical Christian, which I am, 'intolerant of un-Biblical teaching and in particular Freemasonry'. They accused me of being un-compassionate, which presumably meant I had upset Masons' and their relatives' feelings. It was said that membership of my church was going down, but I had had about fifty of the elderly members die and had introduced twenty-six new members. They said I was not ecumenically minded enough in that I didn't join in local services of other churches, which was not true. It is true that I have reservations about the present moves towards church unity but we did have ecumenical meetings with local churches roundabout. And I was accused of allowing the children's work to decline when it is actually expanding. I knew then that the rest of the charges had been trumped up by Masons determined to end my opposition to Masonry. I was not allowed to answer the charges. And then when I next met them a month later on 20 June 1980 they presented a report before the governing body without any warning – and I was dismissed.

'I received information several days later from a member of my other church who made some enquiries of some masonic friends that a Lodge meeting had taken place in March at which it was decided that pressure had to be brought to bear to have me removed. I have made this charge in public and it has never been rebutted.

'I was dismissed from the pastorate, not from my ministry. These are technically different, in practice the same. I then appealed to the highest body in the church, the Association, which appointed a panel of men to look into it. They said that a period of twelve months should be allowed to see if a reconciliation could be achieved between me and the local people who wanted me sacked. I agreed to this but they made no attempt at reconciliation.

'I won my appeal but it was not implemented because my local church would not accept it. I was sacked and told to leave my house within six weeks.'

The elders of the church claimed before the industrial tribunal that Davies had not been an employee of the Church but self-employed, and as such ineligible to claim unfair dismissal. They cited the case of a minister dismissed from Scunthorpe Congregational Church in 1978 as a precedent. But the non-masonic tribunal decided that Davies had been an employee and therefore had the right to seek a ruling.

Meanwhile, after six months on the dole, he works (at the time of writing) as minister for an independent church he has formed at Whitchurch along with members of both his former churches.

PART SIX

The KGB Connection

The Italian Crisis

A masonic conspiracy of gigantic proportions rocked Italy to its foundations in the spring and summer of 1981. Known as the 'P2' case, this imbroglio of corruption, blackmail and murder brought down the coalition government of premier Arnaldo Forlani and decimated the upper echelons of Italian power.

P2 is the popular abbreviation of Masonic Lodge *Propaganda Due*, which had become, in the words of the leader of Italy's Republican Party, 'the centre of pollution of national life – secret, perverse and corrupting'.

The moment this 'scandal of scandals' hit the headlines, individual members of the United Grand Lodge hastened to point out that English Freemasonry was fundamentally different from that practised in Italy. But in spite of the perfectly sincere disclaimers emanating from Great Queen Street, the mysterious P2 case has a direct bearing on events in Britain today.

If the solution to the mystery of P2 is as I suspect, Britain stands in danger of a social calamity at least as great as that which struck Italy. Data and clues garnered from many sources, including the British Secret Intelligence Service (MI6) and the Security Service (MI5), suggest that without yet knowing it the British government faces an impossible dilemma. Evidence published here for the first time indicates that British Freemasonry, without realizing it, has become a time-bomb which could explode at any moment.

But first P2: how it began, what it seemed, and what it really was.

Freemasonry was introduced to Italy in about 1733 by an Englishman, Lord Sackville, but because of its open involvement in politics and religion Italian Freemasonry was not recognized by the United Grand Lodge of England until 1973.

A 'Propaganda' Lodge was constituted in Turin a century ago under the Grand Orient of Italy. This élite Lodge, which counted among its members the King himself, was in some ways similar to the English Quatuor Coronati Lodge No 2076 in that its purpose was to further research into Masonry. Despite several reports to the contrary, there was no connection save the name between this Lodge and the sinister masonic group of the present day. In fact, Lodge Propaganda Due was not even a Lodge in the true sense. It was a secret grouping of Masons but it was never officially constituted and never held regular meetings of all members.

P2 was formed in 1966 at the behest of the then Grand Master of the Grand Orient of Italy, Giordano Gamberini. The Grand Master's plan was to establish a group of eminent men who would be sympathetic and useful to Freemasonry. The man chosen to create this élite band was a rich textile manufacturer from the town of Arezzo in Tuscany. He had entered Masonry two years before and had risen to the Italian equivalent of Master Mason. His name was Licio Gelli.

Gelli, the first Italian to have been accredited with dual Italian–Argentinian nationality, had fought for the

Fascists in the Spanish Civil War and later been a passionate supporter of Mussolini. Later, having been involved in the torture of Italian partisans, he was forced to flee the country, winding up in Argentina. There he met President Juan Perón and a long and close friendship began. Perón eventually appointed Gelli to the position of Argentina's economic adviser to Italy. Years passed, and Gelli returned to his native country, settled at Arezzo and became a Freemason.

The group of men Gelli was ostensibly getting together on behalf of Grand Master Gamberini was called Raggruppamento Gelli Propaganda Due – P2 for short. The members came to be known as *Piduisti* – 'P2-ists'. Gelli had ambitions for P2 which the Grand Master had never so much as imagined.

By 1969 P2 was being spoken of as a Lodge, and Gelli as its Venerable Master. He had a genius for convincing people he had immense influence in public affairs, and many men joined P2 because they believed the Venerable Master's patronage was indispensable to the furtherance of their careers. By this self-perpetuating process, Gelli's purported power became real. Others joined the Lodge because Gelli used ruthless blackmail. The 'masonic dues' Gelli extracted from the brethren of Lodge P2 were not primarily financial. What the Venerable Master demanded – and got – were secrets: official secrets which he could use to consolidate and extend his power, and personal secrets he could use to blackmail others into joining his Lodge. This most sensitive information from all areas of government was passed to him by his members, who seem to have obeyed him with unquestioning devotion. In 1975 a legitimate Freemason, Francesco Siniscalchi, made a statement at the office of the Rome Public Prosecutor, alleging that Gelli was involved in criminal activities. He was ignored, partly because of Gelli's already formidable reputation, which intimidated two officers responsible for processing the complaint.

Soon after this, Gelli came to the notice of the police after his friend and P2 member Michele Sindona, Italy's most influential private banker, had fled to the United States leaving financial chaos behind him. Wanted on charges of fraud in Italy, Sindona was arrested in New York. Gelli flew to America and testified that Sindona was an innocent victim of Communist intrigue. It was Sindona, widely believed to have links with the Mafia, who introduced Gelli in Washington, DC, to Philip Guarino, a director of the US Republican Party's National Committee and Ronald Reagan's campaign manager in the 1980 Presidential Election. It was thanks to Guarino that Gelli was able to attend the inauguration of Reagan as President in January 1981, two months before the P2 bomb exploded.

In 1980, facing fraud charges in New York following the collapse of his Franklin National Bank – reputedly America's worst banking disaster – Sindona appealed to his Venerable Master for help. Meanwhile in Italy magistrates were still investigating Sindona's fraudulent activities and also the events behind the murder of the liquidator of his financial empire. After the appeal to Gelli, a fake kidnapping was staged in New York and Sindona disappeared. Evidence came to light that implicated Gelli in the escape and on 18 March 1981 two Milan magistrates ordered a police raid on his villa outside Arezzo.

Gelli, as always, had been one step ahead. By the time the police reached the Villa Wanda, named after his wife, they had both disappeared. A warrant was later issued for Gelli's arrest on charges of political, military and industrial espionage, and endangering the security of the state.

Among the documents left behind at the abandoned villa were the membership files of P2. A list of members drawn up by Gelli contained the names of nearly a thousand of Italy's most powerful men. One prosecutor's report later stated: 'Lodge Propaganda Due is a secret sect that has combined business and politics with the intention of destroying the country's constitutional order.'

Among the names were three members of the Cabinet including Justice Minister Adolfo Sarti; several former Prime Ministers including Giulio Andreotti who had held office between 1972 and 1973 and again between 1976 and 1979; forty-three Members of Parliament; fifty-four top Civil Servants; 183 army, navy and air force officers including thirty generals and eight admirals (among them the Commander of the Armed Forces, Admiral Giovanni Torrisi); nineteen judges; lawyers; magistrates; *carabiniere*; police chiefs; leading bankers; newspaper proprietors, editors and journalists (including the editor of the country's leading newspaper *Il Corriere Della Sera*); fifty-eight university professors; the leaders of several political parties; and even the directors of the three main intelligence services.

All these men, according to the files, had sworn allegiance to Gelli, and held themselves ready to respond to his call. The 953 names were divided into seventeen groupings, or cells, each having its own leader. P2 was so secret and so expertly run by Gelli that even its own members did not know who belonged to it. Those who knew most were the seventeen cell leaders and they knew only their own grouping. Not even Spartaco Mennini, the then Grand Secretary of the Grand Orient of Italy, knew the entire membership of the Lodge. Only Licio Gelli knew that.

P2 was the very embodiment of the fear that had haunted Italy's Under Secretary of State in 1913 when he had called for a law that 'declared the unsuitability of members of the Masonic Lodge to hold certain offices (such as those in the Judiciary, in the Army, in the Education Department, etc.), the high moral and social value of which is compromised by any hidden and therefore uncontrollable tie, and by any motive of suspicion, and lack of trust on the part of the public'.

In 1976 an official in Italy's Interior Ministry had declared that Gelli controlled 'the most potent hidden power centre' in the country. It took five more years, *and Gelli's own connivance*, for the real extent of his power to be revealed. As the magistrates ploughing through the files from the Villa Wanda stated, Gelli had 'constructed a very real state within the state', and was attempting to overturn the Republic.

Of the many political groupings in Italy, Gelli's files showed that only the Communist Party had no links with P2. All the others – Christian Democrats, Socialists, Republicans, Radicals, Neo-Fascists – had members in the Lodge.

When the magistrates finally presented the Gelli papers to the Italian Parliament in May 1981, they had sorted them into ten heavy piles. There was immediate uproar and calls for the four-party coalition government of Christian Democrat Prime Minister Aldo Forlani to resign. As it became clear how completely Gelli had infiltrated not only the corridors but the most secret and vital centres of power, increasing pressure was applied to Forlani to have the documents published. He was finally forced to agree, but fought to hold on to the premiership by a mere reshuffle that would expel the *Piduisti* from the Cabinet. But the Communists, the second largest political grouping in the country, now doubly strong by virtue of the fact that only they among Italy's parties were completely free of involvement in P2, resisted furiously.

And the Socialists' leader, Bettino Craxi, although he had thirty-five P2 members within his own party, seized his opportunity and refused to be part of any coalition headed by a Christian Democrat. After seventeen days of desperate negotiations with his former political allies, Forlani reached the end of the road. The government fell and Craxi made his bid for the premiership.

When Craxi, too, failed, the eighty-five-year-old President Alessandro Pertini invited Republican Party leader Giovanni Spadolini to attempt to form a new coalition. Spadolini succeeded, becoming Italy's first non-Christian Democrat premier since the Second World War, and heading a government made up of five separate parties.

As more and more documents were scrutinized it became clear that Gelli had his Freemasons in every decision-making centre in Italian politics, and was able to exert significant influence over those decisions. Even top secret summit meetings between the leaders of the coalition had not been secret for Gelli because of the substantial presence at the meetings of Social Democrat leader Pietro Longo, who was P2 member 2223. P2 had reached the very heart of government activity in the Palazzo Chigi. Mario Semprini, the Prime Minister's closest collaborator and his Chief of Cabinet, had been a member of P2 for over four years (membership No 1637), and was regularly passing secrets to his Venerable Master.

Another Christian Democrat officer, Massimiliano Cercelli, a former minister and a friend of masonic Justice Minister Sarti, was also a spy for P2. Lodge member 2180, Cercelli worked at the Office for the Co-ordination of the Secret Services.

Many P2 members were close associates of Forlani.

These included Enzo Badioli, the powerful chief of the Christian Democrat Co-operatives, and Gianni Cerioni, MP for Ancona.

Others were close to the President of the Senate, Amintore Fanfani, who was from Gelli's home town of Arezzo.

The catalogue of the powerful becomes tedious by its very length. A typical example of the enormity of Gelli's own influence over the lives of these men is the case of Mario Pedini who had suddenly been appointed a minister when he joined P2 and as quickly dropped by the government when his Lodge membership lapsed in 1978.

Other P2 members included the Minister of Employment, the Under-Secretary for Industry, the Under-Secretary for Foreign Affairs and the Foreign Commerce Minister.

It became apparent that nothing of vital importance had occurred in Italy in recent years which Gelli had not known about in advance or shortly after. Many vital developments were the result of his covert actions from the centre of his secret web. At the height of his power, the most bizarre actions were taken by successive governments, each of which were in Gelli's pocket.

Magistrates sifting the documents from the Villa Wanda found hundreds of top secret intelligence documents. Colonel Antonio Viezzer, the former head of the combined intelligence services, was identified as the prime source of this material and was arrested in Rome for spying on behalf of a foreign power. Following his interrogation, police raided the offices of a fashionable Tuscan lawyer and two suitcases crammed with incriminating documents were discovered. Dr Domenico Sica, head of the enquiries into P2 in Rome, was confident the papers had belonged to Gelli. They backed up the evidence in the Villa Wanda papers in the form of receipts for subscriptions paid to P2 by its members, and also receipts for bribes paid to Lodge members for 'services rendered'.

The extent to which P2 had destabilized Italy is exemplified by the events following President Pertini's actions immediately he was informed of the scandal. Among the members of the Lodge were two of his own executives, men he had liked and trusted. They were Sergio Piscitello (Master of Ceremonies of the Quirinale) and Francesco Gregorio, Pertini's diligent secretary for many years. Without hesitation the President suspended Piscitello and demoted Gregorio to typist. Three government ministers who believed the P2 lists were genuine wanted to follow Pertini's example. They couldn't. As one observer put it:

The trial of strength with the concealed power of P2 has been exhausting for the weakened Forlani government. For days and days the ministers have been asking for some sign of good will (from Lodge members in high office), even simply to go on leave or to be available to the committee of enquiry, or to delegate their tasks to subordinates.

But the 'Piduisti' have turned down every request, especially those within the military establishment.

On the weekend of 16 and 17 May, generals and admirals included on the membership lists met to work out a common strategy for their own survival. They decided to declare themselves victims of a plot and sit tight, defying the investigators to find concrete evidence against them.

At this point the fearful power of Gelli was found to have undermined not only the national security of Italy, but to have struck at the roots of western strength in southern Europe and the Middle East. NATO was forced to support the attitude of the corrupt Freemasons in Italy's armed forces. Officials in Brussels and Washington suggested discreetly that it was not the right moment to create a vacuum of power in the Italian army, navy and secret services. To replace the Defence Chief of Staff (P2 member No 1825), the Chief of Military Counter-espionage (P2 member No 1603), and the Chief of National Security (P2 member No 1620) might, said NATO, have grave repercussions on NATO's south flank forces, where the Lebanese crisis had taken a dangerous turn.

CHAPTER 27

The Chinaman Report

A bizarre incident occurred in early July 1981. Gelli's daughter Maria flew into Italy under her own name, knowing she would be instantly recognized. She was arrested at Fiumicino Airport, Rome, and her luggage was seized. In a compartment in a false-bottomed suitcase, Customs officers discovered five packages of documents relating to P2. They included statements from several Swiss banks in the names of Italian politicians and political parties, and also a document which appears to have been a forged 'secret report' by the CIA on attempts to subvert western Europe in general and Italy in particular. Why would Signora Gelli return to Italy with incriminating P2 documents that had already been safely removed from the country? What motive was so pressing that she took the step knowing she would be imprisoned on charges of espionage? For an answer to this, and to the question of what Gelli really was up to, we must also look at what was *not* contained in all the bundles of documents from the Villa Wanda, nor in Maria Gelli's suitcase, nor any of the other P2-related papers.

Without the benefit of inside information such as I was later to have, journalist Peter Hebblethwaite came close to the truth in his article 'Gelli's Babies', which appeared in *The Spectator* on 6 June 1981:

We know that he [Gelli] did business with east European countries. . . . As we have already seen, he boasted about his friendship with Ceausescu. Yet there are no names of any Italian Communist politicians or any east Europeans in this vast store of material. But no one can do business with a Communist country without such intermediaries. It follows that their names have been deliberately suppressed. By whom? Not by the Italian Government, which would have every interest in revealing them. By Gelli himself? If so, the suspicion would be aroused that Gelli deliberately 'planted' all this material, arranged for his disappearance, and is now observing the fascinating consequence of his handiwork from some safe villa on the Black Sea coast.

Licio Gelli – ruthless Fascist, torturer of partisans in the Second World War, friend and adviser of Perón and co-ordinator of right-wing corruption in Italy – was an agent of the KGB. This alone answers all the questions that rise up around his sinister figure. It explains how a document describing the structure of the KGB came to be among the Venerable Master's files; why Maria Gelli returned to Italy – to throw the country, and its attempts to recover from the scandal, into further confusion. She even brought with her a forged letter to her father that alluded to purported arrangements for bribing the members of the judiciary actually investigating P2. It explains how the P2 affair, described by many as the most damaging of all Italy's scandals, was linked with the attempted assassination of the Pope on 13 May 1981, even as P2 was coming to the boil. Western intelligence experts are now generally agreed that the attempted killing was inspired by the KGB.

Loyal to no one, obsessed with power for its own sake, Licio Gelli was determined to use whatever means he could to achieve his ambition: the ruin of those colourless weaklings, the Christian Democrats, who for nearly forty years had run the country which had spawned him, then spurned him for his turpitude. A man filled with such hatred can become a precision instrument in the hands of the Soviet Secret Service, intent as it is on implanting the seeds of disruption wherever it can in the West. According to an impeccable source within British Intelligence, Gelli was recruited by the KGB soon after he set about the task of building up *Raggruppamento Gelli Propaganda Due.* Britain's Secret Intelligence Service (MI6) has closely monitored P2 since its inception. It detected KGB involvement in the affair at an early stage.

From the beginning, Lodge P2 was a KGB-sponsored programme aimed at destabilizing Italy, weakening NATO's southern flank, sweeping the Communists into power in Italy and sending resultant shock waves throughout the western world. It achieved its first aim, partially succeeded in its second, came close to realizing the third, and all but failed in the fourth.

MI6 and other western intelligence services have been trying to convince their governments of the enormous growth of the KGB's activities since 1965 (P2 was formed in 1966). Senior officers in British Intelligence regard the KGB as the 'biggest conspiracy in the world', according to one well-placed informant. But their warnings have so far fallen on muffled ears. Even the more hawkish western leaders like Reagan and Thatcher are reluctant to accept the enormity of the threat as it is assessed by MI6 and America's Central Intelligence Agency (CIA).

I have obtained a copy of a secret memorandum written by a British diplomat who worked with MI6 for nearly twenty years during the Cold War, largely in South-East Asia. A First Secretary in the Diplomatic Service, this officer had a secret service training, chaired several sub-committees of the Joint Intelligence Committee (JIC) and worked closely with the legendary former head of MI6, Sir

Maurice Oldfield. He is a specialist in the methods of secret societies and an expert on China, in which he has travelled widely.

The document is fourteen pages long and is typed on ordinary plain A4 paper with a manual typewriter. It is dated 4 June 1981, a time when there was much undercover activity by MI6, the CIA and Israel's Mossad focused on P2. For reasons of security I shall refer to the author of the document by a codename: 'Chinaman'.

By way of background he states:

. . . as a result notably of the loss of the war in Vietnam, and the economic problems of the non-Communist countries which have been exacerbated by the cost of oil, the Soviet Union – despite grave and presently growing problems of its own – has embarked on a further phase in its major concerted effort to exploit to its own advantage the weakness and confusions in the non-Communist world by all means short of war. It can be argued that the Soviet leadership itself has come to regard the Cold War as a race to determine who buries whom – accepting that *both* sides, not just the 'capitalist' side, suffer severe internal 'contradictions' and vulnerable areas.

Writing on information received up to 4 June 1981, Chinaman was unable then to state with certainty that the KGB had been behind P2, but merely confirmed that 'the affair has so far been to the considerable advantage of the Soviet Union and of the Communists, which alone of the political parties has no known members among the listed names published by order of the [Italian] Prime Minister'.

Since then I have had many long meetings with him and developments have persuaded him that the original strong suspicion that the KGB was responsible for P2 is now inescapable.

Freemasonry has been a factor in Russian political thinking since long before the establishment of the Soviet state.

The February 1917 Revolution was provoked by Freemasons and was operated from the few masonic Lodges left after decades of persecution from Tsarist Secret Police. Alexander Kerensky, Justice Minister in the provisional government of Prince Georgi Yevgenievich Lvov, was a Freemason. After the Petrograd uprising in July 1917 which led to the resignation of Lvov, Kerensky took over as Prime Minister and appointed exclusively Masons to the government. When, chiefly because of Kerensky's inability to control the economy and his refusal to withdraw from the European war, the Bolsheviks took over the country in October, Kerensky and most of the Masons involved in the earlier revolution fled to France, where they established Lodges under the aegis of the Grand Orient of France.

As soon as the Bolshevik State was declared, Freemasonry was proscribed. This anti-masonic stand was enshrined in a resolution of the fourth Congress of the Communist International:

It is absolutely necessary that the leading elements of the Party should close all channels which lead to the middle classes and should therefore bring about a definite breach with Freemasonry. The chasm which divides the proletariat from the middle classes must be clearly brought to the consciousness of the Communist Party. A small fraction of the leading elements of the Party wished to bridge this chasm and to avail themselves of the masonic Lodges. Freemasonry is a most dishonest and infamous swindle of the proletariat by the radically inclined section of the middle classes. We regard it as our duty to oppose it to the uttermost.[*]

[*]Quoted by Eugen Lenhoff, *The Freemasons*, 1934.

Freemasonry was thoroughly investigated by the CHEKA, the first Soviet intelligence organization, as a matter of priority. This enquiry led to the formal outlawing of the Brotherhood in 1922. It is known that in its successive incarnations as GPU, NKVD, GUKR ('Smersh'), KGB and the rest, the Soviet espionage machine has made a priority of infiltrating every kind of organization in every country of the world. Its prime target, in every country where it existed, was inevitably Freemasonry. 'Any organization, and in particular any secretive organization,' says Chinaman, 'must come to the notice of the KGB, whatever its political, social, spiritual, criminal or subversive aims.'

There is abundant evidence not only that this has been true from the very beginning of the Soviet state, but that it is a continuing phenomenon, and that the Russian government is pouring ever more funds into the KGB coffers to expand this penetration and manipulation of foreign organizations. KGB defector Dr Vladimir Sakharov describes modern KGB operatives as the 'crème de la crème of Soviet society', top experts in the language, customs, religion and way of life of the country in which they operate.*

The exploitation of Freemasonry by the KGB is not restricted to Italy. I can reveal that senior officers of British Intelligence are concerned that the KGB has been using Freemasonry in England for decades to help place its

---

*It has recently been revealed that the KGB runs its own religious centres for training appropriate agents to be sent to western and Third World countries. These centres are at Feodosia in the Crimea, Lvov in the Ukraine and at Constanza. In Lithuania there is a school for agents bound for Britain and other English-speaking countries. The Lithuanian centre is almost certain to be the centre of any training in the exploitation of English Freemasonry. Bulgarian defector Mikhail Gloechov has disclosed that Stalin had the centres set up as early as 1936.

agents in positions of responsibility and influence. The areas the KGB is most interested in penetrating are delineated by Chapman Pincher in his controversial study of Russia's infiltration of the West's secret defences, *Their Trade is Treachery*: '. . . when Soviet Intelligence secures a promising recruit, he or she is urged to get a job in MI5, the Secret Service, Government Communication Headquarters (the radio-interception organization), *The Times*, the BBC, the Foreign Office or the Home Office – in that order of preference'.

According to the evidence now available the undoubted 'jobs for the brethren' aspect of British Freemasonry has been used extensively by the KGB to penetrate the most sensitive areas of authority, most spectacularly illustrated in the years since 1945 by its placing of spies at the highest levels of both MI5 and MI6. Even today, members of the security services privately admit that they have no idea of the extent of this penetration.

Although one senior and decorated MI6 officer, based in London, has been actively researching Freemasonry's influence in Britain since the Chinaman Report came into his hands, no investigation has so far been started by MI5, which as Britain's internal security service must conduct any *official* enquiry. MI6 is empowered to act only abroad.

Former KGB officers who have defected to the West confirm the endless patience the organization expends on gathering information on every aspect of life in Britain. Even the tiniest details are filed away at the great KGB headquarters building at 2 Dzerzhinsky Square, Moscow, for possible use in its vast programme of destabilization in the West.

These facts are known, but what MI6 failed to appreciate before the Chinaman Report was the vital corollary to its knowledge that organizations, especially of a secretive nature, were being used by the KGB: a fact so obvious it was never even considered – that the largest and most important organization of a secretive nature in Britain was Freemasonry.

The 'old boy network', the favouritism and the use of Masonry for professional and social advancement – all proscribed by the Constitutions but all nevertheless widespread, as this book has shown – are of obvious value to Englishmen recruited to spy for a foreign power.

I have spoken to five currently serving officers of MI6, two of them senior men but not of the highest stratum. Posed the question, 'If you were a KGB agent in England, given the nature of Freemasonry, what would you do?', four them agreed independently that becoming a Free-mason would be an obvious priority. The fifth said, 'I haven't heard of this, but obviously if there hasn't already been an enquiry there should be now. I know of only two Masons in 6. Naturally, it's not often spoken of.'

This is an interesting point. As I learned from a former Home Secretary (the Home Secretary is responsible for MI5), it is forbidden for any member of either of the intelligence services to be a Freemason.

Pages three to four of the Chinaman document contain this:

I was required when I joined the Foreign Service and when I was given access to increasingly delicate material to 'sign the Official Secrets Act' and make declarations that I was not and never had been a member of certain listed extreme organizations of both left and right wing aims. But I was never required even orally to state whether I was or ever had been a member of any secret society whether of the Masonic type or not. This is less surprising given the social respectability of Freemasonry and the assumption by both members and non-members alike that it could not possibly come to represent in any way a threat to the established order.

This assumption is well illustrated by a comment made by

James Dewar, author of a book on Freemasonry entitled
The Open Secret, when interviewed by the *Sunday Telegraph* in May 1981 at the height of the publicity about
P2. He said, 'Any secret society has in it the seeds of
menace. But it is very unlikely that a similar clique could
operate here, as the movement is headed by so many
people of obviously good repute . . .' And Judge D. H.
Botha, who carried out an enquiry into Freemasonry in
South Africa in 1964, had to rely largely on the evidence
of four Freemasons. He entertained no doubts about their
evidence as to what occurred at masonic meetings because
of the 'exceptionally high esteem in which each of these
persons is held in society and because of their obvious
integrity'. Referring to this, Chinaman states:

This cannot be the view of any trained intelligence officer. It is
of course inconceivable that, given the present composition of
the British Grand Lodges and indeed other Lodges and chapters,
the movement as a whole could possibly be suborned or
persuaded to act consciously in any way to Soviet advantage.
The dangers arise from numerous possibilities for covert
exploitation of a movement which is almost conterminous with
'The Establishment' in common parlance:
(a) Any KGB officer with an agent recruited, say at university,
must be concerned to arrange for that agent to have access to the
highest priority on the list of targets provided by KGB
headquarters that the particular agent is considered suitable to
work against. If it is believed by so many Masons themselves that
recruitment to many organizations, promotion, and other forms
of success can be assisted by membership of Freemasonry, there
can be little doubt but that the KGB shares this view. It must be
expected therefore that the KGB instructs any agent, whom it
believes could benefit from doing so, to become a Freemason.
(b) Equally clearly the KGB, if it recruits an agent who already
has some access to a target, must consider whether membership
of Freemasonry could assist in improving his access.
(c) In any long-term penetration the question of 'the Succession'
is always in a case officer's mind. In addition to the ordinary
risks of life and inevitable ageing, espionage and other covert

activity carries its own risks of being 'blown', and mental strain leading to breakdown. Therefore an agent in place who is a Mason may very well be considered more likely to be able to assist in placing his own successor to best advantage.

(d) The KGB must consider in each case whether membership of Freemasonry would afford any particular agent increased protection. For example, whether membership would confer on the agent additional respectability which would stifle or help to stifle suspicion, and whether membership could provide useful cover for other secret activities; or indeed, whether membership would assist in any necessary cover-up – other members of the Fraternity doubtless believing they were only assisting a brother over some dereliction of duty or other relatively minor infringement.

(e) The KGB will also consider whether Fraternal relationships can be used to obtain information or to cause actions desired by its headquarters. That is to say, to use the masonic bond apparently for the normal purposes of mutual advancement and mutual protection, but in fact for the benefit of the KGB. In particular the KGB will be aware that Masons may well be less on their guard when talking outside the Lodge to other Lodge members and other Masons generally than they would be speaking to others about their professional and personal concerns.

(f) It follows from this that the KGB may through masonic contacts come by information which would greatly assist in any blackmail attempt against an individual. Indeed, were the KGB to become aware of any improper actions by two or more Masons in regard to cover-ups, e.g. in the administration of justice, such blackmail could be applied to a group. The threat of exposure could then lead to further masonic involvement in order to preserve the movement's good name. As Watergate showed, cover-ups generally start small but tend to grow uncontrollably.

(g) An agent in any movement enjoying such diverse support at such varying levels of the social hierarchy provides (a) ideal opportunities to 'talent spot', and (b) the means to contact some specialist in almost every field where assistance may be needed, and in a manner most conducive to obtaining any 'favour' required.

It will be noted that in all these cases there is no need for Freemasonry as an institution, or indeed for any other member of the movement to be 'conscious' to KGB's use of Masonry. KGB will simply be riding the 'lift' that Masonry supplies ready installed to enable its members to arrive at higher floors more quickly and with less effort than those, perhaps better qualified, who are hurrying up the stairs. During the 'lift ride', others in the 'lift' may be examined and contacted in a relaxed atmosphere. It is clearly unlikely that once KGB found . . . the masonic 'lift' they would not use it again several times. But once again there is no need for one conscious KGB agent within Masonry to know or even know *of* any other. Unless there is some overriding 'need to know', the KGB will obviously make every effort to prevent this happening.

Through an intermediary, I asked former KGB spy Ilya Grigevich Dzhirkvelov, who defected to the West in 1980, about Freemasonry. The Soviet authorities are well aware of the size and influence of Masonry in the West. Dzhirkvelov was based in Geneva for most of his thirty-year career as a KGB agent, so was not in direct touch with espionage activities in Britain. Switzerland's Grand Lodge 'Alpina' is based at Lausanne. The entire country has only fifty-two Lodges – compared with London's 1,677. There are about 3,450 Swiss Masons. Dzhirkvelov spoke of the 'vast' scale of the KGB's espionage activities in the UK, and said that if Freemasonry was such an important part of the Establishment as I said, *there was no doubt at all that the KGB was exploiting it, even to the extent of instructing its British recruits to become Masons.*

Among the currently serving and former officers of both services I met was one much respected officer of MI6, recently retired, who was more cautious. We met next to the fish pond on the first floor of Coutts & Co in the Strand early in 1982. He had agreed to meet me only on the understanding that we did not discuss matters covered by the Official Secrets Act. He was not a Freemason. He said that he had never been aware that Freemasonry could be an advantage in government service, nor felt the need to become a Mason to advance his career. He added, 'But perhaps that is because I have never thought about it.'

He told me that he had never come across a case of the KGB using Freemasonry in England, and added, 'But of course that does not mean it has not happened.' The fact that he had never even considered such an obvious possibility did not surprise me. It seems that nobody prior to Chinaman had. Even Sir George Young, former Vice Chief of MI6, told me that the extent of his knowledge about Freemasonry was that 'the Royal Family are all in it'.

My contact pointed out that Masonry would not be used by a KGB agent as a cover, in the sense that Guy Burgess joined the Anglo-German Fellowship before the war to conceal his Communist sympathies, because by its very nature membership of Freemasonry is not something one can boast about without giving rise to suspicion. He paused and set his mind to work on the problem. At length he said: 'The records of Freemasonry in Tsarist Russia would have fallen into the hands of the CHEKA, the KGB's predecessor, in 1917. A close study of Freemasonry would certainly have been made by Soviet intelligence officers then.*

'If the KGB had a target in England – somebody they wanted to "turn" or from whom they wanted to obtain information by one of a number of means – and this person was a Freemason, I have no doubt that it would instruct an agent to join the same Lodge. That would be an obvious move. If being a Freemason makes a man more likely to bare his soul to another Freemason than to an outsider [there is ample evidence that this is the case], any intelligence service worth its salt would exploit that. Once

*This was the case, as already explained.

again, I have no evidence that this has happened. The fraternity most often exploited of course is the homosexual one – the homintern we used to call it.'

Towards the end of our meeting, my contact said, 'Is there any evidence that any of the known people were Freemasons?'

By 'people' he meant traitors, British subjects who had been recruited by the KGB either before they were in positions where they had access to delicate material, while they were rising in their careers towards such positions, or after they had arrived.

One case particularly bears examination.

Few people in MI5 now doubt that Sir Roger Hollis, director-general of the service in the crucial years 1956–65, was a Russian spy for nearly thirty years. This has been convincingly demonstrated by veteran investigative journalist and espionage expert Chapman Pincher. The government in the person of Margaret Thatcher has denied this, and a number of Hollis's old colleagues have jumped to his defence, but their evidence is weak and contradictory.

I shall not rehearse the case against Hollis here. It is proven beyond reasonable doubt in the revised edition of Pincher's book, which appeared in fuller form after various official attempts to discredit the evidence and arguments contained in the first edition.

As one MI5 officer of long standing confided to me: 'We've known about Hollis for years. Pincher has excellent sources within the service and an excellent brain. He is *so close* to the truth.'

Hollis was not a member of the 'homintern'. The same MI5 source told me baldly, 'Hollis was certainly a Mason.'

Of the many mysteries surrounding Sir Roger Hollis, one of the most baffling is how he was ever accepted into MI5 in the first place. He was quite *the opposite* of what was required. In MI5, as opposed to MI6 which operates abroad, there is a reluctance to accept candidates who have travelled widely out of the UK. In the 1930s when Hollis was recruited this stipulation was more easily met than it is today. For this and other reasons, Hollis was a most unlikely recruit. Doing badly at university, he threw in the towel in 1926 after only two years, worked in a London bank for a while and set off for China. Stranded with only £10 in his pocket in Malaya, he got a job with an international tobacco company in Penang and was later transferred to the company's offices in Shanghai. He moved around China for the next nine years, working at Peking, Hangkow and Dairen. After this, he became tuberculous, and travelled to a Swiss sanatorium by way of the Trans-Siberian Railway from Vladivostok, spending some time in Russia. All this, especially his time in Russia, should have been an insuperable obstacle to any hopes he had of joining MI5.

And so it proved . . . at first. Even after his treatment his health was not strong enough for him to continue working for the tobacco company, so early in 1936 he was back in England. 'Even his friends agree that he was not particularly talented,' wrote Chapman Pincher, who describes him at the time of his return to England as 'basically a broken man': 'Though surprisingly athletic, he was to retain the look of someone who had been tuberculous and became progressively so round-shouldered that he looked almost hunched . . . He had no degree, his health was suspect and his experience in China was not likely to be helpful in securing a post in England. The only work he could find was as a clerk–typist.'

However, through an army major he met, he secured an interview with MI5. He was turned down and told that his experience abroad might be useful to MI6. He applied and was turned down for health reasons by that service.

When he applied to MI5 for the second time later that

year nothing had changed . . . except the mind of MI5. This time he was taken on. The director-general of MI5 then was Major General Sir Vernon Kell, who happened to be a Freemason.

With almost everything going against him, Hollis got in. What is even more remarkable was the rate at which he was promoted within the service once he had got in. This astonished his colleagues then, and still cannot be explained by any of the MI5 officers, current and retired, with whom I have had contact either directly or through intermediaries. This is one of the great mysteries of Roger Hollis, even to those who, because they were not involved in particular events and because they liked the man, are not convinced that he was a spy.

Even though it was against the regulations for any officer to be a Freemason – and this, incidentally, must presumably indicate that membership was regarded as a threat to security – several officers were in the Brotherhood. Among them was a man called Potter, who was in charge of the huge MI5 card index, now computerized. Such a man would be good to have as a friend.

But was it Freemasonry that got Hollis against all odds into the service and took him, the unlikeliest of all its officers, to the very top? I believe it was. The likeliest key to the mystery of Hollis is Shanghai and the time he spent there working for the British American Tobacco Company in the 1930s.

The European community in Shanghai was small. The English-speaking community was of course smaller and very tight-knit. Virtually every Englishman arriving in Shanghai gravitated to the Masonic Hall at 1623 Avenue Road. Freemasonry had flourished among the British expatriates here and at the previous Masonic Hall at 30 The Bund, Shanghai, since the mid-1800s. In the twenties and thirties, when Hollis was in Shanghai, the tradition of Freemasonry there was at its zenith. A man who was not a Mason was at a grave disadvantage in achieving whatever social or professional ambitions he had.

Almost everyone I have contacted who knew Hollis, including MI5 officers past and present, has reacted similarly to the suggestion that the former director-general was a member of the Brotherhood – that he was just the kind of man, extremely secretive by nature, with few open friendships and with small prospect of advancement – who would join Masonry in order to exploit its covert advantages. Freemasonry, said the contacts, offered the first explanation to the Hollis mystery, his otherwise inexplicable acceptance and his phenomenal rate of promotion. This would be especially likely, I was told, if Hollis's immediate predecessor as director-general of the Security Service, Sir Dick Goldsmith White, had been a Mason. The one notable voice of dissent was that of Sir Dick White himself, whose own formidable career contains one striking anomaly. White is the only man ever to have been head of both MI5 and MI6. He moved from 5 in 1956 to take over the Secret Service from Sir John 'Sinbad' Sinclair. Despite his impressive record and qualifications, the unprecedented transfer was viewed by many within MI6 as dangerous and as something which, once again breaking all the traditional rules governing the secure operation of the two services, should never have been allowed. It was White who, on his appointment as Secret Service Chief, recommended Hollis as his successor to premier Anthony Eden. When I put it to Sir Dick at his retirement home near Arundel that Hollis's period in Shanghai made it virtually certain that he had been a member of the Brotherhood, he laughed and said, 'Oh dear me, I wouldn't have thought so at all. I can't guarantee it, but it seems to me most unlikely.' When I asked why not, he said exactly the opposite of what others had told me – that Hollis 'really didn't seem the type'. When I asked him if he himself was or ever had been a Freemason, Sir Dick seemed amused, and told me genially that he never had, adding that he hoped I 'reached the right conclusion' about Hollis.

Hollis's treachery should have come to light in the late 1940s when Sir Percy Sillitoe was director-general of MI5. As A. W. Cockerill, Sillitoe's biographer, points out, 'practically the entire effort of the Service from 1946 on, and until long after Sillitoe's retirement, was directed at identifying and weeding out Communists from positions in which they posed a threat to national security'. Cockerill states that one of Sillitoe's first actions after getting settled into the job as MI5 chief was to carry out a purge, for which he had something of a reputation in his former career in the police.

In the case of MI5, he was primarily interested in the political reliability of his staff, and a number of employees were forced to leave for one reason or another . . . Beginning with those whose credentials were 'impeccable', he carried out a systematic security check of the entire establishment. This was a programme in which the internal security officers combed through each personal file as though the person concerned was a newcomer; the individuals's history was checked and rechecked, membership in clubs, societies and social organizations was investigated anew to ensure that the service itself was 'clean'.

But Sillitoe, without knowing it, was fighting an impossible battle. With the man in charge of all the personal records being a member of the Brotherhood, Sillitoe would never be allowed to learn that Hollis's means of entry to the service had been by way of a masonic Lodge in China and a masonic director-general.

It is an interesting fact that the membership lists of the

Shanghai Lodges between the wars are among the most closely guarded secrets of the United Grand Lodge. Several attempts by concerned members of the Brotherhood to get hold of these files through the ordinary channels have been blocked. It is evident that those lists of names contain something so explosive, so potentially damaging to the Brotherhood, that it will not permit them to be examined even by senior Masons. Whose name is being concealed, if not Hollis's?

CHAPTER 28

The Threat to Britain

The Chinaman Report goes further than drawing attention to the KGB's almost certain use of Freemasonry for placing operatives in positions of authority, most damagingly achieved, so far as we know, in the case of Hollis. The Report also expresses concern that British Freemasonry as a whole is, quite unknown to its members, a major target for so-called 'Special Political Action' by the KGB. It states:

... sheer prudence demands that the lessons of the P2 affair receive the attention of all who have the interests of the UK and the West at heart, Masons and non-Masons alike ... The affair has so far been to the considerable advantage of the Soviet Union and of the Communists, which alone of the political parties has no known members among the listed names published by order of the Prime Minister. Had P2 continued its secret growth and unacceptable activities, the inevitable eventual scandal could have brought down with it non-Communist government in Italy. Yet Italian Freemasonry has been estimated as of the order of under 100,000 – a mere tenth of the supposed UK total for a roughly similar population.*

---

*This includes England and Wales, Scotland *and* Ireland. Even so, the commonly quoted figure of a million Freemasons in Britain is about 250,000 too high.

It could be argued that Italy's laws regarding secret associations differ from Britain's, and that there is far more prejudice against Freemasonry in Italy because of strong Roman Catholic and Communist opposition than there is in the UK where, on the contrary, the Brotherhood enjoys the inestimable advantage of royal patronage. Thus the reaction in Britain to a masonic scandal would be nothing like so extreme as in Italy. But Chinaman suggests that 'the Italian affair is a serious warning from which important lessons can be drawn . . . The UK could well prove very much more vulnerable to exposure of improper activities by a group of Freemasons than is Italy.'

There are two reasons for this:

First, Masonry so permeates so many revered British institutions from the Crown downwards, that a grave masonic scandal could in modern circumstances involve popular revulsion against the whole established order, Government and business. Second, the proportion of Masons to non-Masons in some professions and other walks of life, including areas of Government, appears to have reached a critical point: the point at which people believe themselves obliged to join Freemasonry, no longer voluntarily, but from a feeling of compulsion.

This statement is certainly accurate, as my own enquiries have revealed.

Masons and non-Masons alike seem increasingly to fear the potential of the fraternity to ruin them. At such a point it becomes hard to find in certain areas vital to the state an adequate number of competent persons who are non-Masons to prevent such a vacuum as now threatens Italy were all the officers of the armed forces of General rank named in the P2 documents to be required to retire. Third, there is much circumstantial evidence that more ruthless elements have joined Freemasonry and are using up the fund of respectability that Royal patronage confers to indulge in activities which reputable members would find quite unacceptable were they aware of the extent of the abuse. This, of

course, is a danger inherent in all secretive societies for their
cellular form devised by the founders for the security of the
movement, can as readily be used to 'hoodwink' the leadership,
who thus become unwitting 'front men' for activities they would
never countenance.

The Report alludes to the argument that there has not
been a masonic scandal of major proportions in modern
times and the contention that should one occur, it could
readily be contained by the Brotherhood by means of both
public expulsions and cover-ups. It continues:

This may possibly be so. But British society as a whole is changing
rapidly. The established order of things developed over the past
thousand years is no longer so widely and so automatically
accepted as in even the recent past. Many, of all political hues,
consider some of our institutions archaic and in need of reform.
This view is fuelled by the loss of national self-confidence and
national pride following from the loss of Empire and our very
poor showing in the list of advanced industrial societies.
Disrespect for those in authority is already considerable and is
increasing at an accelerating rate: such rife dissatisfaction soon
comes to seek a scapegoat, such as 'the Establishment' provides.
But our institutions – both public and private – seem incapable of
reforming themselves and performing the *aggiornamento* the
thoughtful of all moderate persuasions are increasingly coming to
expect.
    Against this worsening background it would be rash to suppose
that the methods of the past to contain scandals and irregularities
in Masonry (or indeed in anything else) will still be adequate by,
say, the end of this decade. And this is to count without the
attentions of the KGB.
    The possibility that the KGB has a long-term interest in British
Freemasonry must be taken seriously. For to any trained
intelligence officer, Freemasonry offers an ideal vehicle for the
destabilization of the United Kingdom. To make two points:
there has for some time been practically no mention of
Freemasonry in the media: for so widespread and important a
movement this almost amounts to a taboo – any serious, well-
documented exposure of substantial malpractices could be

expected to have a disproportionate shock effect. We are not yet
so cynical and so inured to scandal as the Italians. Second, the
KGB – itself growing out of a clandestine movement's seizure of
state power, well understands the organization, motivation and
other problems of secret societies (particularly of communica-
tions, records, and the use of a reputable 'front') and is thus
ideally qualified to exploit Freemasonry for its own ends.

Here Chinaman constructs, from his thirty-year
knowledge of the KGB's political methods and of the inner
workings of British Freemasonry – with the P2 conspiracy
forming a bridge between the two – a scenario which to my
certain knowledge senior officials of both MI5 and MI6
regard with the utmost gravity. The man code-named
Chinaman suggests that the most likely method of attack
would follow the pattern of P2 – in other words, the KGB,
doubtless through Czech intelligence, would attempt to
hive off a promising area of Freemasonry and encourage its
growth.

The more prominent those unwittingly involved, the greater the
ultimate effect – provided the top echelon [of Freemasonry] were
carefully preserved untainted. Another phase would be deliberately to encourage and exacerbate existing abuses for personal
advancement at the expense of non-Masons. Arrogance would be
inflated to a point where the Masons concerned would become
over-confident and incautious . . . the KGB would then obtain
and collate documentary and circumstantial evidence in as many
spheres of activity as possible.
  Once sufficient material had been gathered, the KGB would be
prepared to wait years if required until directed to mount an
exposure at a politically appropriate juncture. Then the 'fuse'
would be lit, for example by arranging for a blackmail operation
to fail, or a Soviet 'defector' to arrive perhaps in the US, and
point conclusively to KGB involvement in Masonry. Media and
Government enquiries could then be fed with supplementary
evidence garnered for the purpose over the years. Names would
be called. Confusion would be sown by including the righteous
(chosen for their effectiveness in opposition to Soviet designs)

with the guilty (chosen for their publicity value): in such circumstances lies mixed with incontrovertible truths would be hard to winnow.

If the right moment for 'ignition' were chosen the disaster could be very great. One need only to remember the effect on each occasion of the news of Fuchs's* espionage, the Maclean and Burgess defections, the Philby case, the Blunt exposure and the recent public allegations regarding the late Sir Roger Hollis, to appreciate the effect of well documented exposures at one time of even fifty prominent persons – let alone nearly a thousand as in the Italian case.

Chinaman makes it plain that short of information from some formerly well-placed genuine defector, there is no certain means of knowing whether the Soviet Union is operating such a plan – nor, if so, how long it has been in preparation. And if it is in preparation, we cannot know how much time is likely to elapse before it could be 'ignited'.

I have no idea whether Communist bloc defectors have been questioned on the subject or what were their replies. I simply suggest that it is self-evident that the possibility should be taken seriously and appropriate defensive action taken if this has not already been done adequately.

I can reveal that no such defensive action has yet been taken because prior to the submission of the Chinaman Report, no one had considered the possible exploitation of Masonry. No one knew enough about the Brotherhood for it to present itself as a possibility. Chinaman suggests measures to minimize the effects of any KGB-promoted exposure in two main ways:

---

*Klaus Emil Julian Fuchs, convicted in 1950 of passing British and American atomic research secrets to the Soviet Union.

First, by ensuring that we are not 'caught' with persons holding certain key delicate positions being Masons . . . From my own experience (as well as reports of the P2 case) I would hope for example that the heads of both the Secret Intelligence Service and the Security Service are not permitted to be Masons, and that the regulations of these two services now provide for any Masons to declare their adherence to the head of the service concerned personally.* I believe that the same should apply to Special Branch. Masons who are members of these branches of Government could however provide a valuable link to Freemasonry in the service of the state if they are not so acting already. In other Departments, arrangements could be made to ensure that heads of personnel sections be non-Masons, and that they have a right of access to the Director-General of the Security Service. The legal profession – presently the object of increasing public disquiet because of its alleged tendency to protect its own – is a particular problem given the large number of Freemasons . . . The second direction I would concentrate upon would be legislation. It seems to me, for instance, far less likely that any deliberately organized exposure would cause serious and lasting damage to the benefit of the pro-Communist left and the Soviet Union, if all citizens had the legal right, if they so elected, to a written assurance that any professional person they consulted is not a member of any secret society, including the Freemasons and similar or related groupings: an untrue denial rendering the professional person liable to criminal proceedings. I appreciate the very great difficulties, but possibly in the not too far distant future in the wake of the P2 affair, some measure along these lines might be passed . . . In the Government service Masons in delicate areas would come to know that for security reasons a few positions were closed to them: this too would help shift the balance of advantage.

Such measures could, I believe, also incidentally lead to a significant improvement in Britain's performance in many places, lessening the possibility that the more dynamic, more forward-looking and better qualified may be passed over to the detriment of governmental and industrial efficiency. I repeat, though, that I am well aware that I have not the qualifications for suggesting counter-measures, that I have for setting out the dangers.

*As already stated, MI5 officers are banned from joining the Brotherhood, but this has not prevented several from doing so.

I have discussed this Report in general terms and off the record with several highly placed officials and with three former Cabinet Ministers, all of whom told me that if such a report came into their hands when they were in office they would have initiated an enquiry. In March 1982, having contacted Foreign Secretary Lord Carrington and been assured by him that he was not nor had ever been a member of the Brotherhood, I was on the point of raising it with him. Then Argentina invaded the Falkland Islands and Britain lost one of its most able ministers.

And here another link is forged between Licio Gelli, his Soviet masters, and the important task P2 had been created to perform in the continuing programme to destablize the West. After his flight from Italy, Gelli did not go into hiding beyond the Iron Curtain as suggested by the perspicacious Peter Hebblethwaite. Most informed sources believed he was in Argentina, where he had exercised so much influence in the past and where, I suggest, General Galtieri was his new Perón. It cannot be a coincidence that Admiral Emilio Massera, the commander of the Argentine Navy and one of the three-man junta that launched the Falklands invasion, and the commander of the Argentine First Army, General Carlos Suarez Mason, were both secret members of Lodge P2.

Epilogue

On 18 June 1982 the dead body of a middle-aged man was found hanging by the neck from a rope suspended from scaffolding beneath Blackfriars Bridge, London. The pockets of his black suit contained nearly £23,000 in various currencies and were weighted with 12 pounds of builder's bricks. He was Roberto Calvi, president of Italy's Banco Ambrosiano, who in 1981 had been named a member of Licio Gelli's illegal Freemasonic Lodge, Propaganda Due. Calvi was later found guilty by an Italian court of illegally exporting $26.4 million to Switzerland and received a four-year suspended prison sentence and ordered to pay a fine equivalent to £7.3 million. A week later he was confirmed as chairman of Banco Ambrosiano. In April 1982 Calvi's deputy at the bank was wounded by a would-be assassin. Known as 'God's banker', Calvi had ben closely linked with Instituto per le Opere di Religione (IOR), the Vatican Bank, for years. A number of highly questionable transactions involving the Vatican Bank, Calvi and Banco Ambrosiano subsidiaries in Latin America and elsewhere led the Bank of Italy to launch an investigation. On the last day of May 1982 the Bank of Italy demanded an explanation for loans of $1,400 million made by Banco Ambrosiano subsidiaries to several companies registered in Panama owned directly or indirectly by the Vatican Bank. This precipitated a run on Ambrosiano's shares, and eleven days later Calvi disappeared in Rome. Using a false passport, he fled to Austria and then England, arriving at Gatwick on 15 June and travelling straight to London where he remained for several days in an apartment in Chelsea Cloisters. On 17 June the Bank of Italy seized control of Banco Ambrosiano and trading in its shares was suspended after they had dropped twenty per cent in value in one day. Ambrosiano's directors resigned and Calvi's secretary, Graziella Corrocher – who kept the books of Lodge P2 – jumped, or was pushed, to her death from a fourth-floor window at the bank. She left behind her what was obviously intended to be taken as a suicide note, although there is more than a small doubt that this was genuine. The note said: 'May Calvi be double cursed for the damage he has caused to the bank and its employees.'

The following night Calvi's body was found hanging from the scaffolding beneath Blackfriars Bridge, four miles from the apartment in Chelsea Cloisters. Even as the *Daily Express* postal clerk who found the body was hastening to call the police, Italian police were busy chartering a plane and a party of high officials arrived at Gatwick a few hours later.

There were many rumours: the Mafia, with whom Calvi had connections, had murdered him; frightened and despairing, he had committed suicide; he had been ritually done to death by Freemasons, a masonic 'cable-tow' around his neck and his pockets filled symbolically with chunks of masonry, the location of the murder being chosen for its name – in Italy, the logo of the Brotherhood is the figure of a Blackfriar.

But a City of London inquest later decided that Calvi had committed suicide, a verdict the banker's family immediately announced its intention to challenge. Italian police, and a number of City of London police associated with the case, are convinced it was murder.

The inquest was told that Calvi had been a 'frightened man, fearful of his life' before flying to London in June. And it was never explained why, even if Calvi had decided to do the work of those he feared, he would travel four miles across London late at night to Blackfriars Bridge, fill his pockets with bricks, climb on to the bridge and over the side on to scaffolding he could not possibly have known was there – all this in a man who suffered extreme vertigo – and perform the elaborate task of arranging a heavy rope, presumably brought with him for the purpose, and launch himself off the scaffolding. It would have been easier by far to throw himself from his office window in Italy, or if the idea of suicide only came to him when he reached London – an awfully long way to go just to kill yourself – why not do it with his belt in the comfort of his Chelsea apartment?

The mystery of Calvi's death deepens rather than clarifies with time. It is inextricably bound up with the riddle of P2, the KGB penetration of Freemasonry, and Freemasonry's penetration not only of the Roman Catholic Church but the Vatican itself.* At the time this book goes to press, investigations are continuing into Banco Ambrosiano's links with the enigmatic president of the Vatican Bank, Archbishop Paul Marcinkus, and into the continuing international reverberations of the P2 conspiracy.

Meanwhile, Licio Gelli has since been arrested in Switzerland where he was attempting to withdraw nearly $100 million from several numbered accounts at Geneva's Union Bank – money belonging to Banco Ambrosiano. Gelli awaits the outcome of extradition proceedings.

*At a second inquest in June 1983, the jury returned an open verdict.

Meanwhile, too, Yuri Andropov, head of the KGB when the P2 plot was hatched, now sits at the pinnacle of Soviet power and diverts ever more funds towards the KGB's activities in the West, the exploitation of Freemasonry included.

There are several clear areas which call for an investigation into the use of Freemasonry's secrets and its network of contacts. Why is it that, although the United Grand Lodge has powers to revoke the charter of any Lodge found to be conducting itself in an unworthy, immoral or criminal way, this provision is never implemented? Why is it that individual Masons, who betray the Brotherhood by proving daily they have joined for pecuniary or other advantage and by constantly exploiting the unique privileges which Masonry confers, are hardly ever expelled, as the Brotherhood's *Book of Constitutions* provides? Grand Lodge remains obdurately silent.

I approached United Grand Lodge early in my investigation explaining my aims and how in its own interests the Brotherhood should surely at least talk of its attitude to those 'bad apples' that all but a few Freemasons readily admit are there. I received a courteous rebuff and was told, nicely but firmly, to mind my own business.

This stubborn refusal to speak to outsiders and Grand Lodge's traditional silence in the face of criticism, even when corruption has been traced to members of a Lodge or group of Lodges abusing Masonry for their own ends, does nothing but heighten suspicion.

It is time for Freemasonry to put its house in order, to operate openly, to comply with the laws relating to it, and to be seen to condemn those within its ranks who are 'traitors' to its stated highly moral aims.

No one who has investigated Freemasonry in Britain

with a clear brain can fail to be impressed by the goodness it contains and which is manifested in many ways. I have met many men who would otherwise be without purpose or self-respect who have found that Masonry brings out all that is most admirable in them.

But the rot must be cut out ruthlessly, because it is spreading. And as it spreads more and more of the 'good' brethren get out and are replaced by the 'bad'.

In the end is the beginning. Although this first edition of *The Brotherhood* has reached its final paragraph, it represents barely a glimpse beneath the surface of Freemasonry in modern society. I am still at the start of my investigations, which will continue, and future editions will not only look at the Brotherhood's influence in fields hardly touched on here – like education, the Civil Service, the Press, agriculture, science and many others – but will include further case histories, and any arguments either in favour of or against Masonry which readers of this edition think relevant and cannot find here.

Information For Candidates

(from *The Universal Book of Craft Masonry*)

Freemasonry consists of a body of men banded together to preserve the secrets, customs and ceremonials handed down to them from time immemorial, and for the purpose of mutual intellectual, social and moral improvement. They also endeavour to cultivate and exhibit brotherly love, relief and truth, not only to one another, but to the world at large.

Freemasonry offers no pecuniary advantages whatever, neither does there exist any obligation nor implied understanding binding one Mason to deal with another, nor to support him in any way in the ordinary business relations of life.

Freemasonry teaches us to remember our common origin; it also distinctly enjoins us to respect all social distinctions, so that while some must rule, others must obey and cheerfully accept their inferior positions.

Freemasonry has certain charities, but it is not in any sense whatever a benefit society, nor is it based on any calculations which would render this possible. The charities are solely for *those who having been in good circumstances* have been overtaken by misfortune or adversity, and they are quite insufficient to meet even these demands now made upon them.

Freemasonry distinctly teaches that a man's first duty is

to *himself, his wife, his family and his connections*, and no one should join the Order who cannot well afford to pay the initiation fees and subscriptions to his Lodge as well as to the Masonic charities, and this without detriment in any way to his comfort, or to that of those who have any claim upon his support.

Freemasonry recognizes no distinctions of religion, but none should attempt to enter who have no religious belief, as faith in a Deity must be expressed before any can be initiated, and prayers to Him form a frequent part of the ritual.

Freemasonry, therefore, demands that everyone before offering himself as a candidate, should be well assured in his own mind:

1. That he sincerely desires the intellectual and moral improvement of himself and his fellow creatures, and that he is willing to devote part of his time, means and efforts to the promotion of brotherly love, relief and trust.
2. That he seeks no commercial, social nor pecuniary advantages.
3. That he is able to afford the necessary expenditure without injury to himself or connections.
4. That he is willing to enter into solemn obligations in the sight of his God.

The Officers of the Lodge

Each Lodge elects the following officers every year:

Worshipful Master Chairman of the Lodge.
Immediate Past Master Last year's Worshipful Master.
Senior Warden Personal officer of WM; next year's WM in most lodges.
Junior Warden Personal officer of WM and next in seniority.
Chaplain The officer who conducts prayers. Can be a man of any profession in the outside world, not necessarily a clergyman.
Treasurer The senior officer in charge of the Lodge funds.
Secretary
Director of Ceremonies In charge of the ritual element of Lodge business.
Senior Deacon   The Deacons – with their wands – play an important part in Lodge ritual,
Junior Deacon   including acting the role of messengers.
Charity Steward Officer in charge of the Lodge's donations to charity.
Almoner Officer in charge of collecting and spending the Lodge's benevolent funds.
Assistant Director of Ceremonies Self-explanatory.
Inner Guard Officer who guards the door of the Lodge on the inside and ensures that only Freemasons enter.
Tyler The outer guard who stands outside the Lodge door with a dagger as the first line of defence against non-Masons trying to enter.

Initiation to the First Degree
up to the end of the Obligation

The Tyler prepares the Candidate in a room outside the Lodge room where he is to be initiated by divesting him of all metal articles. The Candidate removes his outer clothing until he stands in socks, his left shoe, trousers and shirt only. His shirt is unbuttoned to reveal his left breast, his right sleeve is rolled up to reveal the elbow, his left trouser leg is rolled up above the knee and a slipper is placed on his unshod foot. A hangman's noose is then placed around his neck, the end of the rope hanging down behind him. He is blindfolded.

He is then led by the Tyler to the door of the Lodge and the Tyler knocks.

The Inner Guard, moving with the prescribed step and making the First Degree sign, says, 'Brother Junior Warden, there is a report.' After several ritual responses, the Inner Guard opens the door and asks the Tyler, 'Whom have you there?'

'Mr John Smith, a poor Candidate in a state of darkness,' says the Tyler, 'who has been well and worthily recommended, regularly proposed and approved in open Lodge, and now comes of his own free will and accord, properly prepared, humbly soliciting to be admitted to the mysteries and privileges of Freemasonry.'

There follow several repetitious exchanges, the Inner

Guard places the point of a dagger to the Candidate's left breast. He is asked, 'Do you feel anything?'

'Yes.'

The Inner Guard raises the dagger in the air, and the still blindfolded Candidate is led by the right hand by the Junior Deacon to the kneeling-stool before the Worshipful Master, who then addresses the Candidate for the first time.

'Mr John Smith, as no person can be made a Mason unless he is free and of mature age, I demand of you, are you a free man and of the full age of twenty-one years?'

'I am.'

'Thus assured, I will thank you to kneel, while the blessing of Heaven is invoked on our proceedings.'

The Candidate kneels. The Brethren move in the prescribed manner, the Lodge Deacons crossing their wands above the Candidate's head, while the Worshipful Master or the Chaplain prays aloud, 'Vouchsafe Thine aid, Almighty Father and Supreme Governor of the Universe, to our present convention and grant that this Candidate for Freemasonry may so dedicate and devote his life to Thy service, as to become a true and faithful Brother among us. Endue him with a competency of Thy Divine Wisdom, so that, assisted by the secrets of our masonic art, he may be the better enabled to unfold the beauties of true Godliness, to the honour and glory of Thy Holy Name.'

The Immediate Past Master says or sings, 'So mote it be.'

'Mr Smith,' continues the Worshipful Master, 'in all cases of difficulty and danger, in whom do you put your trust?', and the Candidate replies, 'In God.'

'Right glad I am to find your faith so well founded. Relying on such sure support you may safely rise and follow your leader with a firm but humble confidence, for where the name of God is invoked we trust no danger can ensue.'

The Candidate rises to his feet with the help of the Deacons. The Worshipful Master and the Brethren sit. The Worshipful Master then gives a single knock with his gavel. 'The Brethren from the north, east, south and west will take notice that Mr John Smith is about to pass in view before them, to show that he is the Candidate properly prepared, and a fit and proper person to be made a Mason,' says the Master.

There then follows various ritual motions and the Candidate is led in a procession around the Lodge. Arriving at the place where the Junior Warden stands, the Junior Deacon takes the Candidate's right hand and taps the Junior Warden's right shoulder with it three times.

The Junior Warden asks, 'Whom have you there?'

'Mr John Smith,' replies the Junior Deacon, 'A poor Candidate in a state of darkness, who has been well and worthily recommended, regularly proposed and approved in open Lodge, and now comes of his own free will and accord, properly prepared, humbly soliciting to be admitted to the mysteries and privileges of Freemasonry.'

'How does he hope to obtain those privileges?'

'By the help of God, being free and of good report.'

The Junior Warden then takes the Candidate's right hand, and says to him, 'Enter, free and of good report,' and he is led to the Senior Warden, before whom a similar exchange takes place. The Senior Warden moves to the Worshipful Master. 'Worshipful Master,' he says, making the appropriate sign, 'I present to you Mr John Smith, a Candidate properly prepared to be made a Mason.'

'Brother Senior Warden,' replies the Worshipful Master, 'your presentation shall be attended to, for which purpose I shall address a few questions to the Candidate, which I trust he will answer with candour.' He turns to the Candidate. 'Do you seriously declare on your honour that, unbiased by the improper solicitation of friends against your own inclination, and uninfluenced by mercenary or other unworthy motive, you freely and voluntarily offer yourself a Candidate for the mysteries and privileges of Freemasonry?'

'I do.'

'Do you likewise pledge yourself that you are prompted to solicit those privileges by a favourable opinion preconceived of the Institution, a genuine desire of knowledge, and a sincere wish to render yourself more extensively serviceable to your fellow creatures?'

'I do.'

'Do you further seriously declare on your honour that, avoiding fear on the one hand and rashness on the other, you will steadily persevere through the ceremony of your initiation, and if once admitted you will afterwards act and abide by the ancient usages and established customs of the order?'

'I do.'

'Brother Senior Warden, you will direct the Junior Deacon to instruct the Candidate to advance to the pedestal in due form.'

'Brother Junior Deacon, it is the Worshipful Master's command that you instruct the Candidate to advance to the pedestal in due form.'

The Junior Deacon complies, leading the Candidate to the pedestal and instructing him to stand with his heels together and his feet at right angles, the left foot facing east and the right foot south. He continues: 'Take a short pace with your left foot, bringing the heels together in the form of a square. Take another, a little longer, heel to heel as before. Another still longer, heels together as before.'

The Candidate is now standing before the pedestal, with the Junior Deacon to his right and the Senior Deacon to his left.

'It is my duty to inform you,' says the Worshipful Master, 'that Masonry is free, and requires a perfect freedom of inclination in every Candidate for its mysteries. It is founded on the purest principles of piety and virtue. It possesses great and invaluable privileges. And in order to secure those privileges to worthy men, and we trust to worthy men alone, vows of fidelity are required. But let me assure you that in those vows there is nothing incompatible with your civil, moral or religious duties. Are you therefore willing to take a Solemn Obligation, founded on the principles I have stated, to keep inviolate the secrets and mysteries of the order?'

'I am.'

'Then you will kneel on your left knee, your right foot formed in a square, give me your right hand which I place on the Volume of the Sacred Law, while your left will be employed in supporting these compasses, one point presented to your naked left breast.'

This done, the Candidate is then made to repeat the 'Obligation' after the Worshipful Master, 'I, John Smith, in the presence of the Great Architect of the Universe, and of this worthy, worshipful, and warranted Lodge of Free and Accepted Masons, regularly assembled and properly dedicated, of my own free will and accord, do hereby (*WM touches Candidate's right hand with his left hand*) and hereon (*WM touches the Bible with his left hand*) sincerely and solemnly promise and swear, that I will always hele, conceal and never reveal any part or parts, point or points of the secrets or mysteries of or belonging to Free and Accepted Masons in Masonry, which may heretofore have been known by me, or shall now or at any future period be communicated to me, unless it be to a true and lawful Brother or Brothers, and not even to him or them, until after due trial, strict examination, or sure information from a well-known Brother, that he or they are worthy of that confidence, or in the body of a just, perfect, and regular Lodge of Ancient Freemasons. I further solemnly promise that I will not write those secrets, indite, carve, mark, engrave or otherwise them delineate, or cause or suffer it to be so done by others, if in my power to prevent it, on anything movable or immovable, under the canopy of Heaven, whereby or whereon any letter, character or figure, or the least trace of a letter, character or figure, may become legible, or intelligible to myself or anyone in the world, so that our secret arts and hidden mysteries may improperly become known through my unworthiness. These several points I solemnly swear to observe, without evasion, equivocation, or mental reservation of any kind, under no less a penalty, on the violation of any of them, than that of having my throat cut across, my tongue torn out by the root, and buried in the sand of the sea at low water mark, or a cable's length from the shore, where the tide regularly ebbs and flows twice in twenty-four hours, or the more effective punishment of being branded as a wilfully perjured individual, void of all moral worth, and totally unfit to be received into this worshipful Lodge, or any other warranted Lodge or society of men, who prize honour and virtue above the external advantages of rank and fortune. So help me, God, and keep me steadfast in this my Great and Solemn Obligation of an Entered Apprentice Freemason.

Further Reading

BEHA, Ernest, *A Comprehensive Dictionary of Freemasonry* (Arco Publications, 1962).

BOX, Hubert S., *The Nature of Freemasonry* (Augustine Press, 1952)

CAHILL, E., *Freemasonry and the Anti-Christian Movement* (Gill and Son, Dublin, 1952).

CARLILE, Richard, *Manual of Freemasonry* (Wm Reeves, London, 1845).

CARR, Harry, *The Freemason at Work* (Lewis Masonic, 1976).

COVEY-CRUMP, Rev, *The Hiramic Tradition*, (London, 1937).

COX, Barry, SHIRLEY, John and SHORT, Martin, *The Fall of Scotland Yard* (Penguin, 1977).

DEWAR, James, *The Unlocked Secret* (William Kimber, 1966).

FITZWALTER, Raymond and TAYLOR, David, *Web of Corruption* (Granada, 1981)

GOULD, R. F., *History of Freemasonry* (Caxton, 1951).

HANNAH, Walton, *Darkness Visible* (Augustine Press, 1952); *Christian by Degrees* (Britons Publishing Co 1954).

JONES, Bernard E., *Freemasons' Book of the Royal Arch*

(Harrap, 1957); *Freemasons's Guide and Compendium* (Harrap, 1950).

'JUBELUM', *Freemasonry and the Church of England Reconciled* (Britons Publishing Co 1951).

KNIGHT, Stephen, *Jack the Ripper: The Final Solution* (Harrap, 1976).

LAWRENCE, Rev John, *Freemasonry - A Way of Salvation?* (Grove Books, 1982).

LAWRENCE, Rev John T., *Masonic Jurisprudence* (A. Lewis, 1923).

LENNHOFF, Eugen, *The Freemasons* (A. Lewis, 1934).

LEPPER, J. Herron, *The Traditioners* (Ars Quatuor Coronatorum, vol 56, Quatuor Coronati Lodge, no 2076).

LEO XIII, POPE, *Humanum Genus, 1884* (Britons Publishing Co, 1952).

MACKENZIE, Norman (Editor), *Secret Societies* (Aldus, 1967).

MACKEY, Albert G., *Encyclopaedia of Freemasonry* (3 vols) (Macoy Publishing and Supply Co, Richmond, Virginia, 1946).

MORGAN, William, *Freemasonry Exposed* (Glasgow, 1836).

NEWTON, Joseph Fort, *The Builders: A Story and Study of Freemasonry* (Hogg, 1917; Allen and Unwin, 1918).

PICK, Fred L. and KNIGHT, G. Norman, *The Pocket History of Freemasonry* (Frederick Muller, 1953).

PINCHER, Chapman, *Their Trade is Treachery* (Sidgwick and Jackson, 1981).

RAINSBURY, Rev A. W., *Freemasonry - of God or the Devil?* (substance of a sermon preached in Emmanuel Church, South Croydon, 1959).

RUMBLE, Dr L., *Catholics and Freemasonry* (Catholic Truth Society pamphlet).

THURSTON, H., *Freemasonry* (CTS pamphlet).

'VINDEX', *Light Invisible, A Freemason's Answer to Darkness Visible* (Britons Publishing Co, 1952).

VOORHIS, H. V. B., *Facts for Freemasons* (Macoy Publishing Co, 1951, revised 1979).

WHALEN, William J., *Christianity and American Freemasonry* (Bruce Publishing Co, Milwaukee, 1958).

MASONIC PERIODICALS

Freemasons' Magazine and Masonic Mirror
Freemasons' Monthly Remembrancer
Freemasons' Quarterly Review
Masonic Square

CONSTITUTIONS of the Antient Fraternity of Free and Accepted Masons under the United Grand Lodge of England (UGL, London, 1917).

Index